CENTRE OF EUROPEAN LAW
KING'S COLLEGE LONDON

The United Kingdom Parliament and European Union Legislation

Adam Jan Cygan

KLUWER LAW INTERNATIONAL
THE HAGUE/LONDON/BOSTON

Published by Kluwer Law International
P.O. Box 85889
2508 CN The Hague, The Netherlands

Sold and distributed in the USA and Canada by
Kluwer Law International
675 Massachusetts Avenue
Cambridge, MA 02139, USA

Sold and distributed in all other countries by
Kluwer Law International
Distribution Centre
P.O. Box 322
3300 AH Dordrecht, The Netherlands

A C.I.P. Catalogue record for this book is available from the Library of Congress

Printed on acid-free paper

Cover design: Alfred Birnie bNO

ISBN: 90 411 9650 1

© 1998 Kluwer Law International

Kluwer Law International incorporates the publishing programmes of Graham & Trotman Ltd,
Kluwer Law and Taxation Publishers and Martinus Nijhoff Publishers

The United Kingdom Parliament and
European Union Legislation

STUDIES IN LAW

*A series of publications issued
by the Centre of European Law,
King's College London*

General editor
Mads Andenas

Volume 2

The aim of this series is to publish studies in the broad
area of European Community Law and Comparative
European Law. Each publication will provide an
important and original contribution to the development of legal scholarship in its field and will be of
interest to the legal practitioner, academic,
government and Community official.

*The titles published in this series are listed at the end
of this volume.*

For Basia

THE UNITED KINGDOM PARLIAMENT AND EUROPEAN UNION LEGISLATION

ABSTRACT

The aim of the book is to analyse the role of the United Kingdom Parliament in the law making procedures of the European Union.

Part one considers the constitutional position of Parliament in the European Union and examines the formal and informal relationship between Parliament and the European Institutions and their effect upon the legislative process.

Part two focuses on the House of Commons scrutiny of European Community legislative proposals. It examines the work of the Select Committee on European Legislation, the two European Standing Committees and the Departmental Select Committees. A particular point of focus is their primary task, of influencing the minister before he gives final agreement to a legislative proposal in the Council of Ministers.

Part two concludes with an analysis of how developments post Maastricht have affected the scrutiny process. Particular attention is paid to the co-decision legislative procedure and its impact on scrutiny.

Part three focuses on the arrangements in the House of Lords for scrutiny of European decision making. The two core chapters examine and evaluate the Select Committee on the European Communities and the five subject related Sub-Committees. Where relevant, comparative analysis with procedures in the Commons is drawn.

Developments post Maastricht are also considered by inquiring into the scrutiny arrangements for legislation proposed under the Inter-Governmental Pillars – the political cooperation forum within the European Union. Part three concludes by an appraisal of current proposals for reforming the Lords and their potential impact on scrutiny.

Part four, the conclusion, evaluates the evidence presented and proposes detailed reforms to the scrutiny process. The final paragraphs focus specifically on the outcome of the 1996-97 Inter-Governmental Conference whose agenda included the role of national parliaments in the European Union. Within this context, the prospects for, and future likely developments to, the scrutiny process are considered.

PREFACE

The book aims to provide an analysis of the developments that have taken place since 1973 which provide for the scrutiny of secondary European legislative proposals (i.e. regulations and directives) within the United Kingdom Parliament. Over this period, Parliament has sought to hold the minister accountable for decisions taken in the Council of Ministers by influencing him prior to the legislative proposal being confirmed. This is the central element of the scrutiny process.

Law making by the institutions of the European Union has undoubtedly become more significant in terms of volume and its impact on domestic policy. However, unlike domestic legislation where Parliament is the Sovereign law-maker, in the European sphere Parliament cannot amend the legislation once agreed in Council. Thus the scrutiny process is the only opportunity for Parliament to influence the minister. For the UK, with its long tradition of Parliamentary democracy and accountability of the executive, it is vital that the effectiveness of this process is maximised. In particular, this means ensuring the effectiveness of the internal arrangements within both Houses of Parliament.

I have therefore endeavoured to investigate and explain the importance of this law-making process, which has so far not been the object of any extensive academic research study. Whilst certain aspects of this process have been the subject of academic research and examination, for example, Professor St J.N. Bates 1991 analysis of the introduction of the two European Standing Committees published in the Statute Law Review (Vol. 12 No.2 p.109), the legislative process as a whole, and in particular how developments post Maastricht have affected ministerial accountability, have not been the subject of any comprehensive research such as that undertaken for this book.

The research has required detailed analysis of Parliamentary papers, principally Select Committee reports from both Houses of Parliament, dating back to the 1960s. It has also necessitated my attendance at numerous Select and Standing Committee meetings where practical experience of the functioning of the scrutiny process was obtained. In addition, the investigation greatly benefited from oral evidence of, and correspondence with Parliamentary Clerks and Officials who provided invaluable information relating to the procedures in the various Committees. Finally, a complete picture of the process was obtained through discussions with MPs involved regularly in the scrutiny process or those having a particular interest in the relationship between Parliament and the European Union.

I would like to thank all those many persons (see Appendix 1) who freely gave up their valuable time to discuss at length the subject matter of this thesis. Some such as Lord Slynn did this despite their other (more important) commitments. His comments relating to the work of Sub-Committee E in the House of Lords, the scrutiny body of greatest interest to me as a lawyer, provided a unique insight which contributed substantially to my understanding the importance of the work carried out by this Sub-Committee. Without the undoubted generosity of *all* these persons the thesis could not have been possible. I also wish to thank Dr Robert Blackburn without whose continual help, advice and encouragement the thesis would not have been completed. However, any errors in this work remain my own.

I would like to thank Paul Penman and Sarah King at Kluwer Law International for their help and cooperation.

I would also like to thank Barbara Bogusz for her patience and assistance in the completion of this book.

The book describes the law and procedure as at 1 September 1997, with a few later developments which are of particular importance.

PART I:

THE UNITED KINGDOM AND THE EUROPEAN UNION

CHAPTER 1

THE LEGISLATIVE PROCESS OF THE EUROPEAN UNION

INTRODUCTION

The process of law making within the European Community (EC) bears no resemblance to legislative procedures familiar to the UK Parliament. There are two essential differences. The first is the wide and lengthy consultative process embarked on by the Commission. This includes consultation not only with each Member State, but also with a variety of specific interest groups. This is a small part of an extremely wide and well developed lobbying process which has become an integral part of the EC legislative procedure.

The second and most criticised difference is the fact that the final agreement on a legislative proposal is taken not by an elected Parliament but by the Council of Ministers behind closed doors. For this reason it is often contended that the legislation is devoid of any democratic legitimacy. No national parliament has any involvement in the final legislative stage. In fact it can be argued that the UK Parliament is itself only a small part of the lobbying process.

The role of the UK Parliament is limited to an attempt to influence the minister prior to him casting his vote in the Council of Ministers. Thus, any influence Parliament may have comes solely through the existing scrutiny arrangements within Parliament. A similar point was made by the House of Commons Select Committee on Procedure in its Fourth Report of 1989:[1]

> "...the scrutiny procedures keep Members well informed on Community legislative proposals....and together with the vigilance of pressure groups and other affected organisations, should make it highly unlikely that the House will be caught unawares as regards the existence of a particular item of Community legislation once it has been formally adopted by the Commission."

What the Procedure Committee is in fact saying is that Parliament should not isolate itself in this legislative process. There is an acceptance by the Procedure Committee that Parliament has neither the time nor the expertise to be involved in every aspect of Community legislation. It advocates a consensual approach, such as a partnership with other interested groups and a pooling of resources to ensure that the UK plays its full part in the Community legislative process.

The lobbying of government by interest and pressure groups at the pre-legislative stage is an integral part of the legislative process in the United Kingdom. When the government publishes its consultative Green Paper this is an opportunity for interested parties to inform the government of their views on a particular policy or proposed Bill. This procedure works well within our Parliamentary democracy. The government, though under no legal or

---

1   See HC (Session 1988-89) 622-1 p. xi, para. 18.

constitutional obligation to take on board the views presented to it, will nevertheless not ignore powerful groups such as The British Medical Association or The National Farmers Union. Even those groups that may be considered as naturally hostile, for example the TUC to the present government, will all make an informed and reasoned contribution to the debate.

Lobbying in a European context, is not too dissimilar from the procedures used in the national context. However, the main difference is that the lobbyists can participate at two levels. Influence can be brought both on the national government and on the European Commission, the key institution in the development of EC legislative proposals. At a national level, pressure groups must have good relations with the government of the day. If the government can be persuaded to adopt the line taken by the pressure group, then there is greater potential to influence. In the final analysis, the government may decide to use its veto and block a proposal. However, this is remote in today's political arrangements. The growth of Qualified Majority Voting (QMV) means a Member State's ability to veto has been removed in many important areas.[2]

The most effective form of influence is where a pressure group and the government working together in a partnership forge a strong negotiating position which the minister may then take into the Council of Ministers meeting. This reflects the views held by the Procedure Committee who felt that such a partnership was the most productive way forward.[3]

At the European level,[4] by far the most important institution to influence is the Commission. As already stated this organisation acts as a civil service and develops legislative proposals. Therefore, it is essential for all pressure groups who have interests in European affairs to have direct access to the Commission. Since 1986, the Single European Act (SEA) has increased the powers of the Commission to initiate legislation in a number of key areas and most importantly for the completion of the Single Market. This introduced a welter of new legislation in areas such as free movement of goods and persons, the majority of which was proposed by the Commission.

There are twenty Commissioners who are appointed by the Member States (Article 158 EC). Each Commissioner is responsible for a particular area of policy. Most importantly, this includes proposing legislation. For example, the UK's two Commissioners Neil Kinnock and Sir Leon Brittan are responsible for Transport and for Trade policy respectively. Developing strong links with the office of each Commissioner is vital for any interested party.

Thus the SEA 1986, shifted much of the regulation in these areas from the national to the European level, and as a consequence a need to influence a supra-national organisation. This changed fundamentally the lobbying pro-

---

2   For example, all legislative proposals leading to the implementation of the Internal Market in 1992 were taken by QMV.
3   See n. 1 above.
4   For more detail and an in-depth discussion of these issues see Mazey and Richardson (eds.) *Lobbying in the European Community* Nuffield European Series, (OUP, 1993) pp. 3-26.

cess within the EC. The emphasis now shifted from the national to the European level. Organisations developed close and direct links with the Commission, a relationship that does not exist between Westminster and the Commission.

According to figures published by Mazey and Richardson[5] in 1993, there were 525 interest groups who had developed strong official links with the Commission. They ranged from organisations such as European Trade Unions, to consumer groups, to individual companies such as Imperial Chemical Industries (ICI) and British Aerospace. This development is evidence that the European Community is now accepted as being as important as national institutions in the legislative process.[6]

One final point to note in this area is that lobbying at the European level is not limited exclusively to the European Commission. Though it does not initiate legislation, the European Parliament has, since the Maastricht Treaty, a greater ability to propose amendments. Most importantly, the Parliament is active in areas of social policy and environmental protection. Even though the Council may reject their amendments, the Parliament may slow up the process which can lead to compromise. It has not yet been fully appreciated by many in the UK that the Parliament is now an integral part of the legislative process with a positive input. Thus, closer links with the Parliament are essential and should be developed.

THE LEGISLATIVE PROCESS

Treaty provisions

Legislation in the European Community is made either by the Council of Ministers, on a proposal from the Commission, under powers conferred by the Treaties,[7] or by the Commission itself under powers given to it directly by certain Treaty Articles,[8] or under authority delegated to it by the Council. In addition, the Single European Act placed a further obligation on the Council of Ministers to extend the powers of the Commission to enable it to implement the rules which the Council lays down, subject to certain exceptions.

It remains here to describe the basic nature of each form of Community act. As far as this secondary legislation is concerned, the preliminary point to note is the hierarchy of Community acts with regulations ranking as the strongest form and non-binding recommendations as the weakest. By far the most common are directives which leave the form of implementation to each

---

5   *Ibid.* p. 6.
6   See Grant "Pressure Groups in the European Community" in *Lobbying in the European Comminity* (OUP, 1993) pp. 27-46.
7   EC Treaty Articles 145-154 (as amended by the Single European Act 1985, Article 10).
8   EC Treaty Articles 155-163.

Member State. However, the crucial point is that it is the content of a measure which is the key in deciding its nature and not the form which it is given by the adopting institution (See *International Fruit Company v. Commission* [1971] ECR 411).

Though there are various procedures by which legislation can be made, the Treaty lays down the form which any legislation should take:[9]

> "In order to carry out their task, and in accordance with the provisions of this Treaty, the European Parliament acting jointly with the Council and the Commission shall make regulations, issue directives, take decisions, make recomendations or deliver opinions.[10]
>
> A **regulation** shall have general application. It shall be binding in its entirety and directly applicable to all Member States.
>
> A **directive** shall be binding, as to the result to be achieved upon each Member State to which it is addressed, but shall leave to the national authorities the choice of form and methods.
>
> A **decision** shall be binding in its entirety upon those to whom it is addressed. Recommendations and opinions shall have no binding force."

Reasons for legislation

Any regulation, directive and decision whether emanating from the Council of Ministers or the Commission must state the reasons on which they are based, including most importantly the legal basis.[11]

A statement of the reasons for introducing the legislation aids any review of the legislation by the European Court of Justice (ECJ). Thus, the Court (or for that matter any other interested party) will know immediately the aims of the adopting institution. In effect, this is an explanation of the policy objectives of the particular institution. In her book, *European Community Law*[12] Josephine Shaw illustrates that the statement of reasons depends upon the type of act adopted.[13] Thus, in her example, she states that a general legislative act requires less specific reasons than an individual act, such as one which imposes a fine on an undertaking for breach of competition rules. This is logical given the impact that such a specific piece of legislation may have on what could be a very narrow group within the Community.

---

9   EC Treaty Article 189 as amended by Article G(60) Treaty of European Union (TEU).

10 This sets out the aim of Article 189b and 189c (both as inserted by Article G(61) TEU). Both these Treaty provisions give greater powers to the European Parliament in the legislative process, by requiring consultation before any final proposal is adopted.

11 Article 190 EC Treaty as amended by Article G(63) TEU.

12 Macmillan Professional Master Series, 1993.

13 See Shaw, p. 76.

The legal basis of legislation

The need to establish the legal basis goes to the heart of whether the legislative proposal is valid or not. Thus, the act must always make reference to the part of the Treaty or the delegated legislation which gives the institution concerned the power to make this legislation. As Josephine Shaw quite correctly points out,[14] the choice of legal basis is an important element of the legislative process. This is because under the Treaty, the power of the institutions is specifically divided such that there is a division of legislative acts between the Commission and Council. This fact has been recognised by the European Court of Justice as being a matter of law:[15]

> "the choice of the legal basis for a measure may not depend simply on an institution's conviction as to the objective pursued but on objective factors which are amenable to Judicial review"

Implementation in the UK

In the UK, regulations are given their direct applicability by Section 2 of the European Communities Act (ECA) 1972. Although regulations are binding in their entirety and directly applicable, supplementary domestic legislation will on occasion be needed to make the legislation fully effective. This is usually the case for enforcement provisions.

Directives are binding upon the Member State as to the results to be achieved, with the form and methods of implementation left to each national authority. In the UK this is achieved by the passage of new primary legislation or by secondary legislation passed under Section 2 ECA 1972. However, whichever method is used, Parliament *cannot* change the substance of the legislation. Failure to implement the legislation in accordance with the aims of the directive will lead to the Commission bringing an action against the UK government in the European Court of Justice (ECJ).

LEGISLATION ADOPTED BY THE COUNCIL OF MINISTERS FOLLOWING A PROPOSAL FROM THE COMMISSION[16]

The function of COREPER

Following any consultation or discussions with national experts or interested pressure groups, the proposal is then considered by official permanent repre-

---

14   *Ibid* pp. 76-77.
15   Case 45/86 *Commission v Council (General Tariff Preferences [1987]* ECR 1493 at p. 1520). This extract was taken from Josephine Shaw *European Community Law* p. 77. For a more general discussion of litigation due to the incorrect legal base being established see also pp. 93-95.
16   For a wider discussion of the issues in this area see Nugent *The Government and Politics of the European Union* pp. 129-152. (Macmillan, 1994).

sentatives of each Member State (COREPER) or in one of a number of Council Working Groups before the formal proposal is submitted to the Council of Ministers.

The work of these advisory bodies is both an essential and integral part of the legislative process. The Committee of Permanent Representatives of the Member States (COREPER)[17] comprises the ambassadors of the Member States to the Communities. Their work, and that of the various sub-committees and Working Groups, is an essential part of the Community legislative process.

Since the Council of Ministers is not a permanent body, meeting only once or twice a month, and the ministers continue to have their various domestic responsibilities, much of the work is taken over by COREPER. The main task of this full time body is to scrutinise and sift proposals for legislation coming from the Commission prior to the final discussion by the Council of Ministers. Such a sifting process is a vital task. It allows the Council to agree the simple proposals with the minimum amount of debate and discussion, and thereby maximising the limited time available for debate of the more controversial proposals.[18]

In addition to COREPER, there is a system of Working Groups (sometimes referred to as Management Committees) which aid the Council by reducing the work-load they face.[19] Under this arrangement the relevant committee (and there is one for each policy area) examines the Commission's proposal for the implementation of an agreed Community policy.

The Working Group carries out its task according to the following procedure. The Commission issues its proposal to the Working Group. If the Working Group decides, by qualified majority, to oppose the Commission's proposal, it will refer the matter to the Council of Ministers for it to collectively arrive at a decision.

In the event of the Working Group not being able to achieve the necessary qualified majority that will ensure a referral to the Council of Ministers, the Commission's original proposal remains intact. However, both COREPER and the numerous Working Groups serve the additional function of acting as a check upon the Commission's executive powers. But the question of their effectiveness in performing this task must be raised.

---

17 EC Treaty Article 4 provides for the establishment of Permanent Representatives to the European Community.

18 The legality of this Working Party procedure was questioned in the European Court of Justice in *Firmer Koster Berodt and Co.*(Case 25/70). The Court upheld this procedure as being a legitimate form of delegation of the Council of Ministers law making powers.

19 These were introduced in 1967. See Reg. 120/67, Official Journal No.117, 19 June 1967 p. 2269/7.

Limitations of COREPER

The obvious criticism to be levelled at this arrangement is that it lacks any democratic credentials. Neither COREPER nor the Working Parties are elected, and furthermore their ability to scrutinise the work of the unelected Commission is also questionable. The fact that the Working Parties must act by qualified majority before any referral is made to the Council of Ministers makes such a referral unlikely. Obtaining the agreement of enough Member States to muster the necessary majority is difficult especially if the Member States with the larger share of the votes do not support such a review of the proposal.

Furthermore, if the Member State holding the Presidency of the Council is reluctant to slow up the legislative process, then political horsetrading will usually ensure a compromise that leads to the adoption of the legislation with the minimum of disruption to the legislative timetable.

The contrast with established practices in the UK cannot be greater. Most importantly, legislation is only made in the UK by elected representatives answerable to Parliament and their constituents. In effect, the European legislative process is one of legislation being made by an unaccountable Executive body. This is the "democratic deficit" so often referred to by critics of the structure and role of the European institutions. Aware of this criticism the European Community has responded by increasing the role taken by the European Parliament in the legislative process. This, in itself however, has been an extremely slow task, and one further complicated by the reluctance of national parliaments to be cast in the role of a "bit player" in the formulation of legislative proposals, with the European Parliament taking the lead.

THE INVOLVEMENT OF THE EUROPEAN PARLIAMENT IN THE LEGISLATIVE PROCESS.

Since the implementation of the Maastricht Treaty in 1993, the role of the European Parliament in the legislative process has been significantly extended.[20] The Parliament now can provide its input in one of three ways:

(i)   Through consultation;
(ii) Via the cooperation procedure; and
(iii) Via the co-decision procedure.

These will now be examined in turn.

Consultation

In those circumstances where consultation is prescribed (this will depend on the nature and content of the legislative proposal) the Council is under an

---

20   For an analysis of the impact of this extension on the domestic scrutiny arrangements of the UK Parliament, see chapter 6 "The Scrutiny of European Legislation by the House of Commons after Maastricht".

obligation to consult with the European Parliament as to its views on the relevant Commission proposal.[21] Furthermore, in a majority of cases, the views of
the Economic and Social Committee (ECOSOC) must also be sought.[22] The
purpose of ECOSOC is to provide representation within a formal Community structure for disparate regional and economic interests. Under Article
193 of the Treaty, ECOSOC is given advisory status and this means being
consulted by the Council and the Commission where the Treaty provides, e.g.
Article 100A.

However, the Council of Ministers are under no corresponding obligation
to take account of the views of the Parliament. Hence, there is potential for
conflict between the two institutions where there is a substantive disagreement. However, the Council being mindful of criticism that it operates very
much in isolation, will rarely dismiss outright any opinion of the European
Parliament. In fact, the practice has developed in recent years that the European Parliament will be consulted by the Council beyond that which is legally
required by the Treaty. The Council being ever aware of political considerations, does not wish to give the appearance of being an inflexible and isolated
institution that ignores the views of Europe's elected representatives.

Through the way it conducts itself in the consultation process, the European Parliament can increase its ability to influence. Most notably, if the
European Parliament delays in the delivery of its opinion it can influence the
Council of Minister's negotiations. The Council will informally be aware of
the Parliament's opinions but according to the Treaty cannot make a final
decision until it has received an official opinion. With the President of the
Council adding to the pressure of coming to an agreement, the Council will
be forced to reflect at least some of the views of the Parliament in its deliberations and final opinion on the proposal. Following this consultation process
the Commission may if it wishes amend its proposals.

The cooperation Procedure

The cooperation procedure[23] was introduced by the Single European Act
1986. Under this process, the European Parliament, which had been directly
elected since 1979, would for the first time have a direct input in the legislative process. The aim of the co-operation procedure was to address the much
debated democratic deficit which was seen as undermining the credibility of
the European Community. It went to the heart of the issue, that despite electing its MEPs, the European Community was still fundamentally undemocratic and unaccountable for the legislation it passed.

The cooperation procedure works in the following way. The Commission
submits a proposal for legislation to the Council of Ministers, and at the same

21   See EC Treaty Articles 137-144 (as amended by Article G(41) TEU), in particular
     Article 138b.
22   See EC Treaty Article 4 (as amended by Article G(6) TEU).
23   Article 189c EC Treaty as inserted by Article G(61) TEU.

time seeks the opinion of the European Parliament on the proposal. In some circumstances the Economic and Social Committee will also be consulted. At this stage, following deliberations, the Council will adopt its common position by qualified majority. The common position expresses the collective view of the Council on the proposal and this is communicated to the European Parliament, who can accept it, reject it, or propose its own amendments to it.

If the European Parliament does propose any amendments to the Council's common position, the Commission will then submit a further re-examined proposal based on the common position and taking into account the proposed amendments of the European Parliament. The Commission also forwards to the Council those amendments of the European Parliament it has not accepted, together with the reason for not accepting them. The Council may then adopt either the Commission's re-examined proposal as it stands by a qualified majority, or adopt it in an amended form. If the Council chooses the latter, it may also, by unanimity, accept those amendments of the European Parliament which have been rejected by the Commission.

However, if the Council takes no action within three months, the Commission's re-examined proposal will be deemed not to have been adopted. A failure by the European Parliament to accept the Council of Minister's common position, will require unanimity by the Council for its adoption.[24]

The co-decision procedure [25]

The co-decision procedure was introduced by the Maastricht Treaty.[26] The process is based upon the pre-Maastricht cooperation procedure and is a further attempt by the European Community to address the democratic deficit. Therefore, the main difference between the two procedures is that co-decision gives greater powers to the European Parliament and limits the role of the Commission in the legislative process. Furthermore, though the two legislative processes operate independently of each other, covering decision making in different policy areas, there are some common areas e.g. environment policy where legislation can be passed by either procedure. Where this is the case, co-decision now appears to be the favoured vehicle.

The main change introduced by the co-decision procedure is to introduce an extra stage into the legislative process. On second reading, the European Parliament may by an absolute majority reject or amend the common position. This is identical to the position under the co-operation process. However, the difference lies in the options now open to the Council.

---

24 All the stages post the adoption of the common position are subject to prescribed time limits.

25 For a more detailed discussion of the workings of the co-decision procedure see Nugent *The Government and Politics of the European Union* pp. 314-323, or alternatively Josephine Shaw *European Community Law* pp. 76-97. A brief outline of the stages in the co-decision procedure may also be found in *The House of Lords and the European Union, Information Sheet No.4* produced by the Journal and Information Office in the House of Lords.

26 Article 189b EC Treaty.

Under cooperation, the Council will need to act by unanimity to proceed on a second reading where the European Parliament has rejected the proposal. However, under co-decision, if the proposal is rejected, the Council may convene the Conciliation Committee.[27] This is commonly referred to as the "third reading". Similarly, if the European Parliament has only proposed amendments to the common position, the Commission issues its opinion on those amendments and the text is forwarded to the Council which may amend the proposal accordingly or convene the Conciliation Committee with a view to reaching a joint text. The Conciliation Committee comprises fifteen representatives each from the Council and the European Parliament. When any votes are taken, the Council acts by qualified majority and the Parliament by simple majority.

The aim of the Conciliation Committee is to reach a compromise on the proposed legislation and approve a joint text. The Conciliation Committee has only six weeks to complete its deliberations.[28] If the deliberations lead to the adoption of a joint text then the proposal is adopted. However, if they end in failure, then the Council acting by a qualified majority may approve the original common position by qualified majority. At this stage, the European Parliament may only reject the common position by an absolute majority.

QUALIFIED MAJORITY VOTING[29]

Operation of Qualified Majority Voting

The process of decision making by Qualified Majority Voting (QMV) has developed substantially since its inception in 1965. Despite initial difficulties, which were to some extent overcome by the Luxembourg Accords,[30] QMV is today the main form of decision making in the Council of Ministers.[31] This is largely due to the changes brought about by the Single European Act 1986 which laid the groundwork for the completion of the Internal Market Pro-

---

27   See Article 189b (3)-(6).
28   In fact the whole co-decision process is subject to a very strict timetable. See also n. 22 above.
29   Article 148 EC Treaty (as amended by TEU).
30   The Luxembourg Accords were an attempt by the European Community to confront French concerns in 1966 when QMV was extended into the area of agricultural policy. De Gaulle saw this movement as potentially damaging to French national interests and this led to their withdrawal from the work of the Council of Ministers from June 1965 to January 1966. The accords were an informal understanding with no legal status within the Community, but provided that where a decision was to be reached by QMV that was important to the interests of a Member State, the Council would attempt to reach a decision that could be adopted by unanimity. For further discussion of this see, *The Government and Politics of Europe* by Neil Nugent pp. 142-151.
31   The entire Internal Market Programme was completed by the use of QMV.

gramme. Furthermore, the Single European Act signified a shift in the attitude of Member States to a greater acceptance of the need for QMV if the European Community was to move away from the period of legislative stagnation which characterised the years in which the Luxembourg Accords prevailed.

Qualified Majority Voting works by each Member State having a weighted number of votes according to population size. Thus the United Kingdom and Germany have 10 votes each but Luxembourg has only 2 and Belgium 3. In the Council, each Member State votes on the proposal by casting their weighted vote and if a qualified majority is reached the proposal is adopted.[32] The weighted votes of each Member State are as follows:[33]

Austria	4
Belgium	3
Denmark	3
Finland	3
France	10
Germany	10
Greece	5
Ireland	3
Italy	10
Luxembourg	2
Netherlands	5
Portugal	5
Spain	8
Sweden	4
United Kingdom	10
Total	**87**

Adoption by the Council of an act by a qualified majority requires at least:

- 62 votes in favour (out of 87) where the Treaty requires the act to be adopted on a proposal from the Commission; or
- 62 votes in favour, cast by at least ten members in other cases.

Implications of Qualified Majority Voting

Qualified Majority Voting can be viewed as a double edged sword. Without its extension in the Council of Ministers it is unlikely that a legislative pro-gramme such as the Internal Market could have been completed. If unanimity was required on each occasion, Members States would use their veto to block

---

32   An analysis of the impact of the growth of QMV on scrutiny by National Parlia-ments can be found in the Chapter 6 "The Scrutiny of European Legislation by the House of Commons Scrutiny after Maastricht."

33   See HC 239-I Session (1994-95) p. lvi.

legislation which from a domestic point of view may prove unpopular. Furthermore, unanimous agreement between 15 Member States would be unlikely. However, as Article 148 EC Treaty now requires 62 out of 87 votes for a proposal to be adopted, at least three Member States must oppose the proposal. On the basis of the weighted votes, it is almost certain that a legislative proposal will only be defeated if at least two of the Member States with the largest share of the weighted vote, vote against the proposal. Such a proposition today is unlikely, given the fact that France and Germany are the driving forces behind further European integration.

From a domestic scrutiny perspective however, the extension of QMV is potentially very damaging. The aim of the scrutiny process in the House of Commons is to "influence" the minister[34] prior to giving final approval to a legislative proposal in the Council of Ministers.[35] The influence is exercised via the scrutiny process with the minister taking into account the views of Parliament when negotiating in Council.

However, the ability to hold a minister accountable for decisions taken in Council has been eroded by the extension of QMV. In a number of increasing policy areas QMV is now the norm. Thus, if the minister following Parliament's opinion on a particular proposal is outvoted, because of QMV, by other Member States in Council he or she cannot readily be held accountable to Parliament for a piece of legislation which they disapproved of and subsequently voted against. In effect ministerial accountability is removed. The power to make legislation has been transferred away from Parliament and to an executive body which is not readily accountable to, either, any domestic legislature or the electorate. In addition, the fact that negotiations in Council are secret and usually involve a degree of political horsetrading, Parliamentary control of ministers is further undermined. The Council will always try to achieve a compromise in order to save a proposal and so the final piece of legislation will be different to that originally scrutinised by Parliament.

To conclude, Qualified Majority Voting appears to be a "necessary evil" of the European Community today. Its importance in ensuring that the Communities legislative programme is carried out cannot be overstated. However, there is a very persuasive argument that such efficiency should not be obtained at the expense of accountability and democracy. This will be too high a price to pay and one not envisaged by the founders of the Community.

LEGISLATION ADOPTED BY THE COMMISSION

Legislation adopted by the Commission constitutes the major part of legislation produced by the EC. Article 155 EC Treaty states that:

---

34 See Fourth Report from the Select Committee on Procedure (Session 1988-89) *The Scrutiny of European Legislation* HC 622 -1 p. xiv, para. 27.
35 See Chapter 3 "The work of the Select Committee on European Legislation."

"In order to ensure the proper functioning and development of the of the Common Market, the Commission shall:
- ensure that the provisions of this Treaty and the measures taken by the institutions pursuant thereto are applied;
- formulate recommendations or deliver opinions on matters dealt with in this Treaty, if it expressly provides or if the Commission considers it necessary;
- have its own power of decision and participate in the shaping of measures taken by the Council and by the European Parliament in the manner provided for in this Treaty;
- exercise the powers conferred on it by the Council for the implementation of the rules laid down by the latter."

However, the majority of Commission legislation consists of measures concerning procedural matters within the European Community such as the management of agricultural affairs within the Common Agricultural Policy or powers relating to competition law and state aids.[36] In all cases, the Commission's power to make legislation comes from powers delegated by the Council that give it the necessary authority to pass legislation. As a legislative body, the Commission does not involve itself in the more controversial or important policy areas which are primarily the domain of the Council.

One further important point to note at this juncture, is that Commission made legislation is *not* subject to the sort of scrutiny given to Council legislative proposals.[37] This is primarily due to the fact that the UK Parliament has no formal link with the Commission and that Standing Orders setting out the Terms of Reference of the Select Committee on European Legislation refer only to proposal for legislation coming from or submitted to the Council of Ministers.[38] From a Parliamentary democracy perspective this is not an acceptable state of affairs as a voluminous amount of legislation is coming onto the statute book without any scrutiny by the UK Parliament.

The principle of Subsidiarity

The meaning of Subsidiarity

This much debated principle of subsidiarity was only introduced into European Community law by the Maastricht Treaty. It reflects a fear held by some Member States, notably the UK, and Denmark, that the rapid increase in the volume of EC law had become unacceptable and infringed upon the attempts made by government in the 1980's to "roll back the frontiers of the state". EC law was viewed as being bureaucratic and eroding the rights of groups

---

36   See Articles 85-90 and 92-94 EC Treaty.
37   See also Chapter 2 "The Constitutional Relationship between the United Kingdom Parliament and the Institutions of the European Union."
38   See Standing Order No. 127 (1) (c).

such as the business community which had long argued against the limiting effect that some EC law had.

Thus Article 3b of the EC Treaty[39] formally introduced the principle of subsidiarity:

> "The Community shall act within the limits of the powers conferred upon it by this Treaty and of the objectives assigned therein.
> In areas which do not fall within its exclusive competence, the Community shall take action in accordance with the principle of subsidiarity, only if and in so far as the objectives of the proposed action cannot be sufficiently achieved by the Member States and can therefore, by the reason of scale or effects of the proposed action, be better achieved by the Community.
> Any action by the Community shall *not go beyond that which is necessary* (my italics) to achieve the objectives of this Treaty."

Therefore, according to Article 3b, the European Community will only legislate where the end cannot be achieved by Member States acting individually and the Community can achieve a better result. Perhaps most importantly, the subsidiarity principle introduces formally the concept of proportionality into EC legislation by providing that when legislating, the Community will do only the minimum necessary to secure the objectives of the Treaty.

Impact of subsidiarity

In practical terms, subsidiarity has changed the thinking within the European institutions.[40] For example, in 1992, a procedure was introduced within the Commission whereby *all* draft legislative proposals to the Council and Parliament have to now be reviewed in terms of subsidiarity. Furthermore, the Commission must now justify each legislative proposal from the point of view of subsidiarity. To help its staff, the Commission has introduced guidelines on how to apply the subsidiarity principle when preparing legal documents. These were drawn up by the Commission after the Edinburgh Council in December 1992 which had at the top of its agenda the development of the subsidiarity principle. The primary guideline involves a consideration of whether the proposal resolves the problem without going beyond that which is absolutely necessary. Similar provisions apply equally to the Council of Ministers and the European Parliament.

---

39   As introduced by Article G(5) TEU.

40   For further information on the development of the subsidiarity principle see *The European Union* published by the Commission of the European Community in 1994. In particular, see pp. 8-12.

THE INTER-GOVERNMENTAL PILLARS[41]

The European Union created after the Maastricht Treaty is comprised of a central pillar formed by the three European Communities,[42] and the two new additional pillars which cover inter-governmental cooperation in the areas of Common Foreign and Security Policy, and Justice and Home Affairs. These two "flanking pillars" as they are known operate independently of the European Community and legislation under them is not subject to the arbitration of the ECJ.

The Common Foreign and Security Policy Pillar

Since 1969 there has been cooperation between Member States in this field. They originally commissioned a report into how they could better co-ordinate both the gathering of information and the formation of foreign policy. This *political* cooperation was viewed as being essential if the economic objectives of the Community were to be achieved. The report published in 1970 recommended procedures that were strictly inter-governmental in nature and not governed by provisions in any of the Treaties.

Under the arrangements as agreed, Foreign Ministers would meet on a twice yearly basis, with other junior ministers and specialist advisers meeting four times a year or when required. This was known as European Political Cooperation. Thus, though there was coordination in the political sphere, the Community was not competent to act in this area. It was not until the Single European Act 1986 that the provisions for European Political Cooperation were codified and given a firm Treaty basis.[43]

The present arrangements for the Common Foreign and Security Policy (CFSP) are contained within Title V, Article J of the Maastricht Treaty.[44] To a large extent, the Common Foreign and Security Policy confirms the arrangements used in European Political Cooperation, but with one important addition. It provides for the first time that the Council will adopt common positions and joint actions which are binding under international law. Furthermore, any disputes will only be subject to the arbitration of the European Court of Justice when the Member States specifically agree. In essence, a whole new legislative process has been created that is distinct from existing arrangements within the European Community.

---

41   See also Chapter 6 and 10.
42   In 1951, the Treaty of Paris established the European Coal and Steel Community with six members - Belgium, Italy, France, Germany, Luxembourg and the Netherlands. In 1957, the same six nations signed the Treaty of Rome that established the European Economic Community and the European Atomic Energy Community. Though these three Communities have separate and distinct powers and functions, the institutions were merged in 1968.
43   See Article 30 Single European Act (OJ 1987, No. L169/1).
44   Articles J.1-J.11.

Under these arrangements, Member States must ensure that their national policies conform with common positions and must uphold these common positions at international conferences. From a national scrutiny perspective, the cooperation under this pillar is problematical. Firstly, commitments that are imposed on Member States by common positions are not subject to national ratification or approval procedures (unlike EC legislation). Secondly, the role of the European Parliament is slight. Though consulted, informed and having its views taken into account, the European Parliament has no right to propose amendments or veto a proposal.[45]

The Justice and Home Affairs Pillar

Title VI Article K of the Maastricht Treaty[46] places inter-governmental cooperation in justice and home affairs on a formal Treaty basis. It provides a detailed list of policy areas which are of a common interest to all Member States.[47] Most controversially this includes the sensitive areas of immigration and asylum policies, but also provides for closer cooperation between national police forces in areas such as drug trafficking and terrorism.[48]

On the initiative of any Member State, or in certain circumstances the Commission, the Council of Ministers may adopt joint positions or joint actions.[49] A joint position by the Council is similar to a common position under the CFSP and similarly are binding only under international law rather than being subject to Community competence. The Council has additional powers of drawing up Conventions that require ratification by national Parliaments and may also adopt measures for these Conventions[50] and give the European Court jurisdiction to interpret and apply them.

In carrying out its tasks, the Council is assisted by a Coordinating Committee of senior officials who act as a civil service. The Commission is fully associated with the work and the European Parliament has only the same rights as under the CFSP, i.e. it will be consulted as to its view but has no right of veto. There is one further point to be noted here. Under Article K9, the Council may by unanimity transfer any area falling under the Justice and

---

45 See n. 46 below.

46 Articles K1-K9.

47 Article K1.

48 For example see House of Lords Select Committee on the European Committees Session 1994-95, HL 51-I *EUROPOL*. This was one of the first major proposals to come forward under the Justice and Home Affairs Pillar and dealt specifically with Police co-operation between Member States. The decision to set up EUROPOL was taken by the ministers alone without any consultation with the European Parliament and thus follows an identical pattern of decision making to that used under the Common Foreign and Security Pillar.

49 Joint actions are subject to the principle of subsidiarity.

50 This may only be done by a two thirds majority unless otherwise provided in the Treaty.

Home Affairs Pillar into the realms of Community competence, with all the effects this has, such as bringing actions before the ECJ. Article 100c EC Treaty[51] provides a gateway to achieve this.

Impact of the Pillars on Parliamentary scrutiny

Both the Common Foreign and Security Policy Pillar, and the Justice and Home Affairs Pillar have established a new method for creating legislation. Though the Council of Ministers and other European institutions are involved in the process to varying degrees, the procedures involved are more akin to inter-governmental negotiation and classical diplomacy.

As already stated, they are both legally *outside* Community Competence. Thus from a scrutiny perspective, these two pillars are not within the terms of the Standing Orders for the House of Commons.[52] In the House of Lords, there has not been the same difficulty in developing scrutiny arrangements to deal with legislation under the Pillars because the Standing Orders are less rigid and structure of the Lords Committee allows for wider investigation than that in the Commons.[53] At this juncture it will suffice to state that the Commons is still having difficulty in scrutinising legislation that is agreed in secret and whose content is not familiar to the Select Committee.

This chapter has outlined the legislative processes of the European Union and signposted some of the more fundamental problems which face both Houses in their scrutiny function, in particular, maintaining the accountability of the Executive. In the forthcoming chapters, these issues will be examined and developed further, along with an assessment of the difficulties Parliament faces in its attempt fulfil its scrutiny role. Where appropriate, reforms to the scrutiny procedures will be proposed which have the potential to enhance the accountability of the Executive to Parliament.

---

51   As inserted by Article G(23) TEU.
52   See n. 38 at p. 15.
53   See n. 41 at p. 17.

CHAPTER 2

THE CONSTITUTIONAL RELATIONSHIP BETWEEN THE UNITED KINGDOM PARLIAMENT AND THE INSTITUTIONS OF THE EUROPEAN UNION

INTRODUCTION[1]

In this chapter, the constitutional position of the United Kingdom Parliament in the European Union will be briefly examined and evaluated. In particular, the focus will be on the relationship that both Houses of Parliament have with the Commission and the European Parliament. This exercise is important in that Parliament, which up until 1973 was the sole legislative body for the United Kingdom, is today not competent to legislate on certain issues without considering European law. Thus the focus will be an investigation in to how far Parliament can move "upstream" and influence the institutions which devise policy – and that means the Commission in particular and to a lesser degree the European Parliament.

The two other institutions of the European Union namely the Council of Ministers and the Court of Justice will not be considered here for the following reasons. The relationship with the Council of Minsters will be the subject of examination throughout the course of the book. In particular, the central issue is to examine how Parliament influences the minister prior to his or her giving agreement in Council and most importantly, how effective this influence is. As far as the Court of Justice is concerned, this is the arbiter of disputes, and thus is not involved in the legislative process. The Court's role is to interpret and apply the legislation and not to develop new policy.

THE COMMISSION AND THE HOUSE OF COMMONS[2]

The House of Commons has no formal relationship with the Commission. This is problematical because the Terms of Reference of the Select Committee on European Legislation require it to examine European Community documents, whose definition includes "draft proposals by the Commission of the European Communities".[3] Thus, the Select Committee is completely reliant on the government, and more precisely the European Secretariat in the Cabinet Office to provide the necessary documents on time and in the correct language. Otherwise, there will be a delay in scrutiny.

The lack of this relationship with the Commission has another potentially greater impact on scrutiny. This is the fact that the scrutiny process does not

---

1   See also Appendix 2 - Structure of the European Union.
2   See Erskine May, *Parliamentary Practice* (twenty-first edition) pp. 766-767.
3   See Standing Order 127(1).

encompass the ever increasing volume of legislation made directly by the
Commission under powers given to it by the Treaties or under implementing
powers delegated in Council legislation.[4] The net effect of this is that a large
quantity of legislative proposals are not subject to any scrutiny. It is true to say
that the overwhelming majority of them are procedural in their nature and
not concerned with major issues of policy. However, constitutionally it is
undesirable that they are not subject to *any* examination.

Developing a relationship with the Commission

The question this issue raises is whether by developing closer ties with the
Commission the scrutiny process will be enhanced? The answer must be a
resounding *yes* and for the following reasons. If through closer ties with the
Commission, documents can be obtained earlier, then the scrutiny process
will undoubtedly be more effective. Practically, this will mean more informed
reports and higher quality debate in the Standing Committee. In addition,
closer links will also gain influence with the Commission. As will be illustrated later, the House of Lords has benefited from such a development.

Some steps have already been taken in this direction. For example, since
1989 the Commissions annual work programme had been placed in the
Library of the House. Furthermore, the Commission will also pass on its three
month forward programme to national parliaments.[5] However, this does not
include working texts. These are texts which are not yet adopted by the Commission but are only in draft form. Though some do make there way to
national parliaments they are unreliable as a basis of scrutiny because being
only in draft they are subject to change.

One undoubted benefit of this is that if the Select Committee becomes
aware of a policy proposal at an early stage, the Commissioner responsible
may be invited to give evidence to the Committee to explain his or her position. Though under no obligation to attend a Commissioner usually will,
because it is seen as an ideal opportunity to explain proposals to perhaps a
sceptical House of Commons.

In its 1989 Report,[6] the Procedure Committee recommended that working texts be submitted to the Select Committee when it required them. They
accepted the evidence that they will on occasion be unreliable but took the
view that the Select Committee could make its own judgment as to how
much reliance will be placed on them.[7] In its response,[8] the government welcomed this proposal and agreed to do all it could to ensure its success.

---

4   Documents of this second type may be compared loosely with domestic delegated
     legislation and thus are not routinely deposited.
5   This information came in a written reply by the Minister of State at the Foreign and
     Commonwealth Office. See Official Report 17 July 1989, Col. 8.
6   See HC 622-I (Session 1988-89).
7   *Ibid.* p. xiii.
8   See Cm1081, p. 2.

A close and productive relationship with the Commission is essentially the key to effective scrutiny. Today there is still no formal link, with the relationship being based on the proposals of the 1989 Procedure Committee report. A new Procedure Committee inquiry has recently been announced and this issue will undoubtedly be looked at again. This time it is vital that the relationship with the Commission is placed at the centre of any proposals for reforming the scrutiny process. Influencing the formulation of policy is as important as influencing the minister prior to agreeing the legislative proposal. Such a development would undoubtedly redress the balance in favour of Parliament and address continuing criticisms of a democratic deficit in the European Union by making the Commission accountable to national parliaments.

THE EUROPEAN PARLIAMENT AND THE HOUSE OF COMMONS

Since the Procedure Committee report of 1989 the influence of the European Parliament has undoubtedly increased. This can be attributed almost exclusively to the introduction of the co-decision procedure which gave the European Parliament a much larger voice in the legislative process.[9] For the House of Commons this is undesirable because it has *no* formal control over the European Parliament. Inevitably this means there are no formal contacts with the European Parliament. Hence Parliament has no influence over what is increasingly becoming a powerful institution.

Developing relations with the European Parliament

At the outset it is necessary to state that any contacts could only be informal. MPs would be reluctant to allow MEPs any formal role within the House. They are "strangers" and thus not eligible to be involved in the daily activity of the Commons. However, two areas can be identified where informal contacts would be most helpful:

1. To act as an early warning of forthcoming legislation; and
2. To provide information on amendments to be proposed by the European Parliament under co-decision.

In 1 above, the House of Commons would undoubtedly benefit from the relationship that the European Parliament has with the Commission. Commissioners regularly speak in the European Parliament and make policy announcements.[10] Thus a sort of scrutiny by proxy could be developed.

In 2 above, the contact will be vital in that it would give the Select Committee some warning of what amendments the European Parliament proposes to the common position as agreed by the Council. This will aid scrutiny as

---

9   For more detail on this see Chapter 6.
10   See HC 622-i, p. xxxv, para. 112.

the Select Committee will have an idea of what the amended proposal will say, and the European Parliament's position in the Conciliation Committee. Thus, scrutiny can centre on these amendments or on the outcome of the Conciliation Committee meeting. Though not perfect this is better than no scrutiny at all – which unfortunately is what currently happens in many instances.

Informal links can be beneficial. The European Parliament itself welcomes closer contact with national parliaments and passed a Resolution to this effect in February 1989. However, the difficulty lies at Westminster. Many MPs view the European Parliament as a threat and challenge to the constitutional position of Parliament as the sole legislative body for the United Kingdom. This is at the core of the reluctance to formalise the relationship between the two institutions. Links with the European Parliament need to be cultivated, in particular, to ensure that all opportunities of acquiring information are maximised. Information on policy developments in the European Union is essential for effective scrutiny. Without it, the House of Commons cannot effectively fulfil its constitutional task of being a check on the Executive when it attends to the Council of Minsters.

THE HOUSE OF LORDS AND THE COMMISSION

Because of the inquiry methods adopted by the Select Committee on the European Communities in the House of Lords, they have developed more informal contacts with the Commission than their House of Commons counterpart. However, there are still no formal links between the two institutions.

As far as informal contacts are concerned, the Select Committee has achieved this in two ways. Firstly, because its Terms of Reference are not limited to just legislative proposals (unlike the Commons) it can carry out free standing inquiries into Commission Green Papers (working texts) and thereby scrutinise policy more effectively than the House of Commons. The Select Committee in the House of Lords regularly moves upstream and investigates policy areas where no legislative proposal has as yet been produced. This inevitably involves regular close contact with the Commission, something which Sir Leon Brittan, a current United Kingdom EC Commissioner has encouraged.[11]

The second type of informal contact comes in the form of Select Committee reports being regularly read by the Commission. This owes much to the high calibre of report produced by the Select Committee which have made the Committee well respected throughout the Community. Practically however, the contacts are more important for the following reason. If the Committee carries out an investigation into a Commission Green Paper, it has, as already said, inquired into policy. But it is in fact more than this. At this point the Committee is involved in the pre-legislative stage. What this means is that its subsequent report may influence the Commission's decision in the final

---

11   See HL 35-I (Session 1991-92) pp. 26-27, para. 74.

proposals which it presents to the Council of Ministers. Now, there is no guarantee that the Commission will accept any of the Committees views, but it will be difficult for it to completely ignore a report produced by such a well qualified and respected Committee.

Ideally, this procedure should be put on a formal footing and the Commission under an obligation to consider the views of any Committee from any national parliament. This would undoubtedly increase the profile of national parliaments in the EU and go some way to address the democratic deficit – that is bring the unelected Commission under some popular control.

The House of Lords and the European Parliament

As with its Commons counterpart, the Select Committee in the Lords has no formal links with the European Parliament. However, there has until recently been one difference. This has been the position that members of the Lords have also been MEPs. Though there is no restriction upon this in the Commons there are no members of the main political parties who take advantage of this.[12] In the Lords though this link was put to good use.

Today however, there are no peers with the dual mandate and it is unlikely that it will happen again. After the European elections in 1994 the last of the peers, Lords Bethell and Kingsland lost their seats as MEPs. Practically, this means a loss of influence. The Select Committee would regularly consult with these peers who would keep the Committee and the Lords generally informed of policy and legislative developments. There is some exchange of information between the Lords and the European Parliament, in particular with reports being read by the MEPs and these MEPs giving evidence to Select Committee inquiries. However, the relationship is essentially *ad hoc* and needs to be reviewed to maximise the Lords influence in the European Union.

Concluding remarks

What this brief discussion illustrates is that for all practical purposes the relationship between the United Kingdom Parliament and the European Institutions is an under utilised one. There is great potential on both sides for developing formal contacts which will undoubtedly benefit all, and most importantly benefit scrutiny in the domestic Parliament. This consideration should be at the core of Parliament's activity and issues of Parliament becoming marginalised or dominated by European institutions put into context. That is to say that both Houses need to react to the changes in the EU. Apathy and indifference will mean they become marginalised with the inevitable detrimental impact this will have on scrutiny. Developing closer cooperation

---

12   The only MPs who are also MEPs can be found among the Northern Ireland parties, e.g. John Hulme.

will have the opposite effect. In the proceeding chapters as well as returning to some of the above issues, the discussion will centre primarily on how Parliament carries out its scrutiny functions today and examine the limitations of the current scrutiny procedures.

PART II:

THE HOUSE OF COMMONS

Chapter 3

The Work of the Select Committee on European Legislation

Introduction

In 1971 the House of Commons voted by 356 to 244 votes for the Motion:

> "That this House approves Her Majesty's Governments decision of principle to join the European Communities on the basis of the arrangements which have been negotiated."

In the next session of Parliament the European Communities Bill passed through both Houses unamended and the Act's provisions became operative on 1 January 1973.[1] As an inevitable consequence of the entry of the UK into the Community, substantial and important parts of law were now to be made in new and different ways, with new and different consequences, e.g.:

(a) by way of Council Regulations which take effect immediately as part of the law of the UK and prevail over any law of the UK which is inconsistent with them; and

(b) by way of Council Directives which place upon Parliament an obligation to make or change the law of the UK in all such respects as is necessary to give legal effect in the UK to the provision of the directives.

A striking difference between these and the existing processes for making or amending the law are that in the case of (a) above, the Executive itself by agreeing with the other Member States to a proposal for legislaton makes law which is immediately binding. Hence the government has assumed the constitutional function and power of Parliament. Whereas in the case of (b) above, whilst there is limited Parliamentary control over the passage of the legislation, it is in fact difficult to exert because Parliament cannot reject the legislation without facing the wrath of the European Court, or propose amendments which change substantially the nature of the directive.

However, it remains central to the UK concept and structure of Parliamentary democracy that control of the law making processes lies with Parliament and ultimately with the elected members of it. It followed therefore that new and special procedures were necessary to counter-balance the inroads made into this concept by the legislative process of the European Community. The scrutiny process which has been developed over twenty four years acknowledges the crucial fact that it is the Council of Ministers which is at the core of this legislative process. In this context, the primary role undertaken by Parlia-

---

1   This is now the European Communities Act 1972 as amended by the Single European Act 1986 and the European Communities (Amendment) Act 1993.

ment is to influence the minister before final agreement to a legislative proposal is given in Council.

This scrutiny process is a complete reversal of traditional law making procedures within the UK. Parliament cannot amend the legislation once the Council of Ministers has formally approved the proposal. In this sense, there is no equivalent to the Standing Committee stage procedure which, because it gives members an opportunity to propose amendments to a piece of domestic legislation, is an integral part to the legislative process in the House of Commons. Though there are two European Standing Committees in existence, their function is not to propose amendments to the legislative proposal, but only to debate its merits. Thus, Parliament cannot amend European legislation. Its sole task is limited to the passing of enabling legislation which has the specific purpose of incorporating the secondary Community legislation (directives) into domestic law.

In his article European Community Legislation before the House of Commons[2] Professor T. St J. N. Bates[3] made the rather astute observation of what the role of the Westminster Parliament is today in the European legislative process. He said:[4]

> "To put it in more negative terms Westminster, in respect of the European Community, finds itself in the unaccustomed and uneasy, although perhaps not unique role of lobbyist"

This is an accurate statement of the relationship between Parliament and the Community. The point Professor Bates is making relates to the legislative process within the Community. Given the wide consultation procedure undertaken by the Commission with a variety of pressure groups in the pre-legislative stage, Parliament (along with other national parliaments) is just one part of this consultation process. Therefore, scrutiny is part of this lobbying process. This is why Parliament must have effective procedures to influence the minister before he goes to give final approval in the Council.

Establishment of the Select Committee

Prior to the UK's accession to the Commuinty in 1973, the House of Commons voted to appoint a Select Committee with the Terms of Reference:[5]

> "...to consider procedures for scrutiny of proposals for European Community Secondary Legislation".

---

2   Statute Law Review 1990, pp. 109-134.
3   Clerk of Tynwald, Secretary to the House of Keys and Counsel to the Speaker.
4   See n. 2 above.
5   Official Journal Thursday 21 December 1972.

The Committee was under the Chairmanship of Sir John Foster (and is more commonly referred to as the Foster Committee).[6] The Committee subsequently published two detailed reports[7] which made a number of recomendations as to how the House of Commons might be kept informed of legislative developments in the Community and how it might develop an effective machinery for the scrutiny of proposals for legislation.

The main recomendation of the Foster Committee was to establish a Select Committee on European Community Secondary Legislation.[8] Its Terms of Reference were such that it only performed the role of scrutiny and made no comment on the merits of a proposal.[9] However, during the 1988-89 session, the Select Committee on Procedure undertook the first major inquiry into the operation of the scrutiny system. This was prompted by the changes in the European legislative process brought about by the Single European Act 1986 and by the ever increasing volume of legislation emerging from the Community. Many of the recomendations of the Report[10] were accepted by the Conservative government in its response[11] and were put into effect at the beginning of the 1990-91 session. Today, these recomendations still form the foundation of the scrutiny arrangements in the House of Commons and will be analysed in this and the forthcoming chapters.

The central issue for the Foster Committee was to put forward a framework for a scrutiny process that would give the Commons the greatest influence in the European legislative process. Legislation in the European Community is introduced primarily by regulations[12] and directives.[13] The main disadvantage of law making by regulation is that in essence it is law making by decree. Once agreed by the Council it is binding immediately. The impact on scrutiny is clear. First, legislation is binding without any Parliamentary approval being necessary, and secondly, the process of agreeing the legislation is not transparent. In these circumstances it is impossible to have any effective democratic control over the minister.

Mr Peter Shore MP, a member of the Foster Committee, argued that regulations were an undemocratic and therefore an unacceptable method of law making. He argued that if there was to be legislation made in the European

---

6   A similar committee was appointed at the same time by the House of Lords with similar terms of reference under the chairmanship of Lord Mowbray-King.

7   See HC 143 and HC 463, 1972-73 session.

8   This Committee is now more commonly referred to as the Scrutiny Committee.

9   Originally the Terms of Reference were set out in Standing Order 105 but these have been amended over the years and are now found in S.O. 127.

10   See HC 622-1 (Session 1988-89).

11   See Cm 108.

12   Regulations are made by the Council of Ministers or the Commission and are of general application. A regulation is binding in its entirety and directly applicable in all Member States.

13   Directives are issued by the Council or the Commission which are binding as to the result to be achieved but which leave the choice of form and methods to the Member States.

Community, the most appropriate method would be through directives.[14] His argument was based on the fact that directives are implemented by the national parliament, by means of some form of enabling legislation. Mr Shore saw this as the vital element of control which is lacking in the implementation of regulations.

Mr Shore makes a valid argument. His observation that European legislation is not subject to the same rigorous scrutiny as domestic legislation is an extremely important point which is still relevant today. However, his secondary argument that directives afford Parliament greater control over the legislation emanating from Europe than that available in respect of regulations, has consistently proved to be flawed.

In their practical effect, there is *no* significant difference between a regulation and a directive. The national parliament in its implementation of the directive cannot change the contents of the directive. Any implementing legislation which is inconsistent with the directive will be a breach of the Treaty and leave the Member State open to an action in the Court of Justice. If the action is successful, the Member State must then change the implementing legislation. All Parliament can do, is to put the directive into force and not alter its content. The *only* control available, as the Foster Committee recognised, is to influence the minister through scrutiny of both the draft regulation and directive before final approval in Council is given. Parliament's role is therefore reduced to that of a mere pressure group lobbying to make its views and concerns known to the minister who will relay them to his counterparts in the Council.

Future developments

Since the Procedure Committee Report of 1989, the UK government has signed the Maastricht Treaty and brought forward the necessary legislation in the form of the European Communities (Amendment) Act 1993 to implement the Treaty provisions in the UK.

This Treaty imposes many changes but perhaps most importantly alters the decision making process within the Community. Most notably it is the co-decision procedure[15] which will have the greatest impact on scrutiny within Parliament. The increased role for the European Parliament in the legislative process will slow-up the scrutiny process by delaying the depositing of documents in the House until after the European Parliament has proposed any amendments and the Council of Ministers has then voted on them. The Scrutiny Committee has recognised these potential problems and produced an initial report highlighting the challenges it will now face.[16] A more detailed discussion of these issues is found in chapter 6.

---

14   See HC 463-II (Session 1972-73), Second Report from the Select Committee on European Community Secondary Legislation pp. 173-175, paras. 723-725.

15   As set out in Article 189b of the amended Treaty of Rome.

16   See HC 99 (Session 1993-94), First Special Report from the Select Committee on European Legislation *Scrutiny after Maastricht.*

FUNCTIONS OF THE SELECT COMMITTEE

It is possible to identify three different functions of the Select Committee:

(i)   The Select Committee as an information and access point;
(ii)   Fulfilling the requirements of the Standing Orders; and
(iii) Scrutinising the executive.

These will now be examined in turn.

The Select Committee as an information and access point

All proposals for secondary legislation come before the Committee and they produce, very rapidly it must be added, a report on the particular document. On average, the Committee have a turnover of at least one document per week. The agenda of the Committee is a short horizon because in most instances, a document is not "hanging around" and waiting for a draft report to be produced detailing its main provisions. This can be contrasted with the work of the Select Committee in the House of Lords. Prior to a report, the Committee conducts an in depth investigation into the document and the wider issues concerning it. In effect, the Lords look at the policy considerations and the merits of the particular document. This is the main difference between the two Committees. Not only does the Standing Order setting out the Terms of Reference prevent investigation of the merits of the document, but so does the time factor within which the Committee works. Yet the Committee does inform the House of the basics of the proposal. It provides the House with a description of the document, indicates its significance and gives the House an understanding which it will not receive from any other source. This allows for an informed debate to take place either in one of the two Standing Committees or occasionally in the Chamber itself.

The Committee is also an access point for the entire Commons as it is constantly in contact with persons who are related to the committee system within the House both here and overseas. Thus, the Committee liaises on behalf of the House with other interested parties to exchange information and discuss legislative developments. However, evidence received from MPs and officials in the Commons suggests that this liaison could be carried out more effcectively if relationships with committees in other Parliaments and other organisations (most notably the European Parliament and the Commission) were put on a formal footing. This cementing of the relationship would allow for easier access to and exchange of information and also recognise that the legislative procedure is really a European one with all Member States contributing to the decision making process.

Fulfilling the Standing Orders

The second identifiable area of activity for the Select Committee is carrying out what Standing Order 127 asks the Committee to do (see pp.36-37 below for a more detailed discussion of this). This is partly informative, and partly acting as a "burglar alarm". If an important document comes along, the House will want to know something about it. It as at this stage that the alarm bells go off and the Committee will issue a report and then recommend what is to be debated and engage the next stage of the scrutiny system.

Scrutinising the executive

The third and final area of activity which involves a substantial amount of the Select Committees time is actually policing the relationship between the House and the government on European matters. This is because there are a whole series of agreements and understandings on how scrutiny is handled.[17] If the Committee discover that some agreement has been reached without their knowledge then they will demand an explanation. If this explanation is unsatisfactory, the Committee will pursue the government until it is given a good reason why Parliament was *not* consulted.

In the same way as the Committee constantly monitor how rapidly documents are deposited in the Vote Office for MPs to read, the Committee pursue very energetically the government's non-consultation of a document with them. This is essential, as any circumventing by the government of the views of the Committee will render ineffectual scrutiny by Parliament. If a document takes so long to arrive at the Vote Office either because it has been agreed in the Council before it is deposited, or if negotiations have progressed to an advanced stage then there is no point in Parliament trying to influence the minister who has already made up his mind. Any scrutiny in these circumstances will be post-legislative and break the terms of Standing Order 127, which states that the Committee will consider European Community documents which are *proposals for legislation*. Once agreed to by the minister in Council, the document is no longer a proposal. If this agreement comes *before* Parliament has had its say via scrutiny by the Committee and debate in the Standing Committee then no effective scrutiny has taken place.

THE POLITICAL, LEGAL AND CONSTITUTIONAL CONTEXT OF THE SCRUTINY PROCESS

Any analysis of the scrutiny arrangements in the House of Commons must begin with a review of the political, legal and constitutional context in which they are set. The starting point for such an analysis is the fact that European legislation is almost exclusively initiated by an executive organisation i.e. the Commission.[18] Most important to this arrangement, is the fact that the

---

17   The most important of these are the Resolution of the House of October 24 1990 and the agreement by the government to make time to debate all those documents which the Committee recommends for debate.

18   See Appendix 2 for a full explanation of the structure of the European Union.

United Kingdom Parliament has *no* formal relationship with the Commission and therefore *no direct control* over legislative proposals emanating from the Commission. Furthermore, the United Kingdom has, as a condition of its membership of the European Union, bound itself to accept the collective decision making and authority of a legislative body (the Council of Ministers)[19] only one of whose fifteen members is accountable to the House of Commons.

The difficulty facing Parliament is clear. Whilst the House may, by changes in its own internal procedures, find ways of increasing the influence and authority it commands over the government and European legislation, it cannot by such means increase that authority nor seek to claw back powers which it has ceded by the Treaty. For example, the extension of the use of Qualified Majority Voting in the Council of Ministers by the Single European Act 1986[20] has placed constraints on the Houses' ability to scrutinise European legislation. These can and have been alleviated but not removed by changes in the practices of the House. These very restrictions were recognised by the Foster Committee Report in 1973. The Report stated that scrutiny would need to develop in parallel with the Community. However, though the House has never throughout our membership of the European Community and now the European Union,[21] ever realistically expected to exercise total accountability in relation to minister's prospective actions in the Council of Ministers, it has *always* demanded explanations and justifications after the event.

The Commons is trying to accommodate two competing principles. That is the legal principle of the primacy of EC law with the constitutional requirement that a minister's primary responsibility is to Parliament. Influencing both of these are political factors – namely that the government is acutely aware of its accountability to a sceptical electorate at home, but also that it cannot appear obstructive in Council. Today, the European legislative process of which scrutiny is a part, can best be described as a balancing act that is becoming ever increasingly more difficult to maintain. Essentially this means that effective scrutiny by the Commons cannot persist if developments in the EC, and in particular the extension of Qualified Majority Voting, continue to occur. The time will undoubtedly arrive when this development will make scrutiny by domestic parliament's irrelevant. Majority voting means that a minister following Parliament's opinion on a legislative proposal can be outvoted in Council. In these circumstances he cannot be held accountable for a decision which he did not support. Scrutiny is malapropos. However, this stage has not yet been reached and Parliament retains some influence. In the next section, the Standing Orders will be examined to establish how they facilitate the Commons objectives in the scrutiny process.

---

19   *Ibid.*
20   See Articles 148-154 Treaty of Rome as amended.
21   Since the Maastricht Treaty the name changed from European Community to European Union to reflect the greater cooperation that takes place between Member States in foreign and judicial affairs.

TERMS OF REFERENCE

The Select Committee on European Legislation is the central element in the arrangements made by the House to keep itself informed of predominantly legislative matters which will be coming before the Communities' Council of Ministers, and enable it where appropriate to seek to influence the position of UK ministers at the Council meeting.

Although the Scrutiny Committee has a pivotal role in the arrangements for examining European legislation in the House, it is important to remember that ministers' European responsibilities are an important aspect of their over-all departmental responsibilities. Besides the *specific* arrangements to be detailed below, all the usual methods of holding ministers to account are available to Members. Therefore, these scrutiny arrangements are *in addition to*, and not a substitute for opportunities such as Parliamentary questions, ministerial correspondence and adjournment debates. Any member can also raise European issues at departmental question time and the Departmental Select Committees will also investigate European issues.[22]

Working arrangements

The Select Committee itself consists of sixteen members who are nominated by the House[23] for the duration of the whole Parliament. From their number the Committee will elect a Chairman.[24] The Committee normally meets once a week on a Wednesday afternoon when the House is sitting. The Committee has power to meet when the House is in recess but rarely exercises this power, which undoubtedly has an impact on the scrutiny process. Because of the occasional fast moving nature of the legislative process it is possible for documents to be agreed in Council before the House has had an opportunity to debate it.[25]

Standing Orders

The Committee is appointed under Standing Order No.127. This provides for the Committee to examine European Community Documents and:

> "(a) to report on the legal and political importance of each such document and, where it considers appropriate, to report also on the reasons for its opinion and on any matters of principle policy and law which may be affected;

---

22   A majority of European issues are dealt with by the Department of Trade and Indus-try and Department of Agriculture Fisheries and Food. Over 60% of legislation affects these two departments. See also Chapter 5.

23   The members are nominated on a motion moved by the Government Whip with the number of members from each party having been agreed by "the usual channels".

24   The present chairman is The Hon. Mr. Jimmy Hood MP who was elected in June 1992.

25   See chapter 4 where the timing of debates is examined in more detail.

(b) to make recomendations for the further consideration of any such document pursuant to Standing Order 102 (European Standing Committees) and;

(c) to consider any issue arising upon any such document or group of documents.

The Standing Order was amended in October 1990 to allow the Committee to consider Community Documents *other* than those which are specific proposals for legislation. In its response[26] to the Fourth Report from the Select Committee on Procedure[27] the government stated that it was:[28]

> "...prepared to propose an amendment of the Terms of Reference which would give the Committee scope for considering, for example, consultative documents embodying important proposals for the future development of the Community, and for examining horizontal proposals."

However, this extended function would continue to be related to specific community documents deposited in Parliament rather than involving free-standing investigations of broad policy issues which might tend to duplicate the work of other Committees. The government is as reluctant today as ever to extend the Terms of Reference beyond those proposed by the Foster Committee in 1973.[29] The Committee is therefore best described as a reactive Committee. Scrutiny is its first responsibility. Policy discussion and consideration lies solely within the remit of the relevant Departmental Select Committee.[30]

Legal and Political Importance

The key phrase of Standing Order 127 is:

> "to report its opinion on the *legal and political importance* of each such document" (my italics).

---

26   See Cm1081.

27   See HC 622-1 (Session 1988-89).

28   See Cm1081 p. 1.

29   In a letter to the Chairman of the Select Committee on European Legislation, the then Leader of the House, John Wakeham, wrote that he was prepared to release documents which were not covered by the Terms of Reference and to consider any requests for *ad hoc* debates to be held on these documents. See Appendix 29 HC 622-I (1988-89).

30   On 17 March 1994 the Select Committee met to take evidence from parties interested in the issue of road safety. At first sight such an evidence session may be regarded as one where policy issues on road safety are being discussed. However, the chairman pointed out at the start of the session that the purpose of it was to establish from experts in the field what they thought were desirable measures to take and then it was up to the Committee to look at the competence issues which are related to documents which are, or will be subject to scrutiny on proposals for European legislation. Thus the evidence session was one of obtaining information to enable the Committee to carry out its scrutiny task more effectively when looking at proposals for road safety legislation.

The Select Committee carries out this principal role by sifting the Community documents deposited in the House by the government and then makes recommendations as to whether they should be debated and on their legal or political importance. The sifting process is vital to the efficient functioning of the Select Committee. The Committee has before it an average of 900-1000 documents per year. Obviously, the detailed scrutiny of each in turn is not possible given the limited meeting time of the Committee and the other demands on the Member's time. The sifting process carried out by the Clerk and his assistants, to select those documents which have legal or political importance, and then for the Committee to scrutinise them and recommend further debate by the House in appropriate circumstances, ensures an efficient use of the limited time available.

For each document (except the most minor) members of the Committee are provided with an advisory brief drawn up by the Committee's staff.[31] This advisory brief is designed to give members *all* the necessary information which they will need in order to enable them to reach a decision on the legal and political importance of the document. The brief concludes with a recommendation on this point.

There are *no* fixed criteria against which the Committee must assess and decide what actually constitutes legal and political importance. Each case must be judged exclusively on its merits. All those documents which the Committee has adjudged not to be of legal and political importance at a particular meeting (this is usually the majority of documents considered at the weekly meeting – approximately two thirds) are listed in a single paragraph at the end of the relevant report. Examples of such documents include *inter alia*:

* routine Common Commercial Tariff and Trade measures
* factual Commission reports
* proposals for consolidation of Community legislation
* minor Commission amendments to legislative proposals

Documents are reported to the House as raising questions of legal or political importance if they deal with matters which the Committee has adjudged that Members of the House would wish to be specifically informed about. For example, *legal importance* may include such things as a doubtful legal base, a questionable assertion of competence on the part of the Commission to propose legislation or the impact of a proposal on existing law. *Political importance* on the other hand, may relate to the sensitivity of a proposal's subject matter or the cost involved in implementation. In these instances, the Committee reports to the House, usually in some detail, about the contents of the document, the government's position, its own reasons for considering that the document raises issues of legal or political importance, and, where it considers appropriate, reactions of those groups or individuals affected by the proposal.

---

31   See Appendix 3 for details of the Committees staff and working methods.

PROVISION OF DOCUMENTS TO THE SELECT COMMITTEE

Official texts

The official text is the final version of the legislative proposal as submitted by the Commission to the Council of Ministers. This will be the document that is debated in the Council and perhaps most importantly from the Select Committee's perspective, it will be the document that is the basis of scrutiny.

It is the lack of this official text which delays scrutiny. In its 1996 report,[32] the Select Committee listed 75 documents which it considered to be of legal or political importance that came before the Select Committee without an official text between 17 July 1995 and 18 July 1996.[33] It also identified a further 222 items that were of lesser importance which were also scrutinised without an official text.[34] In all these cases scrutiny was conducted on the basis of an unofficial text, that is to say a preliminary text published by the Commission. This however, is not ideal because the final version may be different from this preliminary text and what's more the unofficial text cannot be deposited in the House or made public.

The blame for this delay lies essentially with the Commission for providing documents late and the Council for accepting them. This means that the Council, working to a very tight deadline, will want to approve the document as quickly as possible. The net effect of this is that scrutiny will suffer. That is to say, final agreement will be given in Council *before* the Select Committee has completed its task. This is unacceptable, not to say undemocratic.

How can this situation be changed? Obviously, efficient provision of documents in the correct language is the starting point. Anything less makes scrutiny ineffective. However, this itself may not be enough in that the Select Committee is still reliant upon the goodwill of other institutions, in particular the government. Thus the Select Committee has decided to take matters into its own hands. The Committee's Terms of Reference require it "to examine European Community Documents" and to report to the House. This task cannot be done without the appropriate documents.

There are two steps that have been taken by the Select Committee. Firstly, it has called for a four week period to allow for scrutiny between the deposition of the official text and the meeting of the Council of Ministers. This has been endorsed by the government and they are putting it forward at the current Inter-Governmental Conference (IGC). Secondly, and perhaps most significantly, the Committee has taken decisive action. As from the beginning of the 1996-97 Parliamentary session the Scrutiny Committee will not clear a document when no official text has been received. Furthermore, they will expect ministers to impose the scrutiny reserve until the official text has been deposited. Only where the minister believes a delay will damage UK interests

---

32   See HC 51-xxvii (Session 1994-95).

33   *Ibid.* p. lxv, para. 222.

34   *Ibid.* para. 223.

can he or she give agreement, but this must be justified to the House immediately (for more detail on this see p. 49 below).

This development has brought scrutiny to the fore. *The Times* on August 20 1996, ran this story under the headline "MPs plan boycott of European laws to confront Brussels". Sir Teddy Taylor MP, a renowned Eurosceptic, hailed this as a "symbolic victory for the British citizen", and a former chairman of the Select Committee, Nigel Spearing MP, is quoted as saying "We have been pushed too far. It is a mixture of incompetence by ministers and contempt by Brussels for national parliaments. We are not putting up with it."

The issue was also the subject of an investigation by the BBC political affairs programme *On the Record* on October 20 1996. The programme highlighted the very issues discussed above and also provided some interesting anecdotal evidence. In particular one reason given for documents arriving late is that they were sent by second class post or to the wrong address! This is a sad reflection of the state of government today. However, the serious point is inescapable, if documents or information are not supplied on time to the Committee, the whole House is let down. At present it is too early to form any conclusion on whether the Select Committee's tactics will work. The Select Committee feel that they have no other option. What they are doing is protecting Parliament's right to scrutinise the executive and for this they must be applauded.

Explanatory Memorandum

The Explanatory Memorandum (EM) should be provided by the lead government department within 10 days of the date of the deposit of the official text in the Vote Office. The aim of the Explanatory Memorandum is to furnish the Committee with the government's view of the proposed legislation and how it may effect other domestic legislation. However, this part of the scrutiny process illustrates the wider problems faced by the Committee. That is, the reliance of the Committee on the cooperation and goodwill of the government.

If the government delays in the production of the Explanatory Memorandum or it is insufficient in detail then the scrutiny process grinds to a halt. If, as often happens, the legislative process in the Community is fast moving, then Parliament may be rushed into a debate on an important piece of legislation before it has all the necessary facts, or more alarmingly, hold no debate at all. The blame for this lies firmly at the feet of the government department involved. One recent example illustrates this very point. The Committee requested further information on document 6079/95 from the minister on 17 May 1995. He replied on 6 November 1995 that he wished to approve the measure in Council on 6 November 1995. The result no debate and no scrutiny.

Though the government is committed to providing the Explanatory Memorandum as early as possible,[35] this situation is regularly criticised and mem-

---

35   The governments commitment to provide an Explanatory Memorandum as soon as practicable is set out in the governments observations of April 1987, Cm123, on the Second Special Report from the Select Committee on European Legislation HC 264 (Session 1985-86).

bers of the Committee have informed the author of their wish to see this process formalised in the Standing Orders of the House. The recent report of the Select Committee tackled this very issue. They were concerned that the scrutiny process was being held up further by delays in lead departments providing an EM. For example, document no. 8179/95. The English version was received on 7 July 1995 and deposited on 20 July 1995. However, the EM was not received until 9 February 1996. This is unacceptable. The government has pledged to ensure departments respond promptly to this issue. However, the same pledge was made in 1986 and appears to have had little impact. The government must now act firmly. It is within their power to ensure that delays for whatever reason do not occur.

Un-numbered Explanatory Memorandum

There are also special arrangements which apply in the case of fast moving proposals. In such an instance the lead department will provide an un-numbered Explanatory Memorandum based on the information available about the likely content of the formal proposal, from the Commission's preliminary text. This will stand as the main document for the Committee for scrutiny purposes, until it is deposited formally, where it will be treated in the usual way. Once again though, it is the quick response of the government which is essential to the effectiveness of the scrutiny process.

However, if the document is still under discussion in the Council of Ministers it is difficult to ascertain how full an explanation the government has given. This is due in great part to the secrecy which surrounds negotiations within the Council. A minister will be reluctant to give full information on a legislative proposal if negotiations are still in progress because he will not want to reveal his negotiating position, given the "horse-trading" which takes place in Council. In this event, there is the risk that the un-numbered Explanatory Memorandum will be inaccurate by the time the final proposal is decided upon by the Council of Ministers. This is potentially damaging for the scrutiny process as the Committee will have to duplicate their work and delay their final recommendation on the document before them.

The relationship with the government

The power of the House of Commons to influence Community legislation depends of course upon its control over ministers. From the moment of accession to the Community the House of Commons has asserted its right to be informed about proposals for Community legislation and debate them if it thinks fit. This can only be done if the Committee is in possession of all relevant information.

As is evident from the above discussion, the success or failure of the scrutiny system depends upon the adequate and efficient provision of information to the Select Committee. This very issue has been regularly highlighted by the Select Committee since its inception and was brought once again to the government's attention by the Select Committee in its recent report. The current position relates only to the government providing information on "legislative proposals".

In 1973, the government undertook to supply the Select Committee with copies of the documents in English, within forty-eight hours of having received them. However as the Procedure Committee noted in its Report:[36]

> "The English text of a European document is usually deposited in the House about a month after its formal adoption by the Commission followed within a fortnight by an Explanatory Memorandum from the responsible government department."

In evidence which was given to the Select Committee on Procedure in 1989, the Chairman of the Scrutiny Committee stressed the need for early notification of legislative proposals and the increased availability of documents which would provide early warning of future legislative initiatives.[37] He said:

> "...the earlier it can alert the House to a proposal of potential legal or political importance, the greater is the likelihood that the House will be able to influence its outcome."

The most effective way in which this could be achieved would be for the Select Committee to receive Commission documents which give details of the legislative proposals as early as possible, and preferably when the Commission is at its consultative stage. In its response[38] the government undertook to provide the Select Committee with the forward programme of the Presidency of the Council of Ministers, and has done so. In addition the Commission has provided its three month forward programme to national parliaments.[39]

Both these actions are positive steps but availability of other documents is still hampered by the inability of Parliament to contact the Commission formally. The UK Parliament has no direct relationship with the Commission or any other of the institutions in the Community. As well as having no formal input into the legislative process, the Select Committee is reliant on the Executive to provide it with all the necessary documents which it needs to perform its task of scrutiny. The examples given above illustrate that to this day, this issue has not been resolved to the Select Committee's satisfaction and the Executive, still the pivotal player in the scrutiny process falls short in its obligations to the Committee.

---

36   See HC 622-I p. viii, para. 6.
37   See HC 622-2 (1988-89) pp. 52-53, paras. 107-112.
38   See Cm 1081, 1990, p. 2.
39   In its Report HC 622-I, para. 23, the Procedure Committee also identified an internal Commission document, known as the repertoire as a document which would be of benefit to the Select Committee. This document gives a detailed list of pending Commission proposals, including the legal basis of the proposal.

OPTIONS FOR THE COMMITTEE AFTER DELIBERATION

For a document adjudged to raise questions of legal or political importance, the Committee then has to decide whether the document raises issues of sufficient importance to justify its further consideration by one of the two European Standing Committees[40]or exceptionally, by the Chamber itself. In reaching its decision, the Committee will want to consider exactly what specific Parliamentary consideration of the document would achieve. For example, it would be an inefficient use of Parliamentary time to recommend for debate a proposal which the Commission has, in the face of public opinion, decided to modify substantially, or to recommend the debate of a highly technical document which though important could not sustain an informed debate. On the other hand, there would be a very strong argument for debating a document where, for instance, major issues are raised and where there is strong opposition inside or outside Parliament to the government's negotiating position.

It will occasionally be the case that a document is considered to raise questions of legal or political importance, but the Committee is unclear as to whether a recommendation for debate would be appropriate. In this instance, it is the practice for the Committee to recommend "no debate at this stage". It will then attempt to seek further information to enable it to reach a firm view.

There are other documents raising questions of legal and political importance, not of sufficient importance to justify a debate solely on it, but worthy of reference in a wider debate in a relevant policy area. The Committee will indicate this fact in its report. However, the effectiveness of this inquiry will depend exclusively on the debate of this wider policy issue. If this is not debated then it follows that the document is not debated. Once again it is the reliance on the government which is the key. The decision lies with the government business managers and the "usual channels" if there is to be a debate in the Chamber, and what the timing of this debate is to be. Likewise in the Standing Committee, it is the government which decides the timing of the debate and on the motion to be debated. Once the matter comes back to the Chamber from the Standing Committee a similar motion is moved by the government. However, these proceedings are purely formal and the government do not permit further time for debate.[41]

EXERTING INFLUENCE OVER MINISTERS

The Resolution of the House 30 October 1980

Prior to 1980 formal control of the minister was not enshrined anywhere within the procedures of the House. The ability to influence was dependent

---

40   Appointed under S.O. 102.
41   See Chapter 4 for a full discussion on the work of the Standing Committees on European legislation.

on the goodwill of the government of the day. Though the government rarely abused its position, the Procedure Committee's Report of 1978[42] recommended that the government give a formal undertaking to consult Parliament for its opinion whenever the Committee has indicated that a debate needed to be held. This right was enshrined in a Resolution of the House, dated October 30 1980, in the following terms:[43]

RESOLUTION OF THE HOUSE 30 OCTOBER 1980

"That in the opinion of this House, no Minister of the Crown should give agreement in the Council of Ministers to any proposal for European legislation which has been recommended by the Select Committee on European legislation for consideration by the House before the House has given it that consideration unless-

(a) that Committee has indicated that agreement need not be withheld, or

(b) the Minister concerned decides that for special reasons agreement should not be withheld ;

and in the latter case the Minister should, at the first opportunity thereafter, explain his decision to the House.[44]

This Resolution by the House of Commons, recognised the basic precondition of effective scrutiny. That is the requirement that the House will be able to express its views on Community legislative proposals *before* they have been approved in the Council of Ministers.

Perhaps the most controversial aspect of this Resolution was contained in (b), i.e. where the minister decides for *special reasons* that consent need not be withheld. The Resolution itself gave no guidance as to what these special reasons will be. This was left to the government to define without any debate within Parliament. In giving evidence to the Select Committee on European legislation,[45] the then Leader of the House, the Right Honourable John Biffen MP, indicated a number of factors which would influence a minister's decision in such circumstances:[46]

(a) the fact that the Committee may sometimes indicate when they first consider a document that their recomendation for debate need not delay adoption. They may also agree at a later stage to allow adoption of a document before the scrutiny process has been completed;

---

42   See HC 588-1 (Session 1977-78).

43   Official Report (fifth series). Parliamentary debates (1979-80); Vol. 991, Col. 838.

44   An undertaking to substantially the same effect has been given by the government in the House of Lords, but it has not been embodied in a resolution of that House.

45   See HC 527 (Session 1983-84) First Special Report from the Select Committee on European Legislation.

46   *Ibid* p. 3, Q.5, para. 5 of written answers by Lord Privy Seal to questions submitted by the Committee.

(b) the need to avoid a legal vacuum;

(c) the desirability of permitting a particular measure of benefit to the United Kingdom to come into question as soon as possible;

(d) the difficulty, particularly if the negotiations in the Community have been difficult or protracted, of putting a late reserve on a measure which will either have little effect on the United Kingdom or which is likely to be of benefit to the United Kingdom.

The late reserve referred to in (d) means that if it is likely that the Council will attempt to adopt a document on which, exceptionally, scrutiny has not been completed and there are no special reasons for adoption to take place, the normal practice is to place a Parliamentary reserve on the document. In such circumstances, other Member States accept that the proposal should not be adopted until Parliament has completed the scrutiny process. It is, however, accepted that the reserve will be lifted as soon as possible.

Following the Select Committee Report of the 1983-84 Session the government undertook to draw the criteria in (a)-(d) to the attention of all government departments. In their Fourth Report, the Select Committee on Procedure indicated that they had no evidence to suggest that as they are currently defined, the criteria have been improperly invoked by the government departments.[47]

The Leader of the House in his evidence of 16 May 1984, further suggested that he was of the opinion, and that he would advise all government departments accordingly, of the need to interpret criteria (a)-(d) strictly. This need for a more restrictive approach to the adoption of documents prior to the scrutiny process being completed was highlighted after the implementation of the Single European Act in 1986. The increase in the use of Majority Voting by the Council of Ministers eroded the power of individual member countries to block legislation. Given the absence of mandating by the House of Commons, the scrutiny of legislative proposals prior to adoption in the Council is the only influence which Parliament has. This must be protected vigorously if Parliamentary democracy is not to be undermined.

Within the United Kingdom, it is Parliament which ultimately controls the Executive and the Executive is reliant on Parliament for its power. But in the day to day exercise of authority, especially in the context of the European Union it is the Executive which really yields this power without too much constraint from Parliament – except by the Resolution of the House which affords some guarantee of debate and scrutiny.

The Single European Act and the Scrutiny Reserve

The introduction by the Single European Act of the cooperation procedure introduced a complication not envisaged when the 1980 Resolution was agreed to. Under this new procedure, legislative proposals to which this proce-

---

47   See HC 622-1 (Session 1988-89) p. ix, para. 9.

dure applied, were sent to the European Parliament for debate twice instead of once. Where the cooperation procedure applied to a proposal[48] the Council (having consulted the European Parliament) adopted what is known as a "common position" on the proposal.[49] This was then sent to the European Parliament, which could propose amendments to the common position. It was then up to the Commission to decide whether to incorporate these amendments in its "re-examined proposal" to the Council. The implications for scrutiny by this procedure are clear. Any debate which was delayed post the adoption of the common position, though in compliance with the strict terms of the Resolution – i.e. Parliament looked at the proposal prior to final adoption by the Council (but after the European Parliament had proposed its amendments) – had very little prospect of exerting any significant influence on the final outcome because of the amendments which the European Parliament may then propose, which could substantially alter the proposal.

The effect of this procedure, was to diminish Parliament's influence. Any debate delayed post common position and prior to final adoption by the Council could not take into account further amendments by the European Parliament when the proposal went back to them for the so called "second reading". Parliament could not exert any pressure over a minister and ask him not to agree to an amendment proposed by the European Parliament on this "second reading". The debate would have already taken place on the basis of the common position adopted by the Council. The only possibility would be to hold a second debate. However, the use of Parliamentary time to debate an amended proposal, the bulk of which has already been scrutinised was viewed as being a waste of Parliamentary time and should only be carried out in rare circumstances.[50]

The 1980 Resolution and the subsequent statement by the Leader of the House to the Select Committee on European legislation outlining what the "special reasons"[51] are for agreeing to a proposal prior to a debate represented the cornerstone of the scrutiny process. However, following the developments of the Single European Act, most notably in the sphere of Qualified Majority Voting it was acknowledged by all parties involved in the scrutiny process that these provisions were now inadequate.[52] Government undertakings were given in respect of the changes, the most notable being to treat "agreement in the Council of Ministers"[53] as including adoption of a common position under the cooperation procedure. This would thereby give more certainty to

---

48   Article 149 Treaty of Rome.
49   The Common position is adopted by a Qualified Majority Vote in the Council.
50   See HC 400 (Session 1985-86) pp. xv-xvii.
51   See n. 46, at p. 44.
52   See HC 264 (Session 1985-86) First special Report from the Select Committee on European Legislation *The Single European Act and Parliamentary Scrutiny*, pp. 9-11. See also HC 622-1 (Session 1988-89) p. xviii, para. 42. Fourth Report from the Select Committee On Procedure - The Scrutiny of European Legislation. See also n. 37 at p.42.
53   See Resolution of the House 30 October 1980

debates in the House as no further amendments would be agreed to by a minister until scrutiny of the proposal arising from the common position had been completed. This would therefore ensure Parliamentary control over the minister as Parliament would have had its say on the legislative proposal, and perhaps most importantly what further amendments by the European Parliament it would be prepared to accept.

Given the importance of the changes to the scrutiny procedure it was felt that the government undertakings should be made formal and this was recommended by the Procedure Committee in their Fourth Report.[54] They further recommended[55] that the minister should only give consent to a legislative proposal prior to the completion of the scrutiny process if there are "compelling reasons" to do so. They were of the opinion that the presumption should, in the absence of these compelling reasons, always be on the side of withholding consent if scrutiny is not complete. With this in mind, the Procedure Committee "sharpened up" the special reasons outlined by the Leader of the House on 16 May 1984.[56] This included:[57]

(a) the need to avoid a legal vacuum should be justified on the grounds of clear necessity and not merely of administrative convenience;
(b) before voting to agree to a measure considered by the Government to be of benefit to the United Kingdom prior to scrutiny, Ministers should, as far as practicable in the time available, take steps to satisfy themselves (i) that the House would be likely to approve the measure if time permitted a debate and (ii) that the United Kingdom's interests would be materially prejudiced if consent were withheld; and
(c) in assessing the difficulty of placing a late scrutiny reserve on a measure, Ministers should be guided by the likelihood that if consent were withheld, the passage of the measure concerned, or of some other measure, might be jeopardised to the detriment of the United Kingdoms interests.

It is evident from these recommendations that the Procedure Committee along with members of the Scrutiny Committee were eager to ensure Parliamentary accountability was not undermined by the Executive, i.e. ministers taking decisions without consultation or debate, and by Parliament being totally excluded from the decision making process with regards to legislation which would be equally enforceable in the United Kingdom as any other domestic legislation.

The Resolution of the House 24 October 1990

As previously stated the Procedure Committee recommended an amendment to the Resolution of the House of 30 October 1980. This amendment would

---

54   See HC 622-1 (Session 1988-89) para. 42.
55   *Ibid* para. 32.
56   See n. 45, at p. 44.
57   See HC 622-1 (Session 1988-89) para. 32.

be designed to reflect Parliament's concerns following the Single European Act 1986 and how power had by virtue of this Act shifted in favour of the Executive at the expense of Parliament.

In its response to the Fourth Report by the Procedure Committee, the government[58] accepted the Committee's recommendation to formalise the undertakings it had given in respect to changes in the scrutiny system. On the 24 October 1990, on a government motion, a Resolution of the House was passed encompassing the Committee's recommendations.[59] The new Resolution (still in force today) reads as follows:

RESOLUTION OF THE HOUSE 24 OCTOBER 1990

(1) No Minister of the Crown should give agreement in the Council of Ministers to any proposal for European Community legislation:
  (a) which is still subject to scrutiny (that is, on which the Select Committee on European Legislation has not completed its scrutiny); or
  (b) which is awaiting consideration by the House (that is, which has been recommended by the Select Committee for consideration pursuant to Standing Order No. 102 (European Standing Committees) but in respect of which the House has not come to a Resolution, either on a Resolution reported by a European Standing Committee or otherwise);
(2) In this Resolution, any reference to agreement to a proposal includes, in the case of a proposal on which the Council acts in cooperation with the European Parliament agreement to a common position
(3) the Minister concerned may, however, give agreement:
  (a) to a proposal which is still subject to scrutiny if he considers that it is confidential, routine or trivial or is substantially the same as a proposal on which scrutiny has already been completed;
  (b) to a proposal which is awaiting consideration by the House if the Select Committee has indicated that agreement need not be withheld pending consideration.
(4) The Minister concerned may also give agreement to a proposal which is still subject to scrutiny or awaiting consideration by the House if he decides that for special reasons agreement should be given; but he should explain his reasons:
  (a) in every such case, to the Select Committee at the first opportunity after reaching his decision; and
  (b) in the case of a proposal awaiting consideration by the House, to the House at the first opportunity after giving agreement.
(5) In relation to any proposal which requires adoption by unanimity, abstention shall, for the purposes of paragraph (4) be treated as giving agreement.

---

58   See Cm 1081, p. 4.
59   Official Report 24 October 1990 (sixth series) Vol. 178; Cols. 399-400.

It is an accurate statement, that this Resolution is the foundation of the scrutiny process today. Its primary objective is to preserve Parliament's ability to influence the minister before agreement is given in Council. The extensive and detailed nature of the Resolution reflects two things in particular. Firstly, the development of the legislative process within the European Community. It acknowledges the increased role for the European Parliament, a role now even greater after the adoption of the Maastricht Treaty. It attempts to accommodate the need for the European Parliament to be part of the legislative process if the so called democratic deficit in the European Community is to be filled.

However, secondly, and perhaps more importantly, the Resolution endeavours to uphold the notion that Parliament is the Sovereign law maker in the United Kingdom. As paragraph (1) illustrates, Parliament will only acquiesce to a proposal for legislation when and if it has debated the matter fully and made the minister aware of its views. Thus, the authority of the minister to give agreement in the Council of Ministers still flows from Parliament via the Select Committee on European Legislation. This is illustrated by the wording of paragraphs (3)(b) and (4) of the Resolution. In particular, in paragraph (4) it is Parliament which has decided on the limited circumstances in which a minister may give approval without first consulting Parliament.

Furthermore, the element of control is still present in this situation as the minister must explain himself at the earliest opportunity. As suggested, by both the Select Committee and the Procedure Committee in its report[60] the minister concerned should make an *oral* statement at the earliest opportunity to explain his special reasons. In some cases, the Procedure Committee stated that the explanation could come in advance of the Council meeting where they are aware a decision will be made and when there is no time for a debate.[61] Whatever the circumstances of the statement, this statement is only the second best option in comparison to debate prior to final approval. However, if the statement is made at the despatch box by the minister concerned, then there is an opportunity to cross-examine the minister not only on the particular document he has agreed to (or is about to agree to) but also on the policy implications of this proposed legislation. In this case, members of the Select Committee can raise the questions which they and other members would have done had there been a full scale debate,[62] prior to adoption in the Council.

The Scrutiny Reserve and the Parliamentary timetable

Ironically, it is the requirements of this Resolution which can potentially have a significant influence on the effectiveness of scrutiny by the Committee. The working methods of the European Union are such that the Presidency of the Council is held by Member States for six monthly periods beginning 1 Janu-

---

60   See HC 622-1 (Session 1988-89) para. 39.

61   *Ibid.*

62   Any debate would be more likely to take place in Standing Committee (See chapter 4), though on occasion will take place on the floor of the House

ary and 1 July respectively. However, because of the pattern of recesses taken by the House, there is a significant difference between the two halves of the year in the opportunities for debate. In an average year, (i.e. one which is not interrupted by a General Election campaign) the number of sitting days in the second half of the year is likely to be appreciably less than in the first half.[63] Unless the government arrange debates with this factor in mind, there will be difficulties in accommodating debates on major legislative proposals put forward by the Member State holding the Presidency.

The working times of the Scrutiny Committee and those of the Council are for a considerable part of the year not synchronised. Whilst Council of Ministers meetings will continue throughout the summer recess, the Committee, though it has power to meet at the time of recess, has not exercised this power for many years. Beside which, even if the Committee did meet during the recess, any debate which it recommended could not take place until after the recess.[64] This has two major implications for the scrutiny process.

Firstly, there is no opportunity to debate the legislative proposal and thereby influence the minister. The best which can be hoped for is for the minister to put a Scrutiny Reserve on the document and the process be completed when the House meets. Secondly, the potential for a legislative "log-jam" is evident. If many proposals have a reserve on them, then there will be many debates to be held, but in a limited time. Such a shortage of time for debate can only reduce the quality of the debate, and the influence which the House will finally have over the minister concerned.

The Procedure Committee recognised this problem which has faced the Scrutiny Committee from day one. In its 1989 Report, the Procedure Committee recommended that during the recess the government should keep to the spirit of the Resolution and where a debate has been recommended it should only in exceptional circumstances invoke as a special reason for giving consent before scrutiny is completed the fact that Parliament will not meet for several weeks.[65] However, the government in its response,[66] though willing to abide by the Resolution, said that it would have to bear in mind the length of the delay before the debate, and decide accordingly. Any such decision would be informed to the Committee as soon as practicable and the reason given.

Despite this potential difficulty with the Resolution, it is not proposed to amend it to allow for the government to have a free hand in decision making at the Council during a recess. This would yield even more power to an already dominant Executive. However, this raises the wider question, beyond the scope of this work, of the working methods of the House of Commons. Perhaps if these were reformed to give more Parliamentary time, there would not be the controversy which surfaces on the occasions of legislation being passed without proper scrutiny.

---

63   In this average year it will be approximately two thirds of the number of days in the first half of the year.
64   The summer recess of 1996 lasted from 19 July to October 14, a full 86 days between meeting. During this time the Committee did not scrutinise any legislative proposals.
65   See HC 622-1 (Session 1988-89) p. xvii, para. 41.
66   See Cm 1081.

The Scrutiny Reserve Resolution after Maastricht

As far as the Select Committee is concerned, the major development introduced by the Maastricht Treaty has been the co-decision procedure, which
builds upon the cooperation procedure introduced by the SEA 1986. The primary effect of this has been to increase further the role of the European Parliament in the legislative process. In particular it has added on a "third reading" stage whereby a Conciliation Committee is convened, whose task it is to
achieve a compromise on the proposed legislation if the Council and Parliament cannot agree on the amendments put forward by the Parliament. This is
in contrast to the position under the cooperation procedure, where, if agreement could not be reached, the proposal would lapse.

This third reading stage occurs after the Select Committee has concluded
its scrutiny on the basis of the original proposal put forward by the Commission and submitted to the Council (who form their common position) and
may have also included scrutiny of the European Parliament's amendments.
The Scrutiny Reserve has operated up this point and it is now up to Council
to decide whether to accept the proposal as amended.

If the Council reject the amendments, the Conciliation Committee is convened. It tries to agree a compromise proposal between the Council and European Parliament within six weeks. If they succeed (as is likely in a matter of
days) a new proposal will emerge which has not been subject to scrutiny by
the Select Committee. The government have refused to allow the Select Committee the opportunity to scrutinise the compromise proposal by not extending the Scrutiny Reserve Resolution to cover the Conciliation Committee
deliberations. Their argument is based on the fact that once the text is agreed
by the Conciliation Committee no amendment to it is permitted. The Council can only accept or reject it, and on this basis with only two clear options
open to it, the other members of the Council would not accept a further delay
to allow for an additional round of scrutiny by the UK Parliament.

The government have refused Parliament the ability to scrutinise potentially important legislation. It is fair to say that only significant or controversial legislation will find itself before the Conciliation Committee. To refuse
scrutiny is, to undermine Parliamentary democracy. In this event, ministers
cannot be held accountable for their actions. This development raises other
complex issues which together with this one will be discussed further in
Chapter 6, where scrutiny after Maastricht is discussed in detail.

CONCLUDING REMARKS

Widening the Terms of Reference

In the course of an interview with the Clerk of the Select Committee on
European Legislation, the question was put to him of how effective he
thought the Committee was at carrying out the task Parliament has asked it to
do? His reply was that it was "totally effective" at carrying out this task. This

response however poses a further question. Should the task of the Select Committee be different? Almost since day one, the Committee has been concerned that its remit has been too narrow.

This concern has heightened since the passage of the Single European Act, primarily due to the increase of Qualified Majority Voting and the enhanced role for the European Parliament which both this Act and the Maastricht Treaty provide for. In this present climate, there is some *prima facie* value in giving the Committee some latitude to base its reports not just exclusively on a specific proposal for legislation. A Committee which could report on trends and developments in broad policy areas would be particularly valuable especially in policy areas which crossed departmental lines.

However, herein lies the potential difficulty which the Committee could face if it adopted this enhanced role. The fact that this Committee is *not* a departmental committee but a Scrutiny Committee suggests that there will be a possible duplication of work amongst the Committees. Yet given the increase in the number of documents which may be of importance in the context of a wider debate on the development of the Community, and in respect of which the House might benefit from a summary and assessment of the kind made in respect of documents coming within the scrutiny "net", the risk of duplication, is far outweighed by the benefit to the House.

In effect a discussion of merits and policy by the Scrutiny Committee (of the kind which takes place in the House of Lords) will only benefit debate within the House and consequently within the Council of Ministers. As the European Union admits new Member States and sets extravagant goals of Political and Monetary Union for the foreseeable future, the legislation proposed by the Commission will be pivotal in achieving these aims. The policy implications of this legislation must be debated by the House for two important reasons. Firstly, the legislative proposals must be shown to be workable within a European context. That is, the proposals will have tangible benefits for *all* Member States.

Secondly, a discussion of the effect of the proposal on UK policy is vital. Parliamentary approval for a piece of legislation, which may mark a major shift in economic or foreign policy as laid out by the government in its election manifesto is essential. Such a debate would rightly be expected by Members if the government performs a major policy "u-turn" of its own volition. A change to any government policy caused by our membership of the European Union must be scrutinised for the same purposes, i.e. those of accountability to the House and the electorate.

It is at this juncture, that the Select Committee could have a significant role to play. If it was charged with the role of scrutinising the European policy of the government of the day it could provide the House with the necessary nuances involved in that policy being changed by a piece of European legislation. Its role as acting as a source of information for the House would be increased. It would have both the time and expertise to produce a detailed report which would be the foundation of debate within the Chamber. Perhaps most vitally, it would have carried out the in-depth investigation which the Chamber itself does not have the time to do and placed the issue within the European and national context.

The Select Committee on Procedure in compiling its 1989 report[67] took evidence from a number of interested parties including the then Chairman of the Scrutiny Committee Mr Nigel Spearing MP.[68] He very lucidly described the changes which the majority of members of the Committee both then and today view as a positive step forward for the scrutiny process. At the centre of these proposals[69] was the need to extend the Terms of Reference of the Select Committee and allow it to prepare reports into broad policy areas of the kind outlined above.

However, these changes would only be effective if there was a change in the workings of the Commission. The most important of these would be to circulate legislative proposals at an earlier stage, thereby allowing the Committee and the national parliament to have a greater input into the final draft of the legislation. Obviously, these documents would not be final drafts, however, they could conceivably be classed as "working texts" and be part of the wide consultation process which the Commission presently undertakes. This process would fill a significant vacuum. The elected representatives of the Member State, who presently have no formal links with the Commission (other than through the minister of the day) or any involvement in the formulation of legislation, would now be part of this most important of procedures.

There are two identifiable benefits flowing from this involvement. Firstly, the MPs job of scrutiny would be made easier if they were aware of the legislative proposal at an earlier stage. Anything which makes scrutiny more effective must be welcomed. Secondly and perhaps more importantly in the present political climate, any involvement by MPs in the decision making process at an earlier stage, could help in the move away from the present "them and us" mentality which many MPs have expressed. Such involvement could help bridge the gap between not just the UK, but all national parliaments and the European Institutions and remove the sense of isolation felt by many MPs who feel that their role in this process is limited to the time once the legislation has become a *fait accompli*.

Furthermore, it would help the notion held by persons both inside and outside Parliament, that European legislation is in some way alien to us and being imposed on us by an unelected and unaccountable Commission. The European Communities Act 1972[70] gives this European legislation a legitimacy on a par with domestically produced legislation and in cases of conflict, gives this European legislation precedence. Parliament has by due process conceded this aspect of its sovereignty to both the Commission and the Council of Ministers, and, more recently (but not to the same extent) to the European Parliament to propose and pass legislation to be enforced through the UK's judicial process. Such legislation will have a greater understanding and acceptance by the citizens of all European Union countries if the national parliaments and its elected officials played a more active part in the decision making process.

---

67   See HC 622-1 (Session 1988-89).
68   See HC 368-iv (Session 1988-89).
69   *Ibid.* p. 49, paras. 27-28.
70   S.2 (1) - 2 (2).

However, the observations outlined above, remain to a greater extent as aspirations for the Select Committee and do not seem likely to be adopted within the foreseeable future. The Conservative government rejected any extension to the Terms of Reference of the Select Committee in its response[71] to the Fourth Report from the Select Committee on Procedure. The government did, agree to provide as early as possible certain kinds of pre-legislative documents for the Committee[72] but this falls far short of the Committee's objective that it will examine policy issues surrounding legislative proposals and produce detailed reports into the policy. It has been suggested that this will only happen if there were to be a minister at Cabinet rank whose sole area of responsibility was European affairs. In this instance, it would become a Departmental Ministry scrutinised by a Departmental Select Committee, which examines *inter alia* "policy, administration and expenditure".[73] However, no political party has plans to create such a ministry.[74]

Until the government agrees to amend the role of the Committee, it will remain concerned predominantly with the narrow task of scrutinising proposals for European legislation. As has already been stressed, this task is not to be understated. Its importance to the legislative process, in terms of being the only opportunity for MPs to comment upon the Executive's actions at the Council of Ministers, makes it integral to the concept of Parliamentary democracy. That is, Parliament *must* have a say in the passage of legislation, even if that say is in the present limited circumstances. As the author was informed on a number of occasions during his research, some scrutiny is better than no scrutiny at all. The comparison was made with other Member States such as Spain, Greece and Portugal who had not developed any scrutiny process until after the Maastricht Treaty, and where even today the Executive is not held accountable in the vigorous way for decisions taken at meetings of the Council as is seen in the UK. In fact, it can be argued, that perhaps with the exception of the Danish Folketing the UK Parliament is the only one which places this great an emphasis on scrutiny, and which jealously guards the influence it has gained over the years.

Raising the Select Committee's profile

The protection of Parliamentary democracy ultimately lies with the eternal vigilance of MPs. It is the rigour with which they insist on asking the real

---

71 See Cm 1081, p. 1.

72 *Ibid.*

73 Standing Order 130 sets out the function of Departmental Select Committees today. Perhaps most importantly, under the wording of the Standing Order the departmental select committee's are free to choose their own subjects of enquiry and are not concerned at all with Commission documents.

74 Chapter 5 looks at the role of the Departmental Select Committees and how this may be developed to improve scrutiny within the House. This includes a discussion of the benefits to the scrutiny process to be gained by having a European Departmental Select Committee.

questions which get to the heart of an issue, that will determine how influential Parliament will be in the years to come as far as the European Union is concerned. Enlargement of the Union means a dilution of the UK's influence at the Council. However, this could be counter balanced by an increase in Parliament's and more particularly the Committee's power to hold to account at the national level, the decision makers.

Any such step forward, would have to be made as a result of an initiative from Westminster. Perhaps one of the least noticed failures of the Maastricht Treaty was the fact that an increased role for the national parliaments in Europe was relegated to a mere Declaration at the end of the Treaty. This should have been an absolute requirement laid down by the main body of the Treaty itself. With the growth of Qualified Majority Voting in the Council the need for scrutiny is greater than ever.

Thus, more public notice should be given by the Select Committee and in turn more media attention given to what is going on in the Select Committee.[75] Furthermore, the increase in evidence given to the Committee by those who are directly affected by European legislation, e.g trade associations and pressure groups is to be welcomed.[76] However, as has already been stated, this should be extended to allow full discussion and debate on policy by the Committee.

Future reforms

Any increase in the role of the Scrutiny Committee though requiring the cooperation of the government, also requires the cooperation of the European institutions. Most notably, the assistance of the Commission and Council of Ministers is vital. The Commission as already stated should strive to publish legislative proposals as early as possible, perhaps in the form of consultative documents. The Council of Ministers itself must become more open.

However, though the Terms of Reference of the Committee need amending, the manner in which it conducts its work does not. In fact, the consensual approach of the Committee (as with other Departmental Select Committees) is one of its great strengths. It is this concensual approach in Committee, unique to a House of Commons which is based on an adversarial procedure, that allows for effective scrutiny and debate. The Members work together to produce a report which is of benefit for the whole House. Furthermore, as the Committee is carrying out an important task on behalf of the Chamber, this removes to a great extent the party political bickering which usually afflicts discussions on European issues. As a forum for debate the Select Committee cannot be improved upon. To strengthen its powers would only assist to improve its effectiveness.

---

75   A good recent example of such a happening was in the case of the Commission proposals on tobacco advertising where the media widely reported the work of the Committee, thereby illustrating the importance of this legislation to the general public.

76   See n. 30, at p. 37 for an example of how the Committee carries out these limited consultations.

Democracy requires transparency. To hold to account those who make the law, the Committee must know what they are doing. The Committee must be fully aware of the "horse-trading" taking place in the Council. Further progress must be made to achieve this. Members are already told of the votes in the Council, the next step is for them to be fully aware of the deliberations which take place leading up to the vote. This will mean Members of the Scrutiny Committee sitting in on Council deliberations. Given there are no plans to mandate the minister[77] it is essential to know what the minister does in negotiations behind closed doors.

In this chapter, the work of the Select Committee on European Legislation, the integral part of the scrutiny process, has been outlined. However, this is only one part, albeit the first and crucial one, of the scrutiny process. This is why the work of the Select Committee must be thorough. Without it, the further debate which it recommends could not be as influential or informed. A weak Select Committee means ineffective scrutiny. The pressure to reform, cannot in this author's opinion, be ignored any longer. It is within Parliament's own hands to introduce the necessary internal reforms to ensure that accountability is maintained, and scrutiny by the Select Committee strengthened. The Procedure Committee is once again reviewing the work of the Select Committee on European Legislation. It has before it an important and challenging task. Its recommendations will shape the scrutiny process during a very volatile time in the European Union.

---

77 In Denmark, mandating of the Minister is the norm and ensures some control by the national Parliament over his role in Council deliberations.

CHAPTER 4

DEBATING EUROPEAN LEGISLATIVE PROPOSALS IN THE EUROPEAN STANDING COMMITTEES AND ON THE FLOOR OF THE HOUSE

INTRODUCTION

Perhaps the most unique aspect of the whole scrutiny process within the House of Commons is the division of labour between the Select Committee on European Legislation, and European Standing Committees A and B. The limitation in the activities of both the Select Committee and the two Standing Committees is brought about by their narrow Terms of Reference. It is for the Select Committee to decide which European document should be the subject of further debate, but this debate is then carried out by one of the two European Standing Committees or occasionally on the Floor of the House.

The primary function of the debate is to consider the merits of the legislative proposal and most importantly, to *influence the minister* concerned and make him aware of the Houses opinion prior to their giving agreement to the proposal in the Council. It is the process of debate on the Floor of the House, and, perhaps more importantly in the Standing Committees, that will now be the subject of further consideration. The analysis begins with a historical review of the development of the Standing Committee procedure in the House of Commons and the reasons behind the Procedure Committee's recommendations in 1989 for reform of the Standing Committees.

HISTORICAL BACKGROUND

When the Foster Committee considered the arrangements for the scrutiny of European legislation in 1973[1] it recommended that debates on European Community documents be divided between a newly created Standing Committee structure and the Floor of the House. The reason behind this was that members felt that where an important document was to be debated, the whole of the House should be able to attend and vote.

The original Standing Order No. 102[2] provided for the appointment of one or more[3] Standing Committees for the consideration of European

---

1   See HC 143 (Session 1972-73) First Report from the Select Committee on European Legislation; and HC 463-I (Session 1972-73) Second Report from the Select Committee on European Legislation, paras. 53-92.

2   For an account of the Standing Committee Procedure, see Erskine May *Parliamentary Practice* (twenty-first Edition), pp. 595-596. Though this is now out of date after the changes implemented in 1991, it does give an accurate account of the workings of the original European Standing Committees.

3   Prior to the review of Standing Committees in 1988-89, three such committees sat concurrently.

Community documents referred to them. A motion for such a reference to one of the Standing Committees could only be made by the minister. However, the motion could be negatived if twenty or more members rose in their places to signify their objection to the motion. Thus, while the initiative for the referral of the document came from the government, it was a matter for the whole House whether or not the document was actually debated in Standing Committee or whether the debate was to take place on the Floor of the House.[4]

The structure of the European Standing Committees was different from that of other Standing Committees. Perhaps the most important feature (and one retained today) was that in addition to the members nominated to a European Standing Committee, any Member of the House could attend and address the Committee, but was not counted in the quorum and did not vote. This issue will be discussed at greater length when the present Standing Orders of the European Standing Committees are examined. However, it will suffice at this juncture to state that this excellent opportunity for Members to question ministers and debate European policy has, regrettably, been under utilised. Despite European issues being at the top of the political agenda, the vast majority of Members play no active part in the debate of European legislative proposals.

As already stated, the alternative to debate in Standing Committee was for the document to be debated on the Floor of the House. However, for reasons which are explained below, these arrangements proved to be less than satisfactory and their weakness was a factor behind the Procedure Committee's decision to review the effectiveness of the scrutiny arrangements within the House.[5]

Consideration of European Legislation on the Floor of the House

In the evidence that was submitted to the Procedure Committee in their enquiry into the Scrutiny arrangements within the House of Commons,[6] the general consensus which emerged from all witnesses was the inadequacy of the existing arrangements for the debate of European Community documents. It is possible to identify two main criticisms of using the Chamber as a forum for debate.

Firstly, the vast majority of debates took place after 10pm. This posed its own set of difficulties. The previous debate and subsequent vote would often finish later than planned, leaving a start time later than the 10pm scheduled. This in turn would compound the already existing difficulty of poor attendance of these late night debates, which generated little or no public and media interest not say interest among the MPs themselves.

---

4   Evidence which will be present in the Conclusion of this chapter will illustrate that most of the debates actually to place on the Floor of the House and were often perceived to be of little value.

5   See HC 622-I (Session 1988-89) Fourth Report from the Select Committee on Procedure. *The Scrutiny of European Legislation*, paras. 43-74.

6   See HC 622-II (Session 1988-89) Fourth Report from the Select Committee on Procedure - Minutes of Evidence.

The second criticism perhaps carried more weight, because it went to the heart of the problem by illustrating the weakness of the Chamber as the main forum for debate. The then Leader of the House of Commons, The Right Honourable John Wakeham MP, stated that debate in the Chamber centred primarily on the rather tired, old arguments, relating to the principle of our membership of the Community rather than concentrating on the matter in hand, i.e. in examining the detailed merits of a particular legislative proposal.[7] The Clerk of the House, Mr Clifford Boulton CB, further reinforced the point. In his evidence to the Procedure Committee, he illustrated the unsatisfactory nature of these late night debates by stating that they were primarily attended by a "predictable group of Members".[8] The general consensus was that the quality of these debates was not very high.

Amongst the Members themselves, there was great unpopularity with these late night debates.[9] Most backbenchers disliked the fact that a Three Line Whip was placed on divisions that would seldom materialise. The evidence from all interested parties pointed to a high degree of dissatisfaction with the use of the Chamber to consider European legislative proposals.

What role for the Chamber in the Consideration of European Legislation?

The Procedure Committee in its report took the view that the function of debating the merits of a particular document should primarily be within the remit of the new Standing Committees.[10] However, none of the evidence given to the Procedure Committee suggested that the Chamber should have no role in debating European legislative proposals.

The key issue, in deciding upon the future role of the Chamber, was undoubtedly the requirement of ensuring that the limited time available for the discussion of European policies was put to effective use. Despite the establishment of the European Standing Committees, there would still be occasions when important documents would need to be discussed by the whole House. This would be consistent with the general approach towards the use of Parliamentary time. The shift in emphasis was one of making the work of the Commons less Chamber orientated and making greater use of smaller specialist committees.[11] If any debate of a European document were to take place in the Chamber, the Procedure Committee recommended that if at all possible, it would take place in a "prime time" slot. Such a change makes sense for two reasons. Firstly, it would encourage a greater turnout of Members. Secondly, it

---

7   *Ibid.*, Question 70, p. 39.
8   *Ibid.*, Question 371, p. 114.
9   *Ibid.,* Question 71, p. 39.
10   See HC 622-I (Session 1988-89) p. xxxvii, para. 121.
11   This change of emphasis can be traced back to the 1978 Report of the Procedure Committee which recommended the establishment of the Departmental Select Committees. This was implemented by the incoming Conservative government in 1979 and marked a major change in the manner in which the House carried out its scrutiny functions.

is more likely that such a prime time debate on an important European document would achieve greater media attention and so raise the profile of the scrutiny process.

If one examines the subject matter of the debates on the floor of the House, a clear pattern emerges. Debates in the Chamber concentrate on major European legislative and policy proposals which either affect most constituencies or are politically sensitive. This leaves the more "minor" proposals within the domain of the Standing Committee. A closer inspection of the documents recommended for debate since 1991 reveals the following trends:[12]

Documents debated predominantly in the Chamber	Documents debated predominantly in Standing Committee
Budget proposals	Environmental proposals
Fisheries proposals	Transport proposals
CAP Price proposals	Employment proposals
Relations with third countries	Energy proposals

The obvious point from this table is that issues related to major government policies are always debated in the Chamber. The above lists are not exhaustive and merely illustrate a recognisable trend which has developed. There are some occasions when documents which are of more minor policy implication are debated in the Chamber. For example, a debate on Two or Three-Wheeled Vehicles (Docs. 8618/94 and 8037/94) took place in the Chamber on 24 November 1994. However, this was part of a wider debate on transport policy. This is known as "tagging" and occurs when a debate on policy in the Chamber coincides with a debate on a similar subject document in Standing Committee. To ensure efficient use of Parliamentary time the document is discussed as part of the debate in the Chamber.

One effect of the move towards Standing Committees was that more time would now be available for use in the Chamber. The Procedure Committee quite rightly envisaged that this time should be used to debate the government's European policies *prior* to the twice yearly Inter-Governmental Conference (IGC). This would be a major change from the position of there being two retrospective debates on developments over the previous six months. The benefit of making this change is obvious, and it corresponds with the general approach to scrutiny. That is, the aim of the Commons to influence ministers *prior* to their giving acquiescence in the Council of Ministers. In their response to the Procedure Committee Report, the government[13] accepted this change and undertook to be helpful in the provision of texts before each IGC. Today these

---

12   This information was obtained from the twice yearly government publication *Developments in the European Union*. This includes a section on "The Progress of Scrutiny" which details all documents which have been debated in the previous six month Presidency.

13   See Cm 1081 (Session 1989-1990), p. 4.

debates are an important opportunity to scrutinise the Prime Minister and other senior Cabinet Ministers on matters of more general European policy.

This entire discussion on the use of the Chamber emanated from the proposals of the Procedure Committee to shift debate from the Floor of the House to the Standing Committees. The Standing Committees in a revised form were viewed as the appropriate vehicle to tackle the issues of raising the quality of debate, increasing participation by the Members, increasing the media attention and perhaps most importantly ensuring effective scrutiny. The discussion will now concentrate on the working of, and the procedure in the Standing Committees, in evaluating the effectiveness of the present arrangements and in addressing the concerns raised by the Procedure Committee.

REFORMING STANDING COMMITTEES – THE ISSUES

Having considered all the evidence that was presented to them,[14] the Procedure Committee came to the unanimous conclusion that effective scrutiny was best served by the continuation of the Standing Committee process, but in a revised form. The initial recomendation[15] of the Procedure Committee was for five Standing Committees, with each specialising in a particular subject area(s).[16] These Committees would have the power to hear statements from ministers and cross-examine them about the particular proposal *before* any motion relating to that document was made or debated.

Power to obtain evidence and cross examine witnesses

To the undoubted dismay of some enthusiasts of the Standing Committees, the Procedure Committee did *not* recommend that the Committees have the power to send for persons, papers and records. Though proponents felt such a power would give the new Committees greater impact and influence, the Procedure Committee, rightly on reflection, took the view that such an extension of their remit would blur the distinction between the Standing Committees and the already established Departmentally Related Select Committees. The decision can be justified on two grounds.

Firstly, any widening of their Terms of Reference would have led to inevitable duplication with the work of the Departmental Select Committees. Secondly, the main function of these Standing Committees was scrutiny. Any expansion would mean they were carrying out policy investigations, a task which a committee meeting on average once a week for two and a half hours could not hope to carry out. Such a limitation had the effect of deterring the new Standing Committees from straying into the realms of policy evaluation and ensured focus on the important twin tasks of debate and scrutiny.

---

14   See HC 622-II (Session 1988-89).
15   This recomendation was subsequently revised down first to three committees, but the government finally agreed upon two for a variety of reasons that will be explained in the next section.
16   See HC 622-I (Session 1988-89), para. 65.

Procedural Changes

To encourage an increased use of the Standing Committees and help implement the main objectives behind this review of scrutiny arrangements, i.e. the
move away from debates being held predominantly on the Floor of the
House, the Procedure Committee recommended that a motion which referred
a Community legislative proposal to the proposed Standing Committees
could only be defeated, and debated in the Chamber, by forty rather than
twenty members rising in their place.[17]

Other procedural changes which were recommended included the drafting
of more pointed and clearly worded motions for debate, and that the government should be placed under an obligation to table an appropriate motion
that would allow the whole House to pass judgment on the Community document after the Standing Committee has completed its task.[18]

The government in its detailed response to these proposals[19] accepted the
majority of the Procedure Committee's recommendations. However, the government put forward two important qualifications. First, that there should be
three and not five Standing Committees. Second, and perhaps most controversial, was that when the Select Committee on European Legislation recommended that a legislative proposal should be the subject of further debate, the document would stand automatically referred to the appropriate Standing
Committee, unless the government (and no other member) moved a motion
that the proposal would be debated on the Floor of the House. The objection of
twenty members (or forty as the Procedure Committee had recommended) to
prevent a document being referred to Standing Committee was now irrelevant.

This second qualification proved to be most controversial and in a Special
Report[20] the Select Committee on European Legislation strongly opposed the
procedure whereby a document was automatically referred to a Standing
Committee. In fact, the Chairman of the Committee unsuccessfully moved a
number of amendments at the subsequent debate to amend the Standing
Orders of the Standing Committees. The reason behind the Committee's hos-
tility was the justified view that the Executive would have control over which
documents were important enough to warrant a debate in the Chamber, a
task hitherto undertaken by backbenchers.

This was quite rightly viewed as another example of concentrating power
in the hands of the Executive at the expense of the backbencher. In effect, it
would now be left to the Executive to make judgments as to which proposal
was of political significance and they would then frame the wording of the

---

17   *Ibid.,* para. 72.
18   *Ibid.,* paras. 73-74.
19   See Cm 1081 (Session 1989-1990) p. 5.
20   See HC 512 (Session 19889-89) First Special Report Select Committee on Europe-
     an Legislation; and see the subsequent debate on this Report 175 HC Debs., Cols.
     523-586, 28 June 1990.

motion which would subsequently be debated in the Chamber. This would give the Executive the ability to prevent damaging debates on European policy taking place in the full glare of the media and the electorate at large. The Executive would now have a decisive degree of control over the scrutiny procedures which were intended to keep a watchful eye on the government's activities with our European partners.

Not surprisingly, because of its large Commons majority, the views of the government prevailed and the Standing Orders were amended accordingly. However, the new European Standing Committees did not begin work immediately. From the date of amendment of the Standing Order to the first meeting of the new committees was a delay of almost four months.[21] It was reported[22] that this delay in the new Standing Committees beginning their work was due to the difficulty in finding sufficient members to serve on them. Furthermore, the number of Committees was reduced from three to two, confirming the difficulty in securing sufficient membership.

The first meeting of the European Standing Committee took place on January 29 1991, one week after the Standing Orders had been amended to allow for a reduction from three to two Committees. The evidence presented above identifies three primary reasons for reforming the Standing Committees:

1. To bring about a move away from the late night debates on European legislation on the Floor of the House;
2. To provide a more structured and thereby effective forum for debate than the Floor of the House, and for questioning ministers on a particular document; and
3. To build a body of expertise and experience on each Committee by appointing members for a whole session rather than on an ad-hoc basis.

The work of the Standing Committees over the first six years will now be investigated in more detail to establish to what extent these aims have been achieved.

THE EUROPEAN STANDING COMMITTEES IN THE HOUSE OF COMMONS

It can be said with certainty that the new Committees remain firmly as a deliberative part of the House's *legislative* role. They remain totally distinct and separate from the investigating activities of the Departmental Select Committees. As observed above, they have no power to send for persons, papers or records.

The Select Committee on European Legislation receives from the Council of Ministers all legislative proposals. It then decides whether the proposal is of

---

21   Consequently, until the end of January 1991, all recommended debates on European documents took place on the floor of the House.

22   *The Times*, 19 December 1990.

"Legal or Political importance". If it decides that it is, and requires further consideration, the document will then automatically be allocated for debate to one of the two European Standing Committees.[23] The two Committees are divided according to subject matter, and this division is strictly adhered to. Each Committee has a permanent membership of thirteen who are appointed for an entire session. The two Committees are divided in the following manner:[24]

European Standing Committees:	Principal subject matter Matters within the responsibility of the following departments:
A	Agriculture, Fisheries and Food; Transport; Environment;
B	Other Departments

The above division of subject matters is one of the weaknesses of the present arrangements. European Standing Committee A has a much narrower brief and therefore works more effectively than Committee B which covers a far wider remit. For example, Committee A which debates documents concerning agriculture has members sitting on it who are experts in that field and who will represent constituencies where agriculture is an issue. A similar position occurs regarding fisheries issues. However, Committee B covering over ten other departments cannot have the same expertise amongst its thirteen strong membership. The debate will not be as thorough as in Committee A. It is for this reason that the Procedure Committee initially recommended five European Standing Committees. This would have permitted the development of the type of expertise currently enjoyed by Committee A, across all the Committees.

EUROPEAN STANDING COMMITTEES – THE STANDING ORDERS AND PROCEDURE

Standing Order No. 102 which governs the procedure in the European Standing Committees was agreed by the House of Commons on 24 October 1990.[25] However, with the difficulties in securing sufficient Members to serve on the three originally proposed committees, the Standing Orders were amended on January 22 1991.[26] The three amendments introduced the following changes:

---

23   Occasionally if the government feels it is too important a document it will be debated on the Floor of the House. The government must first move a motion to this effect.
24   As of 22 January 1991. See Hansard 22 January 1991, Col. 269.
25   See Hansard 24 October 1990, Col. 393-395.
26   See Hansard January 22 1991, Cols. 269-293. This is a full account of the debate held by the House on the proposed amendments.

(i)   decreased the number of Standing Committees to two;[27]
(ii)   increased membership of each to thirteen;[28]
(iii) divided the subject matter for each committee in line with the table above.[29]

In the forthcoming sections, Standing Order No. 102 will be analysed and the procedure of the two European Standing Committees examined in detail.[30]

Proposing the debate

Standing Order (S.O.) No. 102 (2) provides that if a document is not to be automatically referred to one of the Standing Committees then the minister must move a motion in the House to that effect at the beginning of public business. The question is then put to the House who vote on the motion proposed.

Membership of the Standing Committees

S.O. 102 (3) deals with the membership of the Committees. Each Committee consists of 13 Members, and like all committees, the government will have an in-built majority, which usually ensures the smooth passage of even the more controversial legislative proposals. A unique aspect of the membership of these two Committees is that the thirteen members are nominated for the duration of a *whole* Parliamentary session.[31] This is in stark comparison to other Standing Committees, where the membership is decided upon on an *ad-hoc* basis for each particular Bill. The reason behind this is that the Procedure Committee felt that by appointing the Members for an entire Parliamentary session, they would be able to develop a certain amount of expertise which would otherwise be lacking if they were appointed on an *ad-hoc* basis. It was felt that Members would be able to cope better with the nuances of the Common Agricultural Policy or transport policy if they dealt with these documents on a weekly basis.

One further aspect of this difference, lies in the aim of the government to give the scrutiny process a much higher profile in the Commons. Members with a developed expertise would, it was hoped, become an information point for other MPs and raise the quality of debate within the House. Thus, debates

---

27   S.O. No. 102 (1).

28   S.O. No. 102 (3).

29   *Ibid.*

30   For an outline of the procedure in the two Standing Committee see Bates *European Community Legislation before the House of Commons*, Statute Law Review 1990-91, Vol. 12, No. 2, p.109. However, this article does not take into account the developments that have taken place since 1991 and is somewhat out of date.

31   The Membership of the Committees is decide upon between the two main parties through the "usual channels"

on European Community documents would now concentrate on the issues and not on the dated question of our continuing membership of the European Community.

Attendance by non-members

Standing Order No. 102 (5) is further testimony to the Procedure Committee's aim of raising the profile of the scrutiny of European legislation within the House. This provides that any Member who is *not* nominated to a European Standing Committee, may take part in the Committee's proceedings, but cannot make any motion, vote, or be counted as part of the quorum. Unfortunately, this is a privilege which is under used by all Members of the House.[32] However, the most notable exception lies when European Standing Committee A is discussing a document relating to Fisheries policy. In these instances it has been the case that up to thirty MPs will attend who represent fishing constituencies around the country – but this is the exception rather than the rule. The following table gives figures for non-members attendance at Standing Committee meetings during the last two Parliamentary sessions:[33]

Average Attendance At European Standing Committees

	A	B
1993-94		
Nominated Members (out of 13)	9.4	9.8
Other Members	3.4	3.4
1994-95		
Nominated Members (out of 13)	9.6	8.6
Other Members	3.0	4.2

The figures confirm the poor attendance of non-Members. This issue was highlighted by the Select Committee on European Legislation in its 1996 Report, and they urge the Procedure Committee to review this issue during the Course of its 1996 inquiry into the scrutiny process in the House of Commons.[34] At present, the Leader of the House announces the meeting of the Standing Committee to all Members at Business Questions on Thursday afternoons and informs them what documents will be debated. There is no other information given to the whole House about the Standing Committee meeting.

---

32   On average only two or three MPs will turn up who are not members of the committee.

33   See HC 51 xxvii (Session 1995-96) p. lix. Select Committee on European Legislation *The Scrutiny of European Business.*

34   *Ibid.* paras. 215-217.

However, despite the lack of enthusiasm by non-Members, Standing Order No. 102 (5) illustrates the serious approach taken by the House towards the scrutiny process. The Procedure Committee in making their recommendations in 1989[35] realised that if the scrutiny process was an alien procedure to other Members, there would be resentment, especially if controversial legislation was proposed that may adversely affect their constituents. By allowing *any* Member to attend, it was hoped to bring the scrutiny of European legislation into the mainstream of Parliamentary activity, and not just the concern of the few members who are nominated to attend. Unfortunately, this has not proved to be the case. In short, scrutiny was to be more than just a procedural device. It was and continues to be the cornerstone of the European legislative process, which like the domestic legislative process should be the concern of *all* Members in the House.

The ministerial statement, question time and debate

The main substance of the procedure in Standing Committee is found in Standing Order 102 (7) and (8). Under (7), the Chairman of the Standing Committee may permit (and in practice always will permit) the minister present at the meeting to make a statement, which will last no more than five minutes. He will then answer questions which are put by the Members present. This period of the session will last no longer than one hour.[36]

This aspect of the procedure is, undoubtedly, one of the most valuable of the entire scrutiny process. In this situation, the minister is on his own, and having to face one hour's questioning from Committee Members who are usually on top of the subject. Furthermore, unlike Question Time in the Chamber, the minister has not prepared answers prior to the session with the help of his Civil Servants, or received notification of the question in advance. Furthermore there are no "planted questions". For the minister concerned, the least comfortable aspect of this whole procedure is that he is the *sole* minister present. The task is not shared between the ministers within the department.

This one hour Question Time is an opportunity, which unfortunately the Opposition does not make full use of. This is perhaps the only occasion in the House to question a minister and put him on the spot, and pressure him for an answer. The forum is conducive to this. However, as attendance is usually limited to the Members appointed the government is to a great extent "let off the hook".[37]

---

35   See HC 622-I (Session1988-89) p. xxxix - xl.

36   In a review of the new Standing Committees the Select Committee on Procedure recommended an extension of this one hour period, but this was rejected by the government. See HC 31 (Session 1991-92) and HC 331 (Session 1991-92), the governments reply to HC 31.

37   This was the opinion of one of the Clerks from the Public Bill Office who regularly attends the two Standing Committees. These comments were given in an interview held at the House of Commons on Monday 24 April 1995.

The importance of this procedure cannot be stressed enough. When one talks about influence through scrutiny, this is it in action. The Members of the Committee are acting as representatives of the whole House in putting their views across. This makes the session a political one – but this is in a positive way. Members are acutely aware of the limited time available and strive to use it effectively to procure information from the minister and convey their own views.

On completion of the Question Time, the remaining one and a half hours of the session is given over to debating the document. The document is proposed in the form of a Motion, the wording of which is decided upon by the government. Any nominated Member of the Committee may put forward an amendment(s) to the Motion. The debate is similar to that which may take place in the Chamber, that is, the Member will make a short speech on the issues involved and ask questions of Members from other parties to outline their policies with regards the particular legislative proposal under discussion. The minister will sit and listen to the debate to gauge the opinion of the Committee. In particular, he will ascertain the parameters of the Committee by seeing how acceptable they find the particular proposal. If the Committee has done its task effectively, the minster will attend the Council of Ministers meeting with the Standing Committee's views ringing in his ears.

Once the total two and a half hour period has expired, the Chairman[38] will interrupt the proceedings and ask the Committee to consider the following questions:

> (a) the question on any Amendment already proposed from the Chair; and
> (b) the Main Question (or the Main Question as amended).

At this juncture, the Committee will vote on the Question(s) put before it. The Committee will then report to the House any Resolution which it has passed.

The procedure following debate in Standing Committee

The final part of the Standing Committee procedure, governed by Standing Order No. 102 (9), has proved to be the most controversial aspect of the whole process. It deals with the procedure once the document returns to the Chamber for final approval by the whole House.

After the debate in the Standing Committee has concluded, a vote is taken on the Motion proposed and on any amendments to the Motion. The Standing Committee then reports back to the House as a whole what decisions it came to. It is at this stage that the entire House will have its say on the Motion.

The report made by the Standing Committee is the exact wording of the Motion it has passed (including any amendments). However, because of the

---

38   For a full account of the role of the Chairman, see the section on the role of the Chairman and specialist advisers.

wording of Standing Order No. 102 (9), the government, who propose the Motion in the House, are under *no* obligation to phrase the Motion in the form which the Standing Committee agreed to. A closer analysis of the Standing Order will illustrate the difficulty. S.O. No. 102 (9) reads as follows:

(9) *If any Motion is made in the House in relation to any European Community Document* (my emphasis) in respect of which a report has been made to the House in accordance with paragraph (8) of this Order, Mr Speaker shall forthwith put successively

(a) the Question on any Amendment selected by him which may be moved;

(b) the main Question (or the main Question as amended);
  and proceedings in pursuance of this paragraph, though opposed, may be decided after the expiration of the time for opposed business.

The key phrase of this section is the phrase placed in italics. What this means is that the government can put forward *any* Motion it wants on the document which is before the House. This issue first arose in 1991.[39] Standing Committee A had considered two Commission legislative proposals on the compulsory use of seatbelts.[40] The government moved the following Motion in the Standing Committee:

"that the Committee takes note of European Community Documents Nos. 9228/88 and 1033/90 on the compulsory use of seatbelts; notes that their provision are broadly in accord with present and proposed domestic legislation; and endorses the Government's intention to seek amendment of the proposal so that any adopted directive neither imposes unacceptable constraints nor limits the scope for further action perceived by Parliament to be necessary."

Mr Teddy Taylor MP, a Member of the Committee moved an amendment to the Motion to include the following words at the end:[41]

"... without prejudice to the view of the Government that Article 75 does not cover road safety measures."

The minister indicated that he had difficulty with the amendment because it attempted to make certain the issue on which the government was not yet decided, that is, the competence of Article 75 as a means to introduce this particular legislative proposal. Despite this, with the support of the Opposition, the amendment was agreed without a division.[42]

---

39 For a further discussion of this issue see Professor T. St J. N. Bates *European Community Legislation before the House of Commons* Statute Law Review 1990-91, Vol. 12, No. 2, p. 109.
40 See European Standing Committee A, 13 March 1991.
41 *Ibid.*
42 *Ibid.* Cols. 13-14.

However, when the document came back to the Chamber for final approval by the whole House, the Motion proposed by the government made no reference to Mr Taylor's amendment agreed to by the Standing Committee A. In a subsequent debate, Mr Taylor was scathing about the actions of the government:[43]

> "We passed a unanimous amendment.... What happened? The House of Commons was not told because the Government say that they will report only the decisions of the Committees with which they agree. If they do not agree, they will not tell the House of Commons the decision.... I do not know of any time in the history of Parliament at which a Committee has not been able to tell the House of Commons what it has done."

Though it is still open to a Member to put forward an amendment at this stage, it is unlikely to succeed for two reasons. First, there is no further time for debate and hence no opportunity to try and convince other MPs. Secondly, the government's in-built Commons majority and the heavy handed approach of the Whips means that it will have no realistic prospect of success.[44]

The anger felt by Mr Taylor is quite understandable. The Committee having followed the correct procedure has arrived at a particular opinion which the Executive now choose to ignore. The view has been expressed to the author in the course of his research that this makes a mockery of the scrutiny procedure.[45] The Executive, which is the subject of the scrutiny, is also the arbitrator in the event of any dispute between it and the Standing Committee. In a Parliamentary democracy, this is unacceptable.

In his article,[46] Professor St J.N. Bates[47] appears to discount the impact of the problem on this occasion by stating that "the issue did not raise itself in such stark terms here". He justifies this by stating that the minister in attendance made it clear that the government did not have a clear legal opinion on the matter in issue and that the amendment expressed only the opinion of the Standing Committee and not the government. However, this in itself does not detract from the fact that the Executive completely ignored the view of the Committee which had passed a unanimous amendment.

In the situation where the Standing Committee is doing the work of the Chamber, the government should be expected, at the very least, to debate the Motion passed by the Standing Committee and not adopt a steam roller

---

43   See 193 HC Debs. 26 June 1991, Col. 1109.
44   A more recent example of the can be seen by looking at the debate on the document on External Frontiers. The Motion put forward by the government was different to that agreed to by the Standing Committee in that it contained several amendments put forward by the more Euro-sceptic Conservative MPs.
45   The view was conveyed most strongly by two MPs, both Members of the Standing Committees in interviews held in the House of Commons on Monday March 7 1994 and Monday 21 March 1994.
46   See n. 40, at p. 69.
47   Clerk of Tynwald, Secretary to the House of Keys and Counsel to the Speaker.

approach towards Motions it does not agree with. Anything less diminishes the value of the work undertaken by the European Standing Committees. Even if the analysis of Professor St. J. N. Bates is correct, the question still remains unsatisfactorily answered of what the government will do when a Motion passed in Standing Committee is one with which it does not agree. At present the government will continue to follow the procedure laid down in S.O. 102 (9) and put forward their own unamended Motion before the House.

The Select Committee on Procedure recognised this problem in its Report reviewing the work of the Standing Committees.[48] It was of the opinion that the House having, referred a document to the Standing Committee for its consideration, it is entitled to expect that the Committee's conclusions will form the starting point for the House's decision at the final stage of the scrutiny process.[49] In an attempt to solve this problem, the Committee recommended that the Motion as agreed by the Standing Committee should be the one put before the House. If the government did not agree with it, then it should propose amendments to the Resolution reported by the Committee.[50] However, the Committee acknowledged the procedural difficulty with this, because as the Motion is in the name of the minister, it would be contrary to the practice of the House for the government to seek to amend it.

It tried to overcome this problem by suggesting that any Motion before the House should stand in the name of the Committee as a whole. This would mean a significant departure from the procedure of the House where Motions always stand in the name of an individual.

The government in its response to the Procedure Committee rejected outright this proposal.[51] They viewed it as being too radical a change to the procedures in the House and that the perceived problem was not in itself that big. As the Leader of the House pointed out in his reply, it is still open to the Member to propose his amendments once again in the Chamber. In the end, the only concession made by the government was an undertaking it gave to pay more attention to the views of the two Standing Committees, but reserved the right, as Standing Order 102 (9) provides, to bring forward "any motion" to the House.

However, though the Members find this a frustrating aspect of the process, it is necessary to clarify one important issue which Members of the two European Standing Committees do lose sight of. That is, that the Standing Committees only have delegated powers given to them by the House. The Committees are the forum for debate only, the final decision is one for the entire House. The Standing Committees should therfore not be viewed as supplanting the House in this respect.

Overall, though, this procedure is an improvement on the previous arrangements. The debate is focussed on the issues and the government has

---

48   See HC 31 (Session 1991-92), p. xiv, para. 37.
49   *Ibid.* p. xv, para. 41.
50   *Ibid.*
51   See HC 331 (Session 1991-92), p. vii, para. (x).

been known to be defeated in Standing Committee, which, at the minimum, does cause an embarrassment. However, there still remains the unsatisfactory position once the document returns back to the Chamber. The government are not prepared to change the Standing Orders to provide for the Motion as passed in Committee to be the Motion that must be laid before the House. There is a persuasive argument that the whole House is entitled to debate the informed conclusions of the Standing Committee, to which it has delegated the power of debate. Anything less is an undermining of the whole scrutiny process in the Commons and makes all the hard work undertaken up to this point worthless.

STANDING COMMITTEE OR CHAMBER – WHICH IS MORE EFFECTIVE FORUM FOR DEBATE?

In making such a comparison, the first point to make is that there is in fact very little difference in the way the two forums operate. In fact, it is possible to describe the Standing Committees as a microcosm of the Chamber. The Chairman,[52] who is an MP, is selected from the Chairman's Panel, and takes on the role of the Speaker, by keeping order at the meeting.

The debate itself, follows the same pattern as debates in the Chamber. After, the minister's opening remarks, the Members will ask questions for the first hour and use the remaining one and a half hours to make speeches. The Members themselves sit in the traditional adversarial style on opposite sides of the Committee Room, and adopt the Commons tradition of asking the Member making the speech to "give way" when they wish to ask a question.

Perhaps the main difference between the two forums lies not in the procedure, but rather in the way the Members conduct the actual debate. As previously stated, the quality of debate is generally accepted to be higher in Standing Committee, and the author has found this to be the case both in the meetings he has attended and from talking to actual Members. Furthermore, the fact that there is a specific time devoted each week to the consideration of European legislation means the Members approach their work in a more conscientious manner than might have otherwise been the case if the Chamber was still used as the main debating forum.

However, one universal criticism of the Standing Committee's, is that the time available, two and a half hours in total, is not enough. The main complaint is levelled at the hours question time of the minister, which is generally accepted to be the most valuable aspect of this part of process. The Select Committee on Procedure in its 1991 Report[53] recommended that there should be provision made to extend the time available if necessary. Most importantly, they felt that the period for questions could be extended by 30 minutes at the Chairman's discretion should it be convenient to do so.[54]

---

52   See the next section for a full account of the role of the Chairman of the Standing Committee.
53   See HC 31 (Session 1991-92).
54   *Ibid.* p. xviii.

However, they suggested this extra time for questions should come from the time allotted for debate and not by an extension of the overall time. Though the government accepted this recommendation, they did not view it as a matter of urgency, and have not to this date made the necessary amendment to Standing Order No. 102.

In effect, the Standing Committee procedure is subject to a perpetual guillotine. That is, even if the debate has not been concluded, the Chairman will halt the proceedings after two and a half hours, and a vote on the Motion(s) will be taken. It is this aspect of the procedure which is criticised by both the Members and the Opposition who view it as an opportunity for the government to avoid answering difficult questions on controversial documents. This compares less favourably with the debate in the Chamber which when it takes place in prime time is allotted more time for views to be aired in the debate.

ROLE OF THE CHAIRMAN AND SPECIALIST ADVISERS

The Chairman

As stated above, the Chairman takes on the role of the Speaker in Standing Committee. He ensures that there is order in the debate and that the debate stays focussed on discussing the documents in issue. The Chairman will select a Member to ask a question or make a speech in the same manner as the Speaker does in the Chamber. However, the Chairman has no hand in deciding what the Members will debate or what the Motion(s) for debate are. At the end of the debate, the Chairman puts the question to the Standing Committee who vote on the Motion(s) before them. The Chairman, like the Speaker has the casting vote in the event of a tie. All the votes and proceedings in the Standing Committees appear in the name of the Chairman and the House as a whole is aware of them.

The role of Chairman is not a permanent one on a particular Committee. The Chairman is selected from the Chairmans Panel[55] and only chairs the particular meeting for which he has been chosen. The Committees rotate the Chairman for each meeting.

Is there a case for permanent Chairman?

Many Standing Committee Members[56] have argued that there is a strong case for having a permanent Chairman on each of the two European Standing Committees. It is possible to identify to strong arguments in favour of this change.

---

55 The Chairmans Panel consists of 14 senior MPs who Chair the various Standing Committee meetings in the House. They chair both European and other Standing Committees.

56 Most notably Gwyneth Dunwoody MP in her evidence to the Select Committee on Procedure. See HC 31 (Session 1991-92), Appendix 5.

First, this would ensure a greater degree of consistency in the proceedings, especially with regard to the initial one hour Question Time. Both Gwyneth Dunwoody and Daffyd Wigley[57] in their evidence to the Procedure Committee raised this point. Their main concern was the apparent discrepancy in calling Members to speak. Because the Chairmanship rotates on a weekly basis, the Chairman is not aware of which Member took a more active part in the previous debate and asked more questions. There is a risk, that the same Members may dominate the proceedings each week.

The second argument in favour of appointing a permanent Chairman is that over the period of an entire session, the Chairman would develop a substantial degree of understanding of the issues before the Committee. Furthermore, this expertise could be harnessed by not only Members but by the entire House. In effect, such a change would mean that the role of the Chairman would now be more akin to the Chairman of a Select Committee rather than a Standing Committee.

However, such a change has met with almost universal opposition. In its 1991 review of the European Standing Committees, the Procedure Committee considered this very proposition. Having taken evidence from a variety of interested parties,[58] the Procedure Committee came out firmly against making any such recommendation.

In his evidence to the Procedure Committee, the then Chairman of Ways and Means, Harold Walker MP, stated the following:[59]

> "... the existing arrangement of rotation best suited the chairing of what were basically Standing Committees."

He further reiterated his opposition by stating that the above opinion was the "firm and widespread" view of the Chairmans Panel. The objection stemmed from what Mr Walker said was a recognition that:[60]

> "... the European Standing Committees had been established to transfer a workload from the Floor of the House of Commons – that was the basic reason -and that for that reason the proceedings ought to be very much in a way that would reflect the procedures in the Chamber itself."

He further contended that specialisation was not a real issue for the Committee. The main function of the Chairman was to preside over the proceedings in an efficient, procedurally correct and impartial manner. Thus, the appointment of a Chairman was a purely procedural question.

The rejection of this proposal is justifiable on procedural grounds, but with one important proviso. Any change along the lines supported by Gwyneth

---

57   *Ibid.* Appendix 9.
58   *Ibid.* pp. xiii-xiv, paras. 36-38.
59   *Ibid.* Minutes of Evidence, p. 4, para. 15.
60   *Ibid.*

Dunwoody would inevitably lead to the Standing Committee becoming more akin to a Select Committee. This could potentially cause difficulty with duplicating the work of the Select Committee on European Legislation and the Departmental Select Committees. However, this is an issue which should be kept under review. The increased complexity of many European legislative proposals may require that the Chairman will need to be an information access point for those Members who have not had the time to fully digest the document.

Specialist advisers

The two European Standing Committees have *no* specialist staff to advise them. The only support staff available, comes in the shape of the Clerks from the Public Bill Office in the Commons who have a supervising function in relation to the European Standing Committees. Therefore, the role of the Clerks with regards to the European Standing Committees is tangential, and they are primarily concerned with the Public Bills which are progressing through the numerous Standing Committees in the House.

This lack of specialist support staff is a criticism which has been voiced by many Members in the course of the author's research.[61] It was viewed one of the most frustrating things, when having received the documents for debate less than one week before hand, they had no support staff available to deal with their queries.

In its review of the operation of the Standing Committees, the Procedure Committee looked very seriously at this question of bringing in support staff to aid the Committee Members and/or introducing a permanent secretariat of Clerks skilled in European matters. The Procedure Committee saw the arguments in favour of this change as quite strong, especially in light of the increased flow of legislative proposals emanating from the European Community.

However, the Procedure Committee did not recommend any change, and saw the arguments in favour of this change as flawed in two ways.[62] First, they argued, that by appointing specialist advisers, it would mean a shift in the function of the Standing Committees. These two Committees were set up as an extension of the Houses *legislative* functions. The use of specialist advisers would, they felt, mean that the Standing Committees were mimicking the investigative procedure of the Select Committees in the House. This approach was entirely consistent with that which they took in their earlier Report,[63] where they rejected the suggestion that the Committee should have the power to send for persons and papers. The Chairman of Ways and Means expressed the sole function of these Standing Committees in the evidence he gave to the Procedure Committee:[64]

61   *Ibid,* p. xi and Appendix 5, p. 20. Mrs Gwyneth Dunwoody talked of the "dire need for support staff".
62   See HC 31 (Session 1991-92), p. xi.
63   See HC 622-I (Session 1988-89) p. xxiv, para. 63.
64   See HC 31 (Session 1991-92) Minutes of Evidence, p. 6, para. 23.

"...I believe that one must start from the basic premise that the Committees were
set up to transfer a workload from the Floor of the House."

The second flaw the Procedure Committee identified was that by introducing
specialist staff, this would just mean an increase in the volume of paperwork
for the Committee Member's. Something which they felt was undesirable.

This rejection of the introduction of support staff, which the government
approved in its reply to the Procedure Committee's Report,[65] is on the whole
the correct approach because it ensures the distinct nature of the Standing
Committee's work is maintained. However, it is an important point which
must be kept under review, especially in the light of future legislative developments and major policy changes. This issue will undoubtedly be addressed
once again by the Procedure Committee's inquiry into the scrutiny process
which was commissioned in 1996. Most significantly, since its last major
investigation in 1989 there have been a number of important developments
which could cause the Procedure Committee to alter its view e.g. if the Select
Committee were to scrutinise proposals under the Inter-Governmental Pillars.

Until this issue is addressed by the Procedure Committee, there must with
this lack of specialist staff, be more cooperation with the Select Committee on
European Legislation, the Departmental Select Committees and a greater
understanding on the part of the government, especially in the early provision
of documents. The Members can also help themselves by using the Library
facilities in the House, and being aware of reports by other Departmental
Select Committees and those published by the Select and Sub-Committees in
the House of Lords. Such steps will undoubtedly assist them in what is a challenging task.

ALTERNATIVES TO THE STANDING COMMITTEES

The Grand Committee

One alternative to the Standing Committees has been the proposal to set up a
Grand Committee, similar in structure to the existing Scottish Grand Committee. A Grand Committee operates in similar fashion to a Departmental
Select Committee, except that the membership is larger,[66] and it is more of a
forum for questioning ministers as opposed to specifically debating a particular piece of legislation. In their evidence to the Procedure Committee in
1989, it was the Labour Party Spokesmen on European affairs, George Rob-
ertson and George Foulkes, who were the main proponents in favour of establishing a European Grand Committee. In their evidence they said that the
Grand Committee would provide a forum:[67]

---

65   See HC 331 (Session1991-92) p. vii.
66   The Scottish Grand Committee has 72 Members.
67   See HC 622-II (Session 1988-89) Minutes of Evidence pp. 61-63, Q 163-6 and
     172-3.

"...which might combine the day to day questioning of Ministers which occurred when we had regular oral statements, the flexibility of the House of Lords Select Committee and the necessity of debates which are yet to go to the Council of Ministers."

The view adopted by the Labour Party was that this Grand Committee would have a wide membership and operate as the main forum which the minister was to address after meetings of the Council of Ministers.

However, the idea of a Grand Committee was rightly rejected for two solid reasons. First, the Committee in the form proposed by the Labour Party would resemble more of a Select Committee than a debating forum. There was a substantial risk that if it operated with "the flexibility of the House of Lords Select Committee" it would become more investigative and concerned with policy than with scrutinising legislative proposals. Secondly, and related to the first point, is the fact that the Procedure Committee was taking evidence with the view to improving the scrutiny process. The weak link in the chain was the debate of legislative proposals. They sought to establish a Committee(s) whose *sole* concern was to debate the merits of the legislative proposal before it.

The Procedure Committee were rightly concerned to ensure there was an effective division of labour between the various bodies involved in the scrutiny process. This they correctly concluded would not be best served by the establishment of a Grand Committee. Parliamentary time is scarce, and therfore duplication of tasks must be avoided.

One added difficulty identified with the establishment of a Grand Committee lay with the size of the membership. If it contained a membership of similar numbers to the Scottish Grand Committee, the opportunity for effective debate would be greatly diminished. It would be difficult to give the opportunity to all those who wanted to speak. Furthermore, placing any time limit similar to that now in operation in the Standing Committees (i.e. two and a half hours) would mean that the vast majority of Members would not be able to take part in the debate. Overall, the session would be of little value to the overall scrutiny process.[68] Today the (New) Labour Party have no plans for amending the scrutiny process in the Commons.

---

68   For further information on this point, see the evidence of the Clerk of the House, HC 622-II, Q. 73, who said that the position would be little different to that seen in the Chamber, where the debate degenerated into a pro and anti European discussion. A similar view was expressed by a Clerk from the Public Bill Office who regularly works on matters related to the two European Standing Committees.(Interview Friday 12 May 1995 in the House of Commons).

How effective are the European Standing Committees?

In making any assessment as to the success of the present arrangements for the debate of European Community documents, it is necessary to analyse the impact of the changes which have come into force since 1991. At a basic level, the author has received favourable comments from a variety of interested parties[69] regarding the beneficial impact of the changes. Most notably, there was a general agreement that the quality of debate has been raised by the more structured and systematic approach taken by the Committees to scrutiny. It is the hour's ministerial question time which was seen as being of most value.[70]

The distribution of tasks between the Committees was also viewed as a positive step. There is potential for the development of expertise by Members in the subject matters. However, this has been tempered by the fact that only two Committees are in existence, which results in a large workload for each Committee, and in particular, European Standing Committee B.

The Standing Committees themselves have benefited from the fact that they are appointed for an entire session. If one attends the Committee meetings there is immediately evident a coherence and camaraderie amongst the Members not usually witnessed in the Chamber. The minister who attends is always vigorously questioned, even by members of his own party. Though the members do not vote together, they do give each other space to pursue their own avenues of interest.

The procedure adopted does mean that the quality of debate within Standing Committee is much higher than that seen previously when the Chamber was the main forum for debate. There is less of a tendency to diverge to the pro/anti European debate and a greater concentration on the fundamental issues of the document before them. The smaller turn out means that the one hour question time is utilised effectively by putting challenging questions to the minister. There are no "planted" questions here.

One negative aspect of the process which many Members expressed relates to the limited time available to prepare for meetings. Documents on complex issues such as the Budget or the Common Agricultural Policy often add to a Member's difficulties. The Members of the Committee will know that the document is to be debated but they do not know the exact day. This is because each document recommended for debate by a Standing Committee is placed on the "wait list". However, they will only be notified of the day of the debate the Thursday before it is scheduled. It is at this stage that the Committee Members will receive all the necessary documents for the debate. The

---

69   Very positive comments were received from both MPs and Officials of the House of Commons who were unanimous in their praise for the new Standing Committee arrangements.

70   For a more general discussion of the effectiveness of the present arrangements see HC 31 (Session 1991-92) p. viii. Select Committee on Procedure, First Report, *Review of European Standing Committees.*

Committee itself meets on a Wednesday at 10am. They have less than one week to digest and become familiar with the documents that will be the basis of the debate and on which they are to cross-examine the minister. A task they perform admirably under the circumstances.

Has the move to debate in Standing Committee been successful?

The primary reason for the establishment of the Standing Committee structure was to move debates away from the Floor of the House. It is the success of this development which will now be the subject of further investigation. Making a subjective judgment about the impact of this change will only be of limited value (though it has undoubtedly been a major contribution to the development of an effective scrutiny system). In a previous section it was concluded that the Standing Committees are the preferred forum for the debate of European legislative proposals and evidence cited that there is a higher quality of debate within them. What will now be considered is whether the predominance of debate has actually moved from the Chamber to Standing Committee.

Empirical evidence is of great value in helping one make an authoritative assessment. The following figures are produced by the Cabinet Office and are a six monthly up-date on the progress of the scrutiny process.[71] They give the number of debates held on the Floor of the House, and the number held in Standing Committee. These figures are not separated into Parliamentary Sessions, but rather into the six month Presidency of a Member State:

Year
1989
Jan-Jun.[72]
    (a) Floor of the House – 22 debates held
    (b) Standing Committee – 7 debates held

1989
Jul-Dec.[73]
    (a) Floor of the House – 15 debates held
    (b) Standing Committee – 8 debates held

1990
Jan-Jun.[74]
    (a) Floor of the House – 11 debates held
    (b) Standing Committee – 16 debates held

---

71   These figures are always produced in *Developments in the European Community*. This a six monthly government publication reviewing the recent Presidency held by a particular Member State.
72   Cm 801 (Session1988-89).
73   Cm 1023 (Session1989-90).
74   Cm 1234 (Session1989-90).

1990
July-Dec.[75]
    (a) Floor of the House – 16 debates held
    (b) Standing Committee – 5 debates held

1991
Jan-Jun.[76]
    (a) Floor of the House – 7 debates held
    (b) Standing Committee A – 13 debate
    (c) Standing Committee B – 13 debates held

1991
July-Dec.[77]
    (a) Floor of the House – 5 debates held
    (b) Standing Committee A – 4 debates held
    (c) Standing Committee B – 7 debates held

1992
Jan-Jun.[78]
    (a) Floor of the House – 3 debates held
    (b) Standing Committee A – 6 debates held
    (c) Standing Committee B – 3 debates held

1992
July-Dec.[79]
    (a) Floor of the House – 3 debates held
    (b) Standing Committee A – 4 debates held
    (c) Standing Committee B – 8 debates held

1993
Jan-Jun.[80]
    (a) Floor of the House – 3 debates held
    (b) Standing Committee A – 15 debates held
    (c) Standing Committee B – 15 debates held

1993
July-Dec.[81]
    (a) Floor of the House – 2 debates held
    (b) Standing Committee A – 6 debates held
    (c) Standing Committee B – 8 debates held

---

75   Cm 1457 (Session1990-91).
76   Cm 1657 (Session1990-91).
77   Cm 1857 (Session1991-92).
78   Cm 2065 (Session1991-92).
79   Cm 2168 (Session1992-93).
80   Cm 2369 (Session1992-93).
81   Cm 2525 (Session1993-94).

1994
Jan-Jun.[82]
  (a) Floor of the House – 3 debates held
  (b) Standing Committee A – 7 debates held
  (c) Standing Committee B – 10 debates held

1995
Jan-Jun.[83]
  (a) Floor of the House – 1 debate held
  (b) Standing Committee A – 5 debates held
  (c) Standing Committee B – 16 debates held

1995
July-Dec.[84]
  (a) Floor of the House – 2 debates held
  (b) Standing Committee A – 4 debates held
  (c) Standing Committee B – 11 debates held

The above statistics illustrate that the developments in place since 1991 have had a significant effect in changing the forum for debate of European Community legislative proposals. As the figures show, in the six month period from July to December 1989, 22 debates were held on the Floor of the House, with only 7 being held in the old Standing Committee. Compare these figures with those for the six month period January to June 1993, where only 3 debates were held on the Floor of the House, but 15 in each of the two Standing Committees. Though the number of debates has varied for each six month period (e.g. Jan-Jun 1990), it is now the norm that the two Standing Committees will host the overwhelming majority of the debates.

However, the raw figures given above do not give any indication as to how many documents have actually been debated. At each debate, whether it be on the Floor of the House or in Standing Committee, it will often be the case that more than one document will be debated. In fact, when there is a debate on an EC budgetary document,[85] there may be as many as *seven* documents debated at once. Debates on Environmental proposals regularly focus on three or more documents. Thus, the issue should not be one of the number of documents debated.

The reason for this view, is that the Procedure Committee suggested the establishment of the Standing Committees to relieve the pressure with regards to time available in the House. This they have achieved with great success.

---

82   Cm 2675 (Session1993-94).
83   Cm 3130 (Session 1994-95).
84   Cm 3250 (Session 1995-96).
85   Debates on EC budgetary documents will because of their importance always take place on the Floor of the House. Furthermore, the debate is part of the wider debate on the Budget (or the old Autumn Statement).

The fact is, that whether one document or five grouped together are debated at the same time, only two and half hours are available for the debate in Standing Committee. Debates which on the Floor of the House would have taken four or five hours[86] and often late at night, will now be completed in one two and a half hour sitting on a Wednesday morning. Only the important and controversial debates will now take place on the Floor of the House. But, even these are rarely held as individual debates. They are usually tagged on to a wider debate. For example, the EC budget is always included in the debate on the Chancellors annual budget statement and agriculture proposals as part of regular debates held on CAP.

The evidence illustrates that it can be stated with certainty that the main aim of releasing more time for Chamber to carry out other work and shift the debate of European Community documents to the Standing Committees has been an overwhelming success. The figures prove this.

In 1989, the other major weakness in the debate of legislative proposals lay in the late night scheduling of the majority of debates. A closer inspection reveals the concerns the Procedure Committee had. For example a debate on 11 December 1989 concerning Research and Development began at 12.30am and concluded at 1.47am. Similarly, a debate on Assistance for Asia and Latin America began at 10.58pm and ended at 12.27am. There are other extreme examples like these, though the majority of debates in the Chamber before 1991 took place some time after 10pm. The only exceptions were debates on the EC budget and CAP.

Today the position has undoubtedly improved. Reliance on late night debates is essentially a thing of the past. The relatively few debates which are now conducted in the Chamber begin at a more convivial time to ensure better participation. For example, a debate on Italian Steel Industry Aid on 9 May 1994 began at 7pm and ended at 8.27pm.

Through these developments, the quality of debate has unquestionably been raised and increased the effectiveness of the *entire* scrutiny process. The fact that ministers find the Standing Committee meetings challenging is an indication that they fulfil their specific task – influencing the minister. This must be welcomed, but there is no room for complacency. New challenges face the Standing Committees, most notably the ever increasing workload they face. This itself will further increase if the Select Committee becomes competent to scrutinise proposals under the Inter-Governmental Pillars. A whole new category of documents which require debate will emerge. The Procedure Committee in its 1996-97 review of the scrutiny process must look favourably at increasing the number of Standing Committees and the allocation of their subject areas to ensure that quality debate and scrutiny are preserved.

---

86   For example, a debate on a Fisheries document on 13 December 1990 started at 18.59 and finished at 23.15, lasting a total of 4 hours and 16 minutes.

CHAPTER 5

DEPARTMENTALLY RELATED SELECT COMMITTEES IN THE HOUSE OF COMMONS AND EUROPEAN AFFAIRS

INTRODUCTION

In the previous chapters the discussion has concentrated on the specific arrangements within the House of Commons that are integral to the European legislative process. We have seen how the Select Committee on European Legislation examines a document to consider whether it raises issues of "legal or political importance" that will require further debate and discussion in one of the two European Standing Committees.

However, as already stated, the work of these bodies, in particular that of the Select Committee, is very much dictated by external factors, most notably the fast moving timetable within the European Community. This is why the Select Committee is best described as reactive. Not only does Standing Order No. 102 not permit in-depth investigation of European issues, the time constraints do in any event prevent such activity effectively.

In this chapter, the role played by the Departmentally Related Select Committees in European affairs will be evaluated and the issue of how desirable an extension of this role would be considered. The central issue is whether the present arrangements should be replaced with a Ministry for Europe and all the trappings that go with this, i.e. scrutiny by a Departmental Select Committee which is primarily concerned with policy developments and conducting wide ranging political enquiries as opposed to scrutinising legislative developments.

THE SELECT COMMITTEE SYSTEM

Following recommendations made by the Select Committee on Procedure in 1978[1] existing Select Committees such as the Expenditure Committee were to be replaced by a system of Select Committees that related exclusively to each individual government department.[2] These Departmental Select Committees were first established in the 1979-83 Parliamentary session, and in the intervening seventeen year period have developed into a highly effective machinery for scrutinising the government and holding accountable the individual ministers in each of the departments.[3] Their task is a specific one that compliments the work of the Chamber.

---

1   HC 588-I (1977-78).
2   Generally on Select Committees in the House of Commons see Erskine May *Parliamentary Practice* 21st Edition 1989, pp. 611-662. See also Griffith and Ryle *Parliament - Functions, Practice and Procedure* (Sweet and Maxwell 1989), Chapter 11.
3   It should also be noted that the Departmental Select Committees are part of a wider scrutiny arrangement within the House of Commons. There are other Committees appointed to deal with a diverse list of subjects that include Members Interests or Liaison between the Parties. Each of these Committees has a its own Standing Order.

In the forthcoming analysis a comparison between the work of the Departmental Select Committees and that of the Select Committee on European Legislation will be undertaken. Any such analysis must start with an examination and comparison of the Standing Orders of the Select Committees.[4]

THE STANDING ORDERS

Standing Order No. 130

All the Departmental Select Committees are appointed under Standing Order 130 and their Terms of Reference are as follows:

> "To examine the expenditure, administration and policy of the [relevant department]"

The primary difference between Standing Order 130 and Standing Order 102 (which gives the Terms of Reference for the Select Committee on European Legislation) is that Standing Order 130 gives the Departmental Committees a much wider scope and freedom to conduct enquiries on almost any matter which is (or at some time in the future may be) the concern of the department.

Perhaps of greatest significance is the fact that the Departmental Committee may examine policy. Within the European context, it will be the Foreign and Commonwealth Affairs Select Committee that will be the lead department in considering European policy and not the Select Committee on European Legislation. The practical effect of this will be that the Foreign Affairs Select Committee will consider the important political issues concerning the EU, and the Scrutiny Committee will be concerned with only the narrow task of scrutinising any subsequent legislation. This is indicative of the Select Committee system within the House of Commons. That is, there is a distinct division of labour. Each Select Committee is assigned its own task which it exclusively carries out. The risk of duplication is minimised and effective scrutiny maximised. Or at least, this is the theory.

The consideration of policy

The role of the Departmental Select Committees in the European scrutiny process has been described as "complementary and not an alternative".[5] In practice however, there is strong evidence to suggest that as far as European matters are concerned, this division of labour between the Select Committees can actually be detrimental. This main criticism levelled at the present arrangements is that the Standing Orders lead to the Committees working in isolation. That is, one is purely concerned with the policy and the other with

---

4   See also the Chapter 3 for more about the Standing Orders of the Scrutiny Committee.
5   See HC 622-I (Session1988-89) p. xxvii, para. 75.

the procedural matter of ensuring that the legislative proposal has been properly scrutinised. In the course of his research, the author was informed by members of the various Select Committees that Departmental Select Committees should play a greater part in the Scrutiny of European legislative proposals, perhaps by the establishment of a European Sub-committee in each departmental committee.[6] (This issue will be examined in more detail on p. 100).

The second difference between the Scrutiny Committee and a Departmental Committee that arises out of the wording of the Standing Orders is that in considering a "policy", the Departmental Committee is not limited as to what it may enquire into. For example, the Departmental Committee can carry out an enquiry into an issue which is not within the government's legislative programme. In 1993, the Home Affairs Select Committee carried out a wide ranging enquiry into the controversial area of party political funding.[7] The impetus for this was not because of some government Green Paper prior to legislation, but primarily due to public concern about funding for parties from less than legitimate sources.

Once published, the report did not lead to any significant changes in the law and has probably been of greater use for academics (though it may be of more benefit in the future). However, the point cannot be lost. If the Select Committee on European Legislation had a similar remit, would not scrutiny be more effective? The ability to get behind the issues and investigate the policy which is the driving force behind a legislative proposal would be of immense value. Furthermore, this would be more effective than the present arrangements of the Standing Committee discussing the merits of a document in a two and a half hour session perhaps only days before final approval is given in the Council of Ministers.

In its response to the Procedure Committee, the government[8] rejected any such extension on the grounds that this would lead to duplication of the work of the Select Committees.[9] However, this need not necessarily be the case. If the primary role of the Select Committee on European Legislation continues to be scrutiny of draft proposals, with only an extension of its Terms of Reference to consider in more detail the narrow policy implications of the particular legislative proposal, then the more grandiose considerations of government policy towards European affairs generally could be left to the Foreign Affairs Select Committee, e.g. considering government policy at a forthcoming IGC. In this circumstance, it is unlikely that there would be any significant duplication.

Furthermore, it would address what is viewed as the rather absurd situation seen at present. For example, in 1993, the Health Select Committee pub-

---

6   This suggestion was also put to the Select Committee on Procedure in its 1989 report. See HC 662-I (Session 1988-89) p. xxvii, para 76 and HC 622-II (Session1988-89); pp. 74-76, Q 223-254.
7   See HC 726 (Session1992-93) and HC 301 (Session1993-94).
8   See Cm 1081 (Session1988-89).
9   *Ibid.* p. 6 Recomendation 25.

lished a report on the proposed directive on the advertising of tobacco products.[10] Obviously, there were public health implications in such a report. However, it was a European directive and not initiated as a domestic piece of legislation. Whilst the Health Select Committee Report was concerned with the health effects of tobacco advertising in the UK, i.e. did advertising lead to an increase in the number of people smoking, there was no significant appraisal of European policy to this issue. The report looked at government policy in this area, but no effective investigation was made into European policy which was the driving force behind the proposal (See p. 94 below for more discussion on the work of the Health Select Committee).

The above example illustrates that the Scrutiny Committee has the potential to play a larger role without affecting the work of the Departmental Select Committees. A second example illustrates that the two different types of committee can approach a similar problem but from two different perspectives.

In 1986, The Select Committee on European Legislation produced a report[11] on the impact of the Single European Act (SEA) 1986 on Parliamentary scrutiny. Its primary concern was to evaluate the impact of the Cooperation procedure on the European legislative procedure both within the House of Commons and in the Council of Ministers. The report was very inward looking and paid little attention to the wider political issues of the Single European Act.

In comparison, the 1990 report of the Foreign Affairs Select Committee,[12] was a much longer and wide ranging investigation into the policy issues that resulted from the passage of the Single European Act. Of most interest is the fact that the Foreign Affairs Committee produced its report four years after the implementation of the Act, whereas the Scrutiny Committee made its observations about the impact of the SEA within weeks of its passage through Parliament.[13]

What the above two examples suggest is that the Scrutiny Committee could carry out an enhanced investigative role without duplicating the work of other committees. The fact that it has experience of working to a short time frame, will mean that any investigation will only cover the essential aspects of the problem. The wider policy and political issues can still be left to the Departmental Select Committees in the same way as at present.

In these circumstances, the Scrutiny Committee could play a more active role in the legislative process, with the Departmental Select Committees concerning themselves more with reviewing how the policy has worked. The Scrutiny Committee will no longer be purely reactive. Developing this type

---

10   See HC 221-II (Session1992-93).

11   See HC 264 (Session1985-86).

12   See HC 82-I (Session1989-90).

13   On a closer examination it is evident that the Foreign Affairs Select Committee was more concerned with the effects that institutional and Treaty changes, introduced by the Single European Act, had on government policy towards Europe. Furthermore, it also took account of future developments in the European Community.

of relationship between the Departmental Committees and the Scrutiny Committee will go a long way to making the arrangements for examining European issues within the House of Commons "complementary" and thereby more effective.

POWERS OF DEPARTMENTAL SELECT COMMITTEES

For all practical purposes, there is no difference between the powers of Departmental Select Committees and the Select Committee on European Legislation to send for papers and persons or appoint specialist advisers.[14] The Departmental Committees can, and often do appoint specialist advisers when dealing with complex European issues. This is most common on the Agriculture Select Committee, the Environment Select Committee and the Trade and Industry Select Committee whose departments play perhaps the largest role in European policy issues.

THE ROLE OF DEPARTMENTAL SELECT COMMITTEES IN THE SCRUTINY OF EUROPEAN ISSUES

As has been noted above, the role of the Departmental Select Committees is to consider the "expenditure, administration and policy" of the relevant government department. Their primary function is therefore not to scrutinise in detail government legislative proposals. This is the task of the relevant Standing Committee which has been appointed on behalf of the whole House to scrutinise the Bill. At present the only contact the Departmental Select Committees have with European Legislation will be the Explanatory Memorandum (EM) that will be sent to them by the Scrutiny Committee, if there is a legislative proposal that comes within their department's remit. The minister will prepare the EM for the Scrutiny Committee, who in turn send it to the relevant Departmental Committee.

In the discussion that follows, there will be an examination of the attitudes exhibited by the Departmental Select Committees to European issues generally as well as the specific question of how far these Committees keep abreast of European legislative proposals. The following evidence is taken from letters written by the various Chairmen of the Departmental Select Committees to the Select Committee on Procedure when it was gathering evidence for its 1989 Report.[15] Where appropriate, this has been updated and compared with extracts from correspondence that the author received from the Chairmen and Clerks of the Committees. This will enable a comparison to be made to give a current assessment of the work of Departmental Select Committees in this area.

---

14   See S.O. 130.
15   See HC 622-II (Session 1988-89) pp. 132-145.

The Agriculture Select Committee

In his letter to the Procedure Committee, the Chairman of the Agriculture Committee replied that:[16]

> "The Agriculture Committee's scrutiny of European legislation can best be described as sporadic....We only enquire into new Community proposals where they overlap with current enquiries....There are difficulties in persuading the Select Committee members to inquire into topics which are not just technically complex but the subject of delicate and ongoing negotiations by Ministers."

The above comments are surprising given the central position of agricultural policy in the European Community. It remains the most resource consuming aspect of European policy and is a very controversial area – especially reform of the Common Agricultural Policy (CAP) and Common Fisheries Policy (CFP). However, the Committee feel that their primary consideration is one of policy and not legislation though it will consider legislative proposals where they are part of a wider inquiry. In correspondence with the current Clerk of the Committee he explained the Committees role today as follows:

> "The Agriculture Committee's practice in regard to scrutiny of European legislation remains very much as set out in the Chairman's letter to the Chairman of the Procedure Committee submitted as evidence to that Committees 1988-89 inquiry. In particular, the Committee remains wary of conducting inquiries into specific legislative proposals which are under negotiation within the Agriculture and Fisheries Councils, and it has no systematic procedure for sifting or examining such proposals. It continues to receive information from the European legislation Committee on its consideration of EU documents in the agricultural field. That said, the Committee's work in recent years has been drawn increasingly into consideration of general EU policy and its likely future development. I would cite in particular:
> (i) Sixth Report of Session 1992-93, *The Effects of Conservation Measures on the UK Sea Fishing Industry*, HC 620 – this contains detailed analysis of the Common Fisheries Policy;
> (ii) Fifth Report of Session 1993-94, *Health Controls on the Importation of Live Animals*, HC 347 – contains analysis of the harmonization of health controls and veterinary certification of livestock transported across EU national boundaries and entering the EU from third countries;
> (iii) Fourth Report of Session 1994-95, *Horticulture* HC 61-I – deals in part with the European Commissions proposals for reform of the fruit and vegetables regime;
> (iv) Fifth Report of Session 1994-95, *Pesticides Safety Directorate and Medicines Directorate*, HC 391-I – examines, amongst other things, the harmonization of pesticides registration and veterinary medicines licensing procedures across the EU.

---

16   *Ibid.* p.133 Appendix 2.

This increased focus on EU matters is to be welcomed and encouraged. Comprehensive scrutiny of policy is called for. This cannot be done in isolation from legislation. For example, the last inquiry of the Agriculture Committee was into the UK dairy industry and the CAP dairy regime, in the course of which much evidence was taken on possible reforms of CAP. Similarly, a current inquiry into agri-environmental schemes run by the Ministry of Agriculture Fisheries and Food (MAFF) is based on provisions of Council Regulation 2078/92.

There is a definite identifiable shift in the emphasis of the Agriculture Committee's work. Policy is still central to its role but its inquiries do appear to have a more formal approach to legislative proposals. It can no longer be described as the "sporadic" approach as in the letter to the Chairman of the Procedure Committee in 1989. Furthermore, this increased awareness of legislative proposals is not a coincidence. This change can be attributed to the major EC development that has taken place since 1989 – the introduction of the Single Market.

The Single Market has made European policy a reality in terms of being the most significant step towards European integration. This has undoubtedly influenced much domestic policy and most importantly altered the way in which European policy affects domestic policy. The two can no longer be considered in isolation. Any consideration of domestic policy in the agricultural sphere must now also contain an evaluation of both European policy and European legislation. Only in these circumstances will scrutiny be effectively accomplished. The Select Committee is to be applauded for its positive approach.

The Defence Select Committee

In his letter to the Procedure Committee, the Chairman of the Defence Committee replied:[17]

> "The Defence Committee undertakes no scrutiny of European Legislation."

However, Mr Michael Mates MP, the Chairman of the Committee, felt that there was a need to reform the Select Committee process that would allow for a greater role in the Scrutiny process for the departmental Select Committees.

In the correspondence received it is apparent that there has been no change in the approach of the Defence Select Committee to European issues. In particular, it was pointed out that defence was not an area of European Community competence and thus no need for systematic evaluation of European legislation was called for.

The Education and Employment Select Committee

Before considering the work of this Committee it must be pointed out that this is a newly created Committee, working only since March 1996. In 1989

---

17   *Ibid.* Appendix 3.

only the Education Select Committee gave evidence to the Procedure Committee with the Employment Committee making no submissions.

Back then, the Chairman of the Education Committee described his Committee's role as:[18]

> "...relatively inactive in this field"

He outlined the fact that it is the role of the Clerk of the Select Committee to keep his Committee informed of any relevant European legislative developments but he concluded his letter with the observation that:

> "Members of the Committee are aware that satisfactory consideration of EC matters requires *more than can be done by the Scrutiny Committee alone,* (my italics) as presently constituted"

Since the above evidence was given, the Department for Education has ceased to exist as an individual entity. In July 1995, a new department was created, The Department for Education and Employment, and a new Departmental Select Committee was established that reflected this change.

However, before considering the Employment aspects of the Committee's work there is one further observation to be made. In his correspondence, the Clerk of this new Education and Employment Committee reiterated the point that the old Committee "devoted little of its time to European issues, as there is little European competence in the education field." This is a trend which will continue.

From an employment perspective, the Committee is once again primarily concerned with domestic issues. Furthermore, the UK opt-out to the Social Chapter of the Maastricht Treaty means that the UK enjoys much autonomy over employment matters. There are occasional situations where European legislation will affect employment policy, e.g. via legislative proposals made under the Health and Safety directives, but this is rare.

The Clerk concluded his letter by stating that the Committee does not make any special arrangements for detailed scrutiny of European Community documents and what is more has no plans to develop such arrangements. This task he argues is exclusively one for the Select Committee on European Legislation. The Education and Employment Select Committee will only take account of the European dimension as part of inquiries into specific policy issues. It will not hold separate inquiries.

The Environment Select Committee

The Chairman of the Environment Select Committee in his reply to the Procedure Committee gave an account of how that Committee had come to terms with scrutinising European policy in a policy area which has had more

---

18   *Ibid.* p. 134 Appendix 4.

legislation than perhaps any other. What his letter illustrates is that European policy and legislation cannot be viewed in isolation from domestic political considerations and the Committee have acted accordingly to accommodate this.

The Environment Select Committee has adopted a liberal interpretation of its Standing Orders. Whereas other Departmental Committees have not taken a proactive role in scrutinising the impact of European legislative proposals in their own inquiries,[19] the Environment Committee has done so on a regular basis. The Chairman justifies this by pointing out that only by being aware of the complete picture can effective inquiry be made. Furthermore, there is no duplication with the work of the Scrutiny Committee because the investigation is of a wider policy, of which the European legislative proposal is but one part.

The following extract comes from the letter of the then Chairman of the Environment to the Procedure Committee:[20]

> "The Practice of the Committee has been to consider proposals from the Commission *ad hoc*, as part of specific Committee inquiries, and I feel this policy has been fairly successful. ...in our recent Report on Toxic Waste, the EC Directive on the Transfrontier Shipment of Hazardous waste, Commission proposals for common definitions of Waste throughout the Community and the draft Directive on Hazardous Waste 78/319 EEC.
>
> We have therefore instituted a more formal procedure whereby Members of the Committee will receive regular notice of EC documents relating to the responsibilities of the department of the Environment."

The Committee has taken its own initiative and created a process whereby it is informed of any relevant European legislation which it then incorporates, along with other information, into its inquiry. This approach is to be encouraged amongst the Departmental Committees. This use of specific documents in relevant inquiries can be adopted without any change to the Standing Orders. The approach of the Environment Committee illustrates this.

Since the giving of the evidence to the Procedure Committee in 1989, it is a positive step that the Environment Select Committee has continued to take a proactive approach to European Community issues. If anything, the correspondence from the Clerk and Chairman of the Committee suggest a development in their *modus operandi*. The following is an extract from the correspondence which gives examples of how the Committee have developed their scrutiny techniques in the intervening seven year period:

> "The Environment Committee of the current Parliament has continued to look for opportunities to inquire into EU matters. While many of the Committee's inquiries (such as the recent inquiry into *World Trade and Environment* and last years into *Pollution in Eastern Europe*) will have an EU dimension (and involve the

---

19   For example see the comments of the Chairman of the Agriculture Committee above.
20   See HC 622-II (Session 1988-89) p. 135, Appendix 6.

submission of evidence by the Commission) certain inquiries relate more directly into European policy. For example, the Committee's inquiry into *Volatile Organic Compounds* considered in some depth proposals in respect of VOC emissions from fixed (industry) and mobile (vehicles) sources.

The Committee has also visited the European Commission outside the context of particular inquiries, most recently in November 1995. These visits afford an opportunity to be briefed on the full range of activities both current and planned, and put across the Committee's views to the Commissioner and her officials. A further such visit is likely to be made in the Coming Autumn.
The Committee also receives, *via* the Department of the Environment, the agendas of forthcoming Environment Council meetings and a report of the outcome of such meetings."

Of most interest from the above extract is the outlining of the links the Committee have developed with the Commission. As previously stated, the UK Parliament has no formal links with the Commission. However, the Select Committee has identified the value and importance of the Commission in the area of Environmental policy. In the absence of any such formal links, the Select Committee has developed and nurtured its own links. Most importantly, this means that the Committee is kept fully informed of legislative proposals and can therefore examine their impact on both UK and European environmental policy.

Obviously, this Select Committee has good cause to develop such links, because of the ever increasing competence of the EU in this area. Such an arrangement is plainly not necessary for the Defence Select Committee. However, many other Committees who do have some European input into their investigations could look at the Environment Committee as a model to ensure effective scrutiny and accountability.

However, the correspondence concluded with an unequivocal statement that the Committee did *not* seek a role in the scrutiny of European legislation. The consideration of the merits was to be left with the two Standing Committees and this Committee would continue to concentrate on policy, but within a context of awareness of legislative developments.

The Home Affairs Select Committee

The Home Affairs Select Committee by its very nature would only have a limited role in considering European issues, and has developed no formal procedure for carrying out scrutiny. In his Memorandum to the Procedure Committee,[21] the Chairman was quite certain that there should be a clearly defined role between the Departmental Select Committee's and the Scrutiny Committee:

"Because the impact of European legislation on home affairs is so irregular, it would not make sense to establish a more formalised arrangement to ensure effective scrutiny....

---

21   *Ibid.* p.136, Appendix 8.

> The role of the Departmental Select Committees should be concerned with policy and expenditure involved in any European legislation. The technical scrutiny of legislative proposals should remain with a separate Select Committee, as at present."

This conservative and traditional approach to the workings of the House of Commons is still predominant within Parliament today. The division of labour between Committees and the avoidance of duplication are viewed as the key to successful scrutiny. However, the need for change will be irresistible. Ironically, it will be the Home Affairs Select Committee that will be at the forefront of this change.

These developments will be discussed in greater detail in Chapter 6, "The Scrutiny of European Legislation by the House of Commons after Maastricht". There, an examination of how the introduction of the two new pillars of the European Union, the Justice and Home Affairs Pillar and the Foreign Affairs Pillar, have placed a new burden on the Home and Foreign Affairs Select Committees. Legislation under the new pillars is not made by the European Community and therefore not within the ambit of the Scrutiny Committee. This leads to a requirement of a distinct method of scrutinising these legislative proposals, a method in which the Departmental Select Committees will have to play a greater part.

In the course of his correspondence, the Clerk outlined how this new task will be approached. The Committee is kept informed by the Home Office of any significant proposals under the "Third Pillar". A copy of any of the more important initiatives are sent to the Committee Chairman and the Clerk, and these are then made available to all Committee Members. In addition, prior to the convening of the Justice and Home Affairs Council the Committee receives a copy of the draft agenda and after the meeting a copy of any texts agreed. On rare occasions the Home Affairs Committee will hold oral evidence sessions with the Home Office Minister or Officials concerning a particular document. This is uncommon, primarily due to a shortage of time.

However, when considering these documents, the Committee do not go on to produce a separate report. The issues are considered, where relevant, in other inquiries and reports made by the Committee. For example, the Committee's consideration of the EUROPOL proposals was included in the Committee's report on Organised Crime. Contrast this with the House of Lords where Sub-Committee E produced a very detailed inquiry into EUROPOL.

The Social Services Select Committee

The Social Services Select Committee is another Committee which does not have any major input into European Affairs. European documents relating to Social Security are rare as this is still an area of policy which is within the domain of each Member State. This was a point noted by the Chairman of the Social Services Committee in his letter to the Procedure Committee:[22]

---

22   *Ibid.* Appendix 9.

> ".. I do not think it likely that any Committee concerned with Health and/or Social security will deal specifically with European legislation in any great detail."

Once again, this Departmental Committee favours the *ad hoc* approach to European legislation, and does not have any formal procedures for examining these documents. This is a sensible approach if there is little contact with European affairs.

Correspondence from the Chairman and Clerk of the Committee shows that little has changed for what is now called the Social Security Select Committee. In 1989, the department was split with a new Department of Health being created which is shadowed by its own Committee.

There are occasionally issues which do crop up and are relevant to an inquiry, for example the judgment of the European Court of Justice in the *Barber Case*[23] affected the pensions policy of the UK and so the Committee inquired into its effect. There are other incidental references to European issues, e.g. the Committee's recent Report on Housing Benefit Fraud mentioned the EC Data Protection Directive. In addition, a relaxation of the rules that allow Select Committees to travel to Brussels will now allow the Committee to travel to Brussels (June 24 1996) in connection with an inquiry into saving for retirement, where they discussed European pensions policy with Directorates-General V and XV.

However, the role of the Social Security Committee in European affairs is limited by the fact that the UK government secured an opt-out to the Social Chapter at the Maastricht Treaty negotiations. This ensured, for the time being at least, UK autonomy in these matters, and no formal European perspective in its investigations.

The Health Select Committee

As stated above, the Department of Health was only created in 1990 and thus gave no evidence to the Procedure Committee. However, in the intervening six year period the Select Committee has produced two reports on European issues. These are *The European Community and Health Policy* (HC 180 Session 1991-92) and *The EC's Proposed Directive on the advertising of Tobacco Products* (HC 221 1992-93). However, as emphasised in the correspondence from the Clerk and Chairman of the Committee, it does not engage in examination of European Community documents which fall within its reference as a matter of course.

Two reasons were identified for this. Firstly, because of the limited competence of the EC in health matters and secondly, because this task is viewed as being exclusively within the domain of the Select Committee on European Legislation. Inquiries into European issues as the two given above were carried out because they were part of a wider inquiry which the Committee was engaged in.

---

23   Case 262/88 (1990) ECR I-1889.

The Transport Select Committee

Perhaps the most surprising response came from the Chairman of the Transport Select Committee in his letter to the Procedure Committee.[24] The author's reason for being taken aback by his comments is rooted in the fact that transport and related legislation has grown into one of the largest areas of Community competence. The Chairman wrote:

> "An *ad hoc* rather than a systematic approach is taken to European legislation....In view of our heavy programme I cannot see the Transport Committee being in a position to undertake a more systematic approach."

This is further evidence, if it is needed, that reform of the Departmental Select Committees is now overdue. The lack of co-ordination between them and the Scrutiny Committee must be addressed. It is most unsatisfactory that a Departmental Committee that scrutinises government policy which is so widely influenced by European legislative developments, does not have a more structured response to investigating important European legislation.

The evidence indicates that there has been no substantial change to the way this Select Committee operates as far European legislative proposals go.

The general comment running through all the replies seen above is that each one of the Departmental Select Committees has an extremely heavy workload and therefore, could not carry out any substantial investigation into European legislation. This response has a degree of truth to it. However, the fact must be stated that those Departmental Committees which are at the fore of European policy cannot afford to ignore the important developments. Once again, the view is reiterated that the Standing Orders of the Departmental Committees must be amended to facilitate their scrutiny of European issues and, perhaps most importantly, to encourage them to carry out these investigations. The time has come to stop viewing European legislation as some form of "foreign" legislation which is only peripheral to our legal system. The impact of it is continually growing, and this impact must be effectively scrutinised and reviewed.

The Foreign Affairs Select Committee

The Foreign Affairs Select Committee has the responsibility for oversight of the lead Department for European Community matters, the Foreign and Commonwealth Office. This means that it has the overall duty to review EC policy as a whole and the attitude of the British government towards it. Surprisingly though, there are *no* distinct arrangements for review of European affairs and the Chairman in his letter to the Procedure Committee made the following observation:[25]

---

24   *Ibid.* Appendix 19, p. 144.
25   *Ibid.* Appendix 7, pp. 135-136.

> "Beyond such enquiries into the political and constitutional aspects of the EC, we have considered that it is for other Departmental Select Committees to examine EC policies in the subject areas such as trade, transport etc. or for the European Legislation Committee to keep the machinery of Parliamentary scrutiny under review."

The Chairman's response appears over optimistic given the replies seen by the other Chairmen above. With the exception of the Environment Committee none of the other Departmental Select Committees had any formal method of scrutinising European policy, and some such as the Transport Select Committee stressed their already heavy workload that precluded them from further activity in the area.

The Foreign Affairs Select Committee concentrates exclusively on review of government European policy and has no interest in European legislative proposals. To help in this process it has since 1990 conducted regular oral evidence sessions with Foreign Office Ministers on the future programme of the Council of Ministers, including what the priorities of each Presidency will be. In his reply to the Procedure Committee, the Chairman saw this development as benefiting all other Departmental Select Committees and the Select Committee on European Legislation, who would have an earlier warning of what new European legislative proposals will be brought forward during the following six months and could plan their inquiries accordingly. However, as the Home Affairs Committee has now discovered, the involvement in European Affairs will now increase because of the development of the Common Foreign and Security Pillar. The burden of scrutiny will now fall on the Foreign Affairs Select Committee (This will be discussed in more detail in Chapter 6).

The correspondence received from the Chairman and Clerk of the Committee indicates quite strongly that the position has not altered in the intervening seven year period. The Foreign Affairs Committee still views its primary concern as one of scrutinising government policy towards Europe, especially via the oral evidence sessions where the minister was questioned about developments in the Council.

What the above discussion helps to illustrate, is the point that a review of the Departmental Select Committees is long overdue. The fact that each Committee now has different horizons with regard European issues leads to the conclusion that the time has come for the Standing Orders to be reviewed and tailored to the needs of each individual Committee. This should not pose a major problem. Today, there are a variety of other non-departmental Select Committees which carry out very specific tasks as requested by their Standing Orders. Alternatively, following a comprehensive review, changes could be made to the Standing Orders of all Departmental Select Committees, thereby giving them both the potential and encouragement to assume a greater role in the scrutiny of European affairs. Either way, the change cannot be resisted any longer.

DOES THE UK NEED A DEPARTMENT FOR EUROPEAN AFFAIRS?

One question regularly posed by a variety of persons associated with the scrutiny process is whether we need a Select Committee for European Affairs.

Most recently the Select Committee on Procedure investigated the issue in its 1989 report.[26] However, in this author's opinion, this is only half the picture. In addition to this, the question needs to be asked whether there is in fact a need for a Ministry for Europe? Therefore, whereas a Select Committee for European Affairs could operate independently reviewing European policy amongst all the departments, the creation of a Department for European Affairs would mean that such a Select Committee would now be like any other Departmental Select Committee, focussing on the work of that department exclusively.

The United Kingdom is unique amongst its European partners in that there is no Ministry dedicated exclusively to the task of co-ordinating and developing European policies. Though there is a Minister of State[27] at the Foreign and Commonwealth Office whose brief is concerned entirely with European matters, he does not have a place within the cabinet. The primary concern of the Minister of State is with the political developments in the Community, such as enlargement or the reform of the Qualified Voting Procedure. However, it is not his task to coordinate policy between the various government departments. This lack of coordination has been evident recently where different departments, most notably the Agriculture and Health Departments have been saying different things during the so called "beef crisis". Coordination of the UK policy by one single department could only have been to the UK's benefit.

The issue which needs to be addressed is whether the scrutiny process would be improved by creating a Department of European Affairs, which worked independently of the Foreign Office. Therefore, would the creation of some type of umbrella department enhance the influence of the United Kingdom in the Council of Ministers or would it as many have argued, create another unnecessary level of bureaucracy that merely duplicated the functions of other departments?

The strongest argument in favour of creating such a department is that there would be a greater coordination of European policy because one minster would speak with one voice for the government as a whole. He would have the task of ensuring that European issues within each department were dealt with in a uniform manner. Furthermore, this would be a department that had the time to investigate and discuss policy in a detailed manner that the Foreign Office cannot manage, simply because of its other voluminous commitments. Likewise, the Select Committee that shadowed this department would be able to have a similar freedom in investigating the work of the department, something which neither the Foreign Affairs Select Committee nor the Scrutiny Committee can readily do at the moment. Both these important Committees have a variety of other pressing commitments.

In a Memorandum presented to the Select Committee on Procedure, Professor T. St John Bates[28] identified succinctly three specific and considerable

---

26   See HC 622-I (Session 1988-89)p. xxx1, para. 94.
27   At present the Minister of State is David Davies MP.
28   Clerk of Tynwald.

advantages of establishing a Select Committee for European Affairs, which he felt could be established without any fundamental amendments to the existing Select Committee structure within the House of Commons. He wrote:[29]

"There would be distinct advantages in the establishment of a Select Committee on European Affairs which had an order of reference which would enable it to consider:

(a) the efficacy of domestic arrangements in respect of Community Affairs for example: the arrangements within Whitehall for the co-ordination and preparation of the position of the United Kingdom Government on Commission proposals,

(b) long term legal developments within the Communities: for example the growth of the external competence of the EC, and

(c) major Commission policy proposals and legislative proposals, particularly those which could be identified as having a long gestation period.

A Select Committee on European Affairs would thus be able to consider broader issues than is realistically within the capacity of the Select Committee on European legislation or the present Departmental Select Committees."

However, there is a strong alternative argument that any proposed creation of a Department of European Affairs is not possible within the present Committee framework and therefore the view put forward by Professor St John Bates is open to question. There is merit in the view of the Procedure Committee Report when it said that the introduction of such a Committee would have serious repercussions for the Scrutiny Committee and is unlikely to be possible within the present framework:[30]

"The inevitable result of grafting such a Committee on to the existing structure would be a considerable degree of overlap and blurring of responsibilities, since departmentally related committees would unless their Orders of Reference were amended remain charged with monitoring European documents within their ambit."

In effect what the Procedure Committee is saying is that there would not be the room for both a Scrutiny Committee and a Select Committee for European Affairs. With three Committees being involved (the third being the Departmental Committee) there is potential for conflict and differences of opinion that may be unresolvable.

In the quotation given above from the Procedure Committee report the key words are "...unless their Orders of Reference were amended...". The Procedure Committee is suggesting that Departmental Committees with their present Standing Orders would take over the role of the Scrutiny Committee and monitor documents within their ambit. However, the point is that the Standing Orders could be amended to ensure this did not happen.

---

29   See HC 622-II (Session1989-90), Appendix 38, pp. 168 - 173.
30   See n. 25, at p. 95.

The Standing Orders themselves could be amended to preserve the division of labour essential for effective scrutiny. The Scrutiny Committee could continue with the vital task of scrutinising European legislative proposals, as well as examining the narrow policy issues surrounding it. The Departmental Committees could focus on wider policy objectives, for example the Agriculture Select Committee could concentrate on the important issue of reforming the Common Agricultural and Fisheries Policies. And finally, the newly created Select Committee for European Affairs could be concerned with issues of more general government policy, for example government proposals for the six monthly IGC meeting at the end of the Presidency or the complex issue of enlargement of the European Union and Qualified Majority Voting.

Therefore, what this author is arguing for is development in the scrutiny of European issues by creating a new Department of European Affairs and redefining the roles of the existing Committees by amending their Standing Orders accordingly. This would in fact remove the risk of duplication because each Committee would be charged to do a specific task by its Standing Orders.

This does not appear to be a particularly radical step. Changes could be made after an investigation by the Procedure Committee and a comprehensive debate. However, the central point is that European issues are increasingly at the heart of government policy. Many major policies now have some European aspect to them and domestic legislation itself will often be influenced by some directive or regulation. It is, therefore, appropriate that the Select Committee arrangements in the House of Commons should reflect this by permitting more comprehensive analysis of European issues.

At present, it is highly unlikely that any such reform would take place. During conversations with officials at the Cabinet Office[31] it was pointed out that the Foreign Affairs Select Committee is perhaps the most influential and highly regarded of all Select Committees – a fact that it guards jealously. It would not readily accept any removal or downgrading of its role in European affairs.

STRENGTHENING SCRUTINY BY DEPARTMENTAL COMMITTEES

From the above discussion it can be seen that at present there is little enthusiasm for extending the scrutiny function of the Departmental Committees. This is apparent from both the Committees themselves and the government who are not in favour of reforming the Select Committee system. However, this leaves a gaping hole at the centre of the scrutiny arrangements. How then could more effective scrutiny be achieved within a framework of the present arrangements?

---

31   The author interviewed several officials at the Cabinet Office who work in European affairs. The interviews took place on 19 March 1996.

Appointing Sub-Committees

One solution that has been put forward, is to amend the Standing Orders to allow those Departmental Committees to establish Sub-Committees which could hold more lengthy and detailed inquires into those European issues that merited them. Most significantly, such a solution could allow for the Departmental Committees to play a greater role in considering the impact of European legislative proposals on a wider policy area that may be being considered by the main Committee.

Each Sub-Committee could consist of five to six members, who were either already sitting on the main Committee or were specifically co-opted onto the Sub-Committee for the duration of the inquiry.[32] The advantage of this approach would be to give the Select Committee a certain degree of flexibility to carry out inquiries into more complex or politically controversial areas and develop a degree of expertise which is lacking. It would allow each Committee to develop its own procedure, with those facing more European issues being able to utilise the Sub-Committee on a regular basis.

Though proposals for establishing Sub-Committees on Departmental Select Committees were put forward to the Procedure Committee in 1989,[33] they were rejected by the Committee, the government, advisers and academics.[34] The reason most commonly cited was that there is a lack of time and that the establishment of these Sub-Committees would if anything add to the workload. The Clerk of the House stated that such a development would lead to European business being separated from the mainstream of the House.[35] He felt that it would become isolated and not considered within the context of other domestic policy considerations.

This is a slightly perplexing comment to make. As can be seen above, the response of each of the Chairmen of the Departmental Select Committees strongly suggests that European issues are already within the periphery of the House. Seven years on from the Procedure Committee Report, none of the Committees have any formal or systematic arrangements for scrutinising European issues. If anything, the Select Committees tend to shy away from European issues if possible because of their complex and controversial nature. Though not ideal, the establishment of Sub-Committees could have addressed this reluctance on the part of the Departmental Select Committees and raised the profile of European issues in the House. The production of high quality and informative reports could only assist the House of Commons as a whole.

---

32   This would reflect the sort of arrangements already in existence in the House of Lords. For more information on this see Scrutiny Chapters 8 and 9.
33   See HC 622-II (Session 1988-89) Appendix 18, p. 143 and Appendix 26, p. 156.
34   See HC 622-I (Session 1988-89), p. xxix, para. 85.
35   *Ibid.*

CONCLUDING REMARKS

Despite undertaking this lengthy inquiry, the Procedure Committee made no significant recommendations to reforming the role of Departmental Committees in the scrutiny process. In essence it opted for the *status quo*. A *Status Quo* which, given the evidence from the Clerks of the Select Committees available today, appears to suit all the Committees concerned. One proposal was for the government to make provision for the earlier deposit of documents in the House and for better coordination between the Select Committees on European matters.[36] This proposal appears slightly contradictory. Why make proposals for more effective provision of European documents when the Select Committees by their own admission do not have the time or expertise to deal with them?

Without some reform of the Departmental Committees their role in the scrutiny of European affairs cannot be further developed. In essence, there are two alternatives. Either a wholesale reform leading to the establishment of a Select Committee for European Affairs (the author's preferred option) or the more limited proposals for Sub-Committees to be appointed by the Select Committees. However, in either case there would be a raising of the profile of European issues within the House of Commons, leading to more informed debate of these issues.

---

36   *Ibid.* p. xxx, para. 89.

CHAPTER 6

THE SCRUTINY OF EUROPEAN LEGISLATION BY THE HOUSE OF COMMONS AFTER MAASTRICHT

INTRODUCTION

The Maastricht Treaty signed by the Member States in February 1992 was the first significant review of the European Community since the passage of the Single European Act in 1986. The principal aims of the Treaty were to increase the democratic legitimacy of the European Community and to extend the competence of the European Community into new areas.

These changes created a new organisation which has become known as the European Union. This Union is made up of three separate "pillars" of which the European Community is the central one. The two flanking pillars deal with political cooperation in attempting to establish a Common Foreign and Security Policy ("the second pillar") and increasing collaboration in the fields of Justice and Home Affairs ("the third pillar"). The scrutiny arrangements for the two flanking pillars will be considered later in the chapter. In addition to this, in Chapter 10 the scrutiny arrangements for the inter-governmental pillars in the House of Lords are critically analysed. The issues facing *both* Houses of Parliament are virtually identical and some will be dealt with more comprehensively in Chapter 10.

As far as the central pillar of the European Community is concerned, the most significant development related to the introduction of the co-decision procedure, which is designed to increase the involvement of the European Parliament in the legislative process.[1] At the core of this development was an attempt by the Member States to address perhaps the most frequent criticism levelled at the European Community – that of it being undemocratic in its decision making process. The "democratic deficit" as it became known was criticised by all sides involved in the European debate. In particular, the Commission came in for most criticism, primarily because of its central role in the decision making process, yet it was not elected or accountable in any other meaningful way.

THE MAASTRICHT DECLARATION

Prior to the Maastricht negotiations, the United Kingdom government took the view that democratic accountability within the EC could be strengthened by encouraging the involvement of national parliaments in the European legislative process. In evidence given to the House of Lords Select Committee on the European Communities, the former Minister of State at the Foreign and

---

1   For more detail on the decision making process in the European Community see Chapter 1 - The Legislative Process of the European Community.

Commonwealth Office, Tristan Garrel-Jones MP made the following observation:[2]

> "...the Government greatly values the whole process of parliamentary scrutiny and, indeed in our view the whole question of parliamentary scrutiny is one which we think should be acknowledged throughout the Community, and that would bring considerable benefits to the legislative process in Europe and the Community at large."

Because of this firmly held view articulated very succinctly by the former minister, the UK government insisted on a declaration being added to the end of the Maastricht Treaty to make formal this ambition. In fact in his evidence to the House of Lords, Tristan Garrel-Jones justified the inclusion of such a declaration:[3]

> "...This is the reason why we have proposed in the Inter-Governmental Conference that there should be a declaration attached to whatever Treaty emerges that would enable national parliaments to take the sort of interest in the process which is taken certainly by our Parliament but not perhaps by some of our partner countries."

These sentiments were also expressed to the author when he interviewed the former minister.[4] He stated quite categorically that he felt that some countries were taking the issue of scrutiny "not too seriously". In particular, he cited the southern Mediterranean countries as being the worst offenders. In fact it was not until after the Maastricht Treaty that Spain, Greece and Portugal introduced effective machinery for the scrutiny of legislative proposals within their national parliaments. In retrospect, the Declaration can be hailed as the impetus to addressing this issue.

The actual declaration reads as follows:[5]

> "The Conference considers that it is important to encourage greater involvement of national parliaments in the activities of the European Union.
> To this end, the exchange of information between national parliaments and the European Parliament should be stepped up. In this context, the governments of the Member States will ensure, inter alia, *that national parliaments receive Commission proposals for legislation in, good time for information or possible examination* (my italics). Similarly, the Conference considers that it is important for contacts between the national parliament and the European Parliament to be stepped up, in particular through the granting of appropriate reciprocal facilities and regular meetings between members of Parliament interested in the same issues."

2　See HL 35 II (Session 1990-91) p.121, para. 240.
3　*Ibid.*
4　The interview took place at the House of Commons on 25 April 1994.
5　See EC Treaty as amended by Treaty on European Union (TEU).

In the author's opinion, the most significant part of this declaration is the section that has been placed in italics. The reason for this is that in the UK, the Select Committees of both Houses are solely reliant on the government not only to supply it with the legislative proposals but also to provide the Explanatory Memorandum which will detail the government's response to the proposal. These two documents are the basis of the scrutiny arrangements. If either is missing, effective scrutiny is impossible.

The fact that accountability to national parliaments and the provision of texts to them is placed on a formal footing in the Treaty is, from a scrutiny perspective, a very encouraging development. However, as will be demonstrated later this is not a guarantee to government cooperation at all times. The evidence does suggest that the UK government does not keep to the spirit of the Declaration at all times.

Reasons for the inclusion of the Declaration

As previously stated the government insisted on this Declaration being included because they saw the involvement of all national parliaments in scrutiny as being essential for the EC to become more democratic. In essence, the Declaration is attempting to prevent what may be best referred to as a double democratic deficit. That is to say, one within the institutions and one at a national level. By actively encouraging scrutiny by national parliaments, the UK government saw this as a way to bridge the gulf between the need for accountability, without marginalising the role of domestic legislatures.

From a political perspective, it was also important for the United Kingdom government to sell the Treaty to its own highly sceptical backbenchers. Without their support the Treaty would not have been passed through Parliament. Of most anguish to these backbenchers was the increased role now adopted by the European Parliament through the introduction of the co-decision procedure. This was seen as a challenge to the constitutional position of Parliament in the UK. By guaranteeing some control over the legislative process through the encouragement of scrutiny by national parliaments the government viewed this Treaty as more palatable. However, as history will record in years to come, this Declaration was not in itself enough to silence the critics. In the end, the Treaty was passed only by the threat of a general election if the government lost the vote of confidence in the House.

The above discussion illustrates, that at the Maastricht negotiations the government tried to reconcile two contradictory principles. On the one hand it supported the introduction of the co-decision procedure and on the other pushed strongly for the Declaration. Co-decision as we shall see in the next section was intended to address the democratic deficit. So was the Declaration. However, the UK (and other governments it must also be said) was not prepared to achieve this accountability at the expense of the domestic legislature. What has been created is in fact an unsatisfactory outcome for all sides. Both the European Parliament and national parliaments retain some accountability – yet neither is able to exert effective control over the legislative process and most importantly over the Council of Ministers.

THE SINGLE EUROPEAN ACT 1986: THE CO-OPERATION PROCEDURE

The Single European Act 1986 (SEA) is the beginning of a process which cul-
minated in the signing of the Maastricht Treaty in 1992. Though the SEA was
primarily concerned with establishing the legal framework of the of the Single
European Market it did also address other criticisms – namely the charge that
the European Community was an undemocratic organisation.

At the heart of this democratic deficit was the role of the institutions, and
in particular, the position of the European Parliament. The European Parliament had been elected since 1979, however its powers had not changed in
any significant way. In essence, it was still regarded as a mere assembly. The
cooperation procedure was intended to remedy this by giving the European
Parliament an input into the legislative process of the European Community.

In any discussion relating to the scrutiny arrangements post Maastricht it
is essential to begin with the SEA and the cooperation procedure. The reason
for this is that the SEA can best be described as the foundation of the Maastricht Treaty. This is a process that was concluded at the 1997 Amsterdam
Summit which developed closer links between EU Member States.

The Cooperation Procedure[6]

The cooperation procedure gives the European Parliament an input into the
legislative process. The Commission submits a proposal for legislation to the
Council of Ministers, and at the same time seeks the opinion of the European
Parliament on the proposal. The Council of Ministers will deliberate on the
proposal, which will lead to the adoption of the common position. Prior to
the adoption of the common position the Select Committee on European
Legislation will conduct its scrutiny of the proposal (about which more is said
in the next section). During this time the Scrutiny Reserve will operate and
the UK minister cannot agree to the proposal except in special circumstances.

Once the scrutiny round has been completed the minister can then cast
his vote in the Council which by Qualified Majority Voting, will adopt the
common position. At this stage, the process moves to the floor of the European Parliament. The Parliament has three options open to it with regard the
common position:[7]

(i)   Approve or do nothing;
(ii) Propose amendments to the common position;
(iii) Reject the common position.

As the above three options demonstrate, the avenues open to the European
Parliament are quite limited. Most notably, the European Parliament is not
involved in the formulation of the legislation and its role is essentially consul-

---

6   See Article 189c (as inserted by Article G(61) TEU).
7   See Article 189c TEU (c)-(e).

tative. However, these three options *do* have a much greater impact on the domestic scrutiny arrangements within the House of Commons and in particular on the ability of the Select Committee to conduct effective scrutiny.

Impact of the co-operation procedure on the Commons scrutiny process

As was stated above, the Commons scrutiny process becomes active at the point before the Council adopts its common position. The document will, along with the government's Explanatory Memorandum, be submitted to the Select Committee. If the Committee are of the opinion that the document raises questions of "legal and political importance",[8] they will then recommend debate of the proposal in one of the two European Standing Committees.[9]

Once the scrutiny of the common position is completed the document then goes to the European Parliament which then has the three options open to it. As far as domestic scrutiny arrangements are concerned, options (i) and (iii) above pose least problem. If the European Parliament choose option (i), the Council of Ministers can then adopt the legislative proposal in accordance with the common position when they finally meet. Alternatively, if the proposal is rejected in line with option (iii), then the Council of Ministers may still adopt, by unanimity, the proposal or let it lapse. Either way, the original proposal has not changed.

However, it is the proposal of amendments to the legislation in line with option (ii) by the European Parliament which causes most concern to the Select Committee on European Legislation. Following a proposal of amendments by the European Parliament, the Commission will within one month re-examine the document and forward its views to the Council along with an opinion on the amendments which it has not accepted.[10]

The impact on the Commons scrutiny process is evident. The scrutiny round undertaken by the Select Committee has taken place *prior* to the adoption of the common position and most significantly *before* any amendments have been proposed by the European Parliament. Thus, scrutiny has been conducted on the basis of the *original* document as published by the Commission and submitted to the Council. Therefore, any amendments proposed by the European Parliament will not automatically be subject to scrutiny by the House of Commons.

The position is still complicated further by the options open to the Council of Ministers. It can, *inter alia*, adopt by unanimity the European Parliament amendments that were not accepted by the Commission. In effect, the Council can adopt a substantially different text from that originally proposed by the Commission. The one saving grace, is that unanimity is required for this to occur and a Member State does potentially have a veto.

---

8   See Standing Order 127 (1) (a).
9   For more detail on this procedure see Chapters 3 and 4.
10   See Article 189c (d) TEU.

However, even this is questionable for two reasons. First, the Member State holding the Presidency of the Council may be particularly enthusiastic on the amendments of the European Parliament and will try to force them through. Under these circumstances, it may be extremely difficult for a British minister to resist the amendments if the other fourteen ministers agree. Secondly, because the Council of Ministers meets behind closed doors, it is highly likely that there will be some political "horsetrading" between ministers and the President of the Council to allow the amended proposal to go through.

So where does this leave the Commons scrutiny process? There are two possibilities. First, prior to final adoption by the Council of Ministers of the amended proposal, the Select Committee may wish to re-examine this amended proposal. However, such a second round of scrutiny is difficult because of the limits of time and the quick moving process within the Council.[11] Alternatively, the Select Committee could do nothing and just allow the minister to accept the proposal. Ideally, the first option is to be preferred. However, a further scrutiny reserve is unlikely to be accepted by the Presidency if it is to mean a substantial delay in adoption, or if the Presidency of the Member State is coming to a conclusion. The net result is that the scrutiny process suffers and by implication so does accountability of the Executive, which in the UK is the cornerstone of Parliamentary democracy.

It is apparent therefore that the cooperation procedure works independently of scrutiny arrangements within the House of Commons. It is this fact that contributes most to making the procedure one which is very difficult to follow. However, despite the difficulties with the cooperation procedure, Member States still felt that further reform was needed. Perhaps most significantly, charges of a democratic deficit had not subsided. It was felt that by increasing the role of the European Parliament in the legislative process the European Community could become more accountable. Though the jury is still out as to the success of these changes, their potential impact on the House of Commons and its scrutiny arrangements can already been identified.

THE MAASTRICHT TREATY[12]

The Maastricht Treaty which was so painstakingly negotiated in December 1991 in the town that lends its name to the Treaty came into force on November 1 1993. Within the United Kingdom, the implementation of the Treaty was anything but a straight forward process. The government's Parliamentary majority being only 19 meant that its rebellious backbenchers nearly scuppered the whole Treaty and brought down the government in the process. The Treaty only became part of United Kingdom law when the government tied the fate of the Treaty to its own by putting forward a vote of confidence which its backbenchers, mindful of the government's ever increasing unpopu-

---

11   See HC 400 (Session 1985-86) pp. xv-xvii.
12   Treaty on European Union, Official Journal C224 August 31 1992.

larity, had no alternative but to support. Anything else would have led to the fall of the government – the proverbial turkeys voting for Christmas!

The Maastricht Treaty made a number of significant changes to the institutional framework of what is now called the European Union. From the scrutiny perspective, the two most important changes are the introduction of the co-decision procedure, which gives a much greater legislative role to the European Parliament, and the establishment of the inter-governmental pillars on Foreign and Security Policy, and on Justice and Home Affairs. In the proceeding sections, the impact of these developments on the scrutiny procedures in the House of Commons will be examined, concentrating on how they have affected the ability of Parliament to control the executive.

The Co-decision Procedure[13]

The co-decision procedure is set out in Article 189b Treaty on European Union. Broadly speaking, it is based upon the pre-Maastricht cooperation procedure described above.[14] The principle aim of the co-decision process is to address the democratic deficit still prevalent in the European Community despite direct elections to the European Parliament and the introduction of the cooperation procedure in the Single European Act. The co-decision process aims to do this by enhancing still further the powers of the European Parliament in the legislative process, whilst also limiting the role of the unelected Commission.

The co-decision procedure operates in parallel with the cooperation procedure,[15] but most importantly contains one extra stage. Whereas under the cooperation procedure the Council of Ministers will let lapse a proposal amended by the European Parliament which it did not approve of, under the co-decision procedure, if the Council does not approve the amended text, the Conciliation Committee is convened. This extra step is referred to as the "Third Reading" stage.

The Role of the Conciliation Committee[16]

The Conciliation Committee as its name suggests attempts to reach a compromise between the Council and the European Parliament when there is disagreement on the substance of a legislative proposal. The end result of the Conciliation Committee is for the Council and Parliament to agree a joint text. The Conciliation Committee itself is comprised of fifteen representatives of the Council and an equal number from the European Parliament. When the

---

13 The co-decision procedure is also referred to as negative assent.
14 In fact the co-decision procedure relates to very similar legislative proposals to the co-operation procedure.
15 See n. 6, at p. 106.
16 For more detail on the work of the Conciliation Committee see Nugent *The Government and Politics of the European Unio*n (Macmillan 1994) pp. 37-322.

Committee meets, the Council of Ministers acts by qualified majority and the European Parliament by simple majority when a vote is taken on the joint text.

As stated above, the principal aim of the Conciliation Committee is to reach a compromise on the proposed text within a six week period. Article 189b of the Treaty on European Union provides:[17]

> (5) If within six weeks of its being convened, the Conciliation Committee approves a joint text, the European Parliament, acting by an absolute majority of the votes cast and the Council acting by a qualified majority, shall have a period of six weeks from that approval in which to adopt the act in question in accordance with the joint text. If one of the two institutions fails to approve the proposed act, it shall be deemed not to have been adopted.

> (6) Where the Conciliation Committee does not approve a joint text, the proposed act shall be deemed not to have been adopted unless the Council, acting by a qualified majority within six weeks of expiry of the period granted to the Conciliation Committee, confirms the common position to which it agreed before the conciliation procedure was initiated, possibly with amendments proposed by the European Parliament. In this case the act in question shall be finally adopted unless the European Parliament, within six weeks of the date of confirmation by the Council, rejects the text by an absolute majority of its component members, in which case the proposed act shall be deemed not to have been adopted."

As (6) above illustrates, the Council may act unilaterally in the event of failure by the Conciliation Committee to reach a compromise by resurrecting the original common position. This gives the Council greater power in that only it can revive a proposal if the Conciliation Committee fails to agree a joint text, but this power is checked by the European Parliament which still has to approve this course of action. What this illustrates is that there is the beginnings of system of checks and balances within the European Community, even though this system is rather cumbersome. The democratic deficit has been partially addressed.

Despite this major shift in the functioning of the European Community, the co-decision procedure has been subject to criticism from both sides of the European debate. Those who the media refer to as "Eurosceptics" view this change as the first step to a European Superstate with the European Parliament taking over as the sole legislative body. Their primary fear is that the Westminster Parliament may degenerate into no more than a than a mere local authority, Parliamentary sovereignty being confined to the pages of history. For such Eurosceptics, this is the biggest challenge facing the United Kingdom today – how can Parliament maintain its position as the supreme legislative body?

---

17   See Article 189b (5)-(6) TEU.

However, for pro-Europeans the changes at Maastricht are considered a missed opportunity. Most significantly, they feel that the occasion was not grasped to bring full accountability to the European Community. That is to say, the subjecting of the unelected Commission and the secretive Council of Minsters to the popular control of the European Parliament. In effect their argument is based on the European Parliament becoming the legislative body in a Federal Europe with the other institutions being under the Parliament's control.

The reality though is wholly different. In fact all that was achieved at Maastricht was a political compromise in the true European sense. That is, the Member States accepted the charge of the European Community being undemocratic but, for domestic political reasons, were reluctant for their national parliaments to be completely removed from the legislative process. Countries such as the United Kingdom and Denmark which have developed scrutiny procedures, knew that their national parliaments would not countenance any reduction in their scrutiny activities. With the introduction of the co-decision procedure, a legislative process has been introduced which is cumbersome, complicated and most importantly from a scrutiny perspective, difficult to monitor.

HOUSE OF COMMONS SCRUTINY OF THE CO-DECISION PROCEDURE

The primary difficulty experienced by the Select Committee in its attempt to scrutinise legislative proposals being introduced under the co-decision procedure is that the time frame used by the Select Committee and the one within which the institutions of the European Community work do not readily correspond. To a great extent, this is a problem which has been faced by the Select Committee during the last twenty three years.

The Flow of information

One of the distinctive features of the co-decision process is the rapidity with which decisions may be reached once a joint text is agreed. For scrutiny to be effective, it is essential that the government responds promptly to the needs of the Select Committee by making information about the proposal available. The Select Committee in its report "Scrutiny after Maastricht"[18] made this very observation:[19]

"The scrutiny process is designed to give the House an opportunity to influence Ministers before they participate in Council decision making. A legislative proposal or other document caught by Standing Order 127(1) is deposited in the House....In respect of each deposited document the Government prepares an

---

18   See HC 99 (Session 1993-94).
19   *Ibid.* p. v, para. 5.

Explanatory Memorandum reporting on aspects such as legal base, subsidiarity, financial implications and timetable, and setting out its policy towards the proposal."

In essence, what the Select Committee is saying is that its objectives when scrutinising proposals under the co-decision process are exactly the same as before. The central element of scrutiny is to influence the minister and this can only be done by the government supplying all the necessary information. The European Secretariat within the Cabinet Office which is responsible for the provision of all government documents to the Select Committee performs its task admirably in what can best be described as difficult circumstances. In conversation[20] with two civil servants at the European Secretariat the point was stressed that the government is not always to blame for the non-delivery of information. The government, they pointed out, must wait on both the European Parliament to propose amendments and the Commission to deliver opinions on these amendments before this information can be supplied to the Select Committee. If this is delayed it will inevitably cause a ripple effect. In the meantime though, events will move on and the Council may reach opinions on the amendments long before the Commission does. Only once Commission opinions are given to the Council, will the minister then present these to the European Secretariat who will inform the Select Committee who in turn will conduct their scrutiny.

However, the complication is if the Council has refused to include the amendments proposed by the European Parliament. If this occurs, the Conciliation Committee will be convened. Though it has six weeks to arrive at a compromise, it is likely to do so only in a matter of days. Thus, scrutiny by the Select Committee is squeezed. Whilst it may be considering the European Parliament amendments and Commission opinions, the Conciliation Committee will in fact be agreeing a text that is wholly different. Scrutiny has been pointless. This is because the government has controversially refused to extend the Resolution of the House to cover the Conciliation Committee stage. This issue is dealt with further on page 115 below.

This is the other major difficulty now facing the Select Committee – the increase in the role of the European Parliament. The heart of the problem is that though the European Parliament may propose one set of amendments to the proposal which the Select Committee may scrutinise (time permitting of course), the Conciliation Committee may then agree a revised set. In practice therefore, the Select Committee can not be confident that the amendments it has received from the European Parliament will be the final word.[21]

As can be seen, it is the flow of information to the Select Committee that allows the scrutiny process to function. In its report "Scrutiny after Maastricht", the Select Committee raised several important issues which it viewed

---

20   The conversation was with David North and Les Saunders who work in the Cabinet
      Office in Whitehall and took place on the 19 March 1996.
21   See HC 99 (Session 1993-94) p. vi, paras. 6 and 7.

as central to the maintenance of effective scrutiny procedures. At the heart of these, were the concerns about the increased role of the European Parliament and the effect this will have on scrutiny. In particular, the Select Committee were anxious to safeguard the value of the Explanatory Memorandum – the starting point of scrutiny. In situations where there is some deviation from the original proposal, the Select Committee recommended the following:[22]

1. If the European Parliament proposes amendments to the common position, the amended text plus the Commission opinion should be deposited. This should be done by means of an EM.
2. If the Council does not approve the European Parliament's amendments then the Select Committee should be informed by means of an EM.
3. If the Conciliation Committee approves a joint text, then the text should be deposited and an EM submitted.
4. If the Conciliation Committee fails to approve a joint text then the Select Committee should be informed of the position by a supplementary EM.

The Select Committee in understanding the importance of EM's argues quite forcefully for their continuation during all stages of the co-decision process. In particular they are fighting to maintain the influence which the Select Committee has over the minister.

The government's response

The government provided its response to the report "Scrutiny after Maastricht" as part of the Select Committee's report entitled "Parliamentary Scrutiny of the Co-decision Procedure".[23] The response of the government can at best be described as lukewarm to the four principal recommendations given above.

In particular, in the situations of 2 and 4 above, the government suggested that only a brief letter from the minister should be sent informing the Select Committee and not an EM as suggested.[24] However, this may not be the most appropriate method especially if the Council has changed its common position substantially in the light of stages 2 or 4 above. Following 2 above, the proposal will go to the Conciliation Committee who are likely to agree a substantially different text. Similarly, following 4, the Council may still adopt the proposal and incorporate some of the European Parliament amendments.

In either situation, there is a change from the original common position. An explanation of these changes will require more detailed information than can possibly be contained in a brief letter. Furthermore, an EM could give the Select Committee an up-to-date report of the Council negotiations,

---

22   *Ibid.*
23   See HC 739 (Session 1993-94).
24   *Ibid.* p. x, para. 6(a).

including, most importantly, the government's position regarding the European Parliament's amendments.

Though the government is right to argue that a letter can be despatched more quickly than an EM,[25] it will not be as thorough. Surely, effective scrutiny should not be sacrificed to ensure arbitrary deadlines are met? That is to say, the government should give the House of Commons both the time and information needed to complete its scrutiny functions. As this scrutiny will be focussed on the amendments that have been adopted by the Conciliation Committee, it is unlikely to be a lengthy operation. However, even if it did require additional time this should be given to the Select Committee. Difficult choices need to be made. If the government are serious about scrutiny then they should be not only prepared to accommodate it, but also defend the right of our Parliament to conduct it. After all, this would be in keeping with both the spirit and the wording of the Maastricht Declaration.

THE RESOLUTION OF THE HOUSE AND THE CO-DECISION PROCEDURE

When the work of the Select Committee on European Legislation was discussed in Chapter 3, the importance of the Resolution of the House of 24 October 1990 was stressed. It was referred to as the "cornerstone" of the scrutiny process by restraining a minister from giving agreement in the Council until the scrutiny process is completed. In the report "Scrutiny after Maastricht", the Select Committee recommended the extension of the Resolution to cover what it referred to as the "crucial stages"[26] of the co-decision process. By this it meant not only the stage at which the European Parliament proposes amendments, but also the third reading stage – i.e. the involvement of the Conciliation Committee. To accommodate this, the Select Committee suggested an amendment to the Resolution. It proposed paragraph (2) of the Resolution read as follows:[27]

> "In this Resolution, any reference to agreement to a proposal includes:-
> (a) in the case of a proposal on which the Council acts in accordance with the procedure referred to in Article 189b of the Treaty of Rome (co-decision), agreement to a common position, to a joint text, and to confirmation of the common position (with or without amendments proposed by the European Parliament); and
> (b) in the case of a proposal on which the Council acts in accordance with the procedure referred to in Article 189c of the Treaty of Rome (co-operation), agreement to a common position."

---

25   *Ibid.*
26   See HC 99 (Session 1993-94), p. vi, para. 8.
27   *Ibid.* The full revised Resolution can also be found in Annex D of HC 51 p. xxvii. See also p. 48 for the current wording.

Such an extension is not only logical but also desirable. In particular, it will make formal the relationship between the Select Committee and the Executive which in terms of scrutiny has changed substantially post Maastricht. Also, it will bring the House of Commons into line with the Maastricht Declaration which encourages the involvement of national parliaments in the scrutiny process. The Declaration which it must be reiterated that the UK government insisted on being included. So what has been the UK government's view to this extension of the resolution? Sadly, but perhaps predictably it has been unenthusiastic.

The government's opinion

The Leader of the House, the Right Honourable Tony Newton MP, provoked most controversy in his response to the Select Committees proposal of extending the Resolution of the House. He was prepared to extend the Resolution to cover the amendments proposed by the European Parliament. This is logical and desirable if the House of Commons is to continue to exert influence over the minister and ensure effective scrutiny. Though the evidence suggests[28] that waiting for European Parliament amendments and Commission opinions on those amendments may be a lengthy process, the government to their credit have kept to the limits of the Resolution and delayed giving agreement in Council until scrutiny is completed.

However, this is not as promising as it may initially appear. The reason given for this is that though the Resolution of the House covers the stage up to and including the scrutiny of European Parliament amendments, the government have not permitted its extension to cover the stages that begin with the convening of the Conciliation Committee. This is highly perplexing, because the scrutiny up to this point will now be potentially worthless. If the Conciliation Committee needs to be convened and approves a joint text substantially different to that which was based on the common position and European Parliament amendments, the Select Committee will find it difficult to scrutinise this joint text. This will be due primarily to a lack of time. In essence, this author's argument is one that extending the Resolution only part of the way is fundamentally flawed. In practice it can mean that the Select Committee has wasted its valuable time.

The government based its reasoning on the fact that once the joint text is agreed no further amendment is permitted to it. At this juncture, the Council can only accept or reject it. The Leader of the House stated rather optimistically that:[29]

> "...it is very unlikely that the Council will then decide to throw away all this hard work."

---

28   See HC 51-xxvii (Session 1995-96), p. xlii, para. 149.
29   See HC 739 (Session 1993-94) p. x, para. 7.

The Leader of the House then continues his observations by stating that once the joint text is agreed there will be very little time before final agreement in the Council to allow for a further round of scrutiny. In particular, he stresses that other Member States would not be willing to tolerate any further delay to allow the United Kingdom Parliament to complete scrutiny:[30]

> "…it will often be impossible to operate a scrutiny reserve; other Member States will not countenance a delay of weeks in ratification to accommodate a United Kingdom reserve."

The response to this is that if the government has followed the limits of the Resolution to this stage, any further scrutiny will not be lengthy. It will concentrate exclusively on the changes to the common position and the amendments proposed by the European Parliament. If the government has acted with propriety, the Select Committee's task will be relatively brief.

However, there is a much stronger argument for extending the Resolution, and one which exposes a contradiction in the policy of the UK government to the whole issue of scrutiny. The government continually stresses the importance of national parliaments in the European legislative process. At the time of the Maastricht negotiations the government believed one of its many successes to be the inclusion of the Declaration which was intended to enhance the role of national parliaments. If the government were as fully committed to this as they claim to be, the Leader of the House would not be making such negative remarks. Surely, it would appear to make sense that once a text has been approved by the Conciliation Committee, *every* national parliament and not just that of the United Kingdom would want to take an interest in the amended proposal. If the Declaration is to have any credibility then the Council should wait until all national parliaments have completed their scrutiny. If this is not permitted all that will happen is that one democratic deficit will be replaced by another.

HOUSE OF COMMONS SCRUTINY OF THE INTER-GOVERNMENTAL PILLARS[31]

> "The opportunity for greater openness and democracy offered by the last Inter-Governmental Conference was squandered. It is a sad paradox that, when the democratic deficit was so widely recognised, the Maastricht Treaty should have introduced two areas of inter-governmental cooperation more effectively insulated from democratic control and accountability than almost anything in the existing Treaties."[32]

---

30   *Ibid.* para. 8.

31   For further discussion on this area and explanation of how the pillars function see Chapter 10 "Arrangements in the House of Lords for Scrutiny of the Inter-Governmental Pillars".

32   This quotation is the initial observation on the inter-governmental pillars by the Select Committee in its most recent report *The Scrutiny of European Business.* HC 51 xxvii (Session 1995-96).

The two new inter-governmental pillars created by the Maastricht Treaty are intended to develop inter-governmental cooperation between Member States. In addition to the European Community (the central pillar), there are two "flanking pillars" whose objectives are quite distinct and separate from the central pillar. The second pillar is intended to develop closer political cooperation by means of a "common foreign and security policy" and the third pillar closer cooperation in the field of "justice and home affairs". The aims of the two new Pillars will now be briefly examined.

Common Foreign and Security Pillar (CFSP)[33]

The aim of this pillar is to increase political cooperation between the Member States by forming what will in effect be a single foreign policy for the European Union. Article J.1.2 of the Treaty on European Union (TEU) sets out the primary objectives. Taken as a whole these objectives reflect the ambition of the European Union to become a more self sufficient organisation in this area and more independent of United States influence. This is a reaction to the post cold war situation and the removal of American forces from Europe. In particular, some Member States see this as the first step towards a common defence policy.

Under the CFSP a majority of the documents will be non-legislative and short term, and will not require domestic legislation. Furthermore, a characteristic of documents under this pillar will be that they remain confidential until final agreement has taken place. Although the government has pledged to present all texts of CFSP statements, declarations, common positions and joint actions once they are agreed, it does not consider it appropriate in the vast majority of cases to lay drafts of CFSP texts before Parliament. The reason given by the government is one based on maximising its negotiating strength in the Council by not showing its hand until it absolutely has to. For a similar reason it has rejected extending the scrutiny reserve to cover CFSP texts arguing that once a proposal is agreed there will be little or no time before final approval. This will mean that there can be no wait for Parliament to conduct its scrutiny.[34]

The Justice and Home Affairs (JHA) Pillar[35]

Under this third pillar Member States are developing cooperation in what Article K.1 defines as "matters of common interest". This includes policy areas which up to now have been traditionally within the domestic sphere e.g. asylum policy, immigration policy and external border controls. In addition there is new cooperation to combat *inter alia* organised crime and drug-trafficking.

---

33 See Title V TEU Article J.
34 These issues are discussed in more detail in Chapter 10, where in particular the issue of confidentiality and how this has affected scrutiny has been examined. All these issues affect both the Commons and the Lords equally.
35 See Title VI Article K TEU.

As far as the JHA pillar is concerned, the government has taken a more flexible approach to the provision of documents. The Home Secretary has offered to provide the first full text of any Convention or proposal which would if agreed require later primary legislation in the United Kingdom, and of other documents of significant importance subject to possible security or operational exceptions which would only be used "where absolutely necessary".

The primary reason for this more flexible approach is based on the less sensitive nature of the subject matter being discussed under this pillar. Proposals will not be concerned with diplomatic and military secrets. However, the Home Secretary's proposal for provision of documents only covers situations when primary legislation will be required and not when the Convention or proposal will be implemented by secondary legislation. This is a discrepancy which has been questioned by both the House of Commons and House of Lords.[36]

The initial experience

Scrutiny of the inter-governmental pillars got off to a slow start. As with any new procedure, the Select Committee needed to find its parameters. At the outset, the Commons was influenced quite substantially by developments in the House of Lords which had already conducted a major inquiry into how the pillars could be effectively scrutinised. The Select Committee on European Legislation in the House of Commons noted that new procedures would be needed in this House when it published its report "Scrutiny after Maastricht" in 1993. However, in 1996 there are still no formal procedures within the Commons despite the increased activity under the pillars. In fact, the government has hailed as a success inter-governmental cooperation under the pillars in its White Paper on the IGC called "A Partnership of Nations".[37]

It is apparent therefore that activity under the pillars will grow and is likely to be extended following the IGC. As a result, this will become a growing part of the United Kingdom's domestic and foreign policy which will undoubtedly impose constraints upon the government. This must be subject to democratic control. The European Parliament has only a peripheral role under the pillars with the majority of the work being left to the Commission and Council of Ministers. In this case, the argument for effective scrutiny by all national parliaments of activity under the pillars is irresistible. The quotation from the Select Committee given at the start of this section reflects this increasing isolation that the Committee is feeling with regards European Union legislation. The evidence from the Select Committee contradicts the Maastricht Declaration. The United Kingdom Parliament is excluded from any effective influence in the inter-governmental decision making process. In the subsequent sections the arrangements in the Commons designed to redress this balance will be analysed.

---

36   This issue is also examined more closely in Chapter 10.
37   See Cm 3181 paras. 40 and 52.

ARRANGEMENTS FOR SCRUTINY OF THE PILLARS IN THE HOUSE OF COMMONS

CFSP matters fall exclusively within the Terms of Reference of the Foreign Affairs Select Committee and the JHA is within the domain of the Home Affairs Committee. Both of these Select Committees have taken oral evidence from witnesses primarily as a means of monitoring developments under the Pillars. However up to September 1996, two years since the introduction of decision making under the Pillars, neither Committee has yet reported on a document.

By contrast, the government has so far submitted approximately 30 JHA documents in draft.[38] Copies of these are sent to both the Scrutiny Committee and the Home Affairs Select Committee. However, the Terms of Reference of the Scrutiny Committee are limited to matters coming under the Community pillar and it cannot report on them or even formally consider them. As far as the CFSP is concerned, the government has not yet submitted any document before adoption.[39]

Both the Foreign Affairs and the Home Affairs Select Committees are Departmental Select Committees whose primary task according to their Standing Orders is to examine "policy and expenditure" of the relevant department. In Chapter 5, there was a brief examination of how far these two Departmental Select Committees involved themselves in European issues. The following sections involve a more comprehensive analysis of the work each Committee does.

The Foreign Affairs Select Committee

This Committee is essentially concerned with policy developments in the European Union and in particular government policy. There are no formal procedures for dealing with proposals under the CFSP Pillar, though the Committee is kept informed of developments by means of documents from the Foreign Office. The primary reason for this concentration on policy issues is that the Committee simply does not have the time to carry out such inquiries into legislative proposals. Furthermore, as the evidence shows, there are as yet no CFSP documents that have been submitted to the Committee before adoption. Under these circumstances, scrutiny is not a primary consideration for the Committee.

The Home Affairs Select Committee

The Home Affairs Select Committee as its name suggests is not specifically concerned with European issues. However, it does have primary responsibility for scrutiny of proposals under the JHA Pillar. This is sensible in that such proposals will affect domestic policy and legislation which in the ordinary

---

38   See HC 51-xxvii (Session 1995-96) pp. 5-6 Q 17.
39   *Ibid.* pp. 4-5 QQ 12-15.

course would come within this Select Committee's remit. In addition, the Home Office is the lead department in the Inter-Governmental negotiations and the Home Secretary the principle minister who attends the Council.

As far as the procedures are concerned, the Select Committee itself has no formal process for dealing with such documents. The following, however, is an extract from a letter written to the author by the Clerk of the Home Affairs Select Committee outlining how the Committee functions on a weekly basis in this respect:[40]

> "The Committee maintains monitoring of issues relating to Justice and Home Affairs matters within the European Union as a subject permanently on its agenda. In practice, this means that the Committee is kept informed by the Home Office of significant proposals with copies of the more important initiatives being sent to the Committee Chairman and Clerk. These are made available to Members of the Committee. The Committee is also sent a copy of the draft agenda for each Justice and Home Affairs Council, and a copy of any texts which have been agreed at a Council.

> The Committee sometimes asks for, and receives, special briefing on particular issues. Occasionally, oral evidence sessions are arranged with Home Office officials or Ministers, but the Committee in practice is unable to hold such sessions very frequently."

> The Committee has not agreed any reports specifically on EU matters, but such issues are covered where relevant in other inquiries and reports made by the Committee (as for example, with Europol in the course of the Committee's inquiry into Organised Crime).

The Home Affairs Committee appears therefore to undertake a more active role in the scrutiny of the relevant pillar than its Foreign Affairs counterpart. In particular, it will include JHA proposals as part of an inquiry into a wider policy area and will endeavour to hold oral evidence sessions. The reason for this proactive approach can be traced to the fact that the government provides documents under the JHA Pillar more readily than under the CFSP Pillar. This is exclusively due to the less sensitive nature of the subject matter of these documents. It is logical therefore that unless a Select Committee receives the necessary documents no effective scrutiny can take place.

Despite this more "hands on" approach by the Home Affairs Select Committee, the procedures for scrutinising proposals under the Inter-Governmental Pillars in the House of Commons can only best be described as *ad hoc*. At worse they are ineffective. They are not on any formal footing – the Terms of Reference of these two Select Committees have not been amended. Neither does there appear to be any great enthusiasm for carrying out such scrutiny,

---

40   The letter comes form C J Poyser, Clerk of the Committee and is dated 17 June 1996.

especially by the Foreign affairs Select Committee. Under these circumstances therefore, the argument for reviewing these procedures is now overwhelming. In short the task of scrutiny of the Pillars should, in this author's opinion, be turned over to the Select Committee on European Legislation.

DEVELOPING SCRUTINY OF THE INTER-GOVERNMENTAL PILLARS

"We believe that both inter-governmental pillars should now be brought formally within the House's European Scrutiny System."[41]

This view of the Select Committee on European Legislation in their report published on 18 July 1996 reflects the frustration felt by many in the House Commons that the inter-governmental pillars are not being subjected to the detailed scrutiny which is necessary. The only way this can be remedied is to bring the process within the remit of the Scrutiny Committee. This is logical for two reasons. Firstly, the Scrutiny Committee and the European Standing Committees will have more time to scrutinise these proposals which are both complex and detailed. Secondly, twenty-three years of experience and expertise in dealing with the European Community will be a beneficial factor. The Select Committee in the report put its argument thus:[42]

"We believe that the case for these changes is overwhelming. In the case of both pillars, a clear democratic deficit remains. Activity under them is of great significance to the United Kingdom, and is likely to assume greater importance in the future. The work already carried out by the Foreign Affairs Committee and the Home Affairs Committee will no doubt continue; those Committees are independent and our recommendations are entirely without prejudice to their work. What we wish to see is the extension to Pillars 2 and 3 of the system which now applies to the Community pillar, *involving systematic scrutiny and sifting for legal and political importance* (my italics); rapid analysis and reporting, including seeking further evidence where necessary; a mechanism for debate on the most important proposals; and through the scrutiny reserve, a link between Parliamentary information and assent and Executive decision. We believe this would be welcomed in the House and more widely."

There is one aspect of the Committee's argument which does cause some concern. That is, their contention that both Departmental Select Committees could continue their present functions. This may cause difficulty in that there is a potential risk of duplication which is an inefficient use of valuable Parliamentary time. This would require further consideration, with perhaps the Procedure Committee evaluating this in their current inquiry into the scrutiny process.[43]

---

41   See HC 51-xxvii (Session 1995-96) p. xxx.

42   *Ibid.*

43   Following publication of the Select Committees report *The Scrutiny of European Business* an inquiry by the Procedure Committee into the entire scrutiny procedure in the House of Commons has been announced.

The part of the above extract placed in italics represents the primary function of the Select Committee as it operates today. This is how the Committee would like to scrutinise proposals under the pillars – by concentrating on their legal and political importance. This is desirable as scrutiny of proposals under the pillars will essentially be concerned with their effect on existing UK legislation. It would also fill the vacuum which is left by the rather limited activity of the Departmental Select Committees in this area. The ball is now in the court of the government and their response is awaited to this report and these recommendations. This author strongly supports the Select Committee in its aspirations. The government cannot be allowed to marginalise the Select Committee in what is an important area of European legislation. In this context, the author returns once again, with a rather depressing regularity, to the Maastricht Declaration. This cannot be ignored any longer in the way it is being at present. The current IGC must address the role of national parliaments in the European Union. Given the reluctance of many Member States, including the United Kingdom,[44] to extend the powers of the European Parliament to cover formal scrutiny of any legislative proposal, national parliaments must be placed at the heart of the legislative process – and that means as guardians to ensure democratic accountability for decision making.

The Select Committee's Terms of Reference

At present the Terms of Reference do not permit the Select Committee to engage in any systematic scrutiny of proposals under the Pillars. The Standing Orders[45] only provide for scrutiny of proposals coming forward under the European Community (the central pillar). Obviously an amendment to the Standing Orders is essential. The Committee in its most recent report proposed the following paragraphs to be added to the Standing Orders:[46]

> "127 (1) (c) The expression "European Union Documents" means
> (iii) any proposal to define a common position or the joint action under Title V (Provisions on common foreign and security policy) of the Treaty on European Union which is prepared for submission to the Council and which is not confidential;
>
> (iv) any proposal for a joint position, joint action or a convention under Title VI (Provisions on co-operation in the fields of justice and home affairs) of the Treaty on European Union which is prepared for submission to the Council and which is not confidential"

---

44   See HC 51 (Session 1995-96) p. 21 Q.73. The Leader of the House is not keen on extending the role of the European Parliament in this field.
45   Standing Order 127.
46   See HC 51 xxvii (Session 1995-96) Annex C, p. lxxxi.

These recommendations are designed to put the Pillars formally within the work of the Select Committee on European Legislation. During an oral evidence session the Leader of the House refused to be drawn on the issue of extending the Terms of Reference until the Committee produced its report and he had an opportunity to digest it.[47] It is difficult to speculate on this matter, but it is hoped that the government accepts the recommendations in the form as presented by the Committee. They are not excessive and do not attempt to force the government to present documents which are sensitive or confidential. In fact they are broadly in line with the government's response to the House of Lords report "Scrutiny of the Inter-Governmental Pillars".[48] Furthermore, the Committee are prepared to accept the confidentiality argument providing it is reasonable. They will accept an Explanatory Memorandum at a later stage giving reasons for the confidentiality and are prepared to have this included in their revised Standing Orders if necessary.[49] Thus, the Committee are showing plenty of goodwill. They have accepted the limitations and will work within them. They now need to be given this opportunity.

The Resolution of the House – The Scrutiny Reserve

In Chapter 3 when the detailed work of the Select Committee on European Legislation was examined the fact was stressed that the Scrutiny Reserve is the cornerstone of the entire scrutiny process in *both* Houses of Parliament. At page 51 above it has already been explained how after the introduction of the co-decision procedure the Scrutiny Reserve now has less of an impact. However, as far as scrutiny of the inter-governmental pillars is concerned, the government are not prepared to extend it to cover the pillars. This position is identical to the one in the House of Lords.

The Select Committee is totally unimpressed by the government's refusal to extend the Scrutiny Reserve to cover the pillars and quite rightly so.[50] Failure to agree to this leaves the Committee in a very weak position. They cannot exercise their function of scrutinising the Executive effectively. Together with the difficulties now encountered in scrutinising the co-decision procedure, it can be said that the introduction of the Maastricht Treaty has been primarily a negative development as far as the Select Committee is concerned. The issue of extending the Resolution to the Inter-Governmental Pillars will be dealt with in Chapter 10 following an examination of the work of the only specialist Committee in either House which scrutinises proposals under coming forward the Pillars. It must also be stressed here that as the House of Lords conducts the only detailed scrutiny of the pillars at present the examining of these issues within this context is more appropriate. However, where relevant reference to the procedure in the Commons will be made by highlighting any similarities or differences.

---

47   *Ibid.* p. 20, Q.70.
48   See Cm 2471 (Session 1992-93) p. 5, paras. (iii) and (iv), and p. 5 para. (viii).
49   See HC 51-xxvii, p. xxx, para. 88.
50   *Ibid.* In particular see paras. 93-97.

CONCLUDING REMARKS

The Maastricht Treaty has definitely been a turning point for the European Community. The Community has now become a Union with a much wider field of competence. This has brought new challenges, not least for the national parliaments. Both co-decision and the pillars have successfully challenged the notion that Parliament is the sole legislative body in the UK. If anything these developments have merely confirmed what many have argued for some time – namely that a degree of legislative sovereignty has been surrendered to the European Union. This in itself is not necessarily problematical. As members of the Union we must play by the rules of the club. The issue is not one of whether the UK should be a member, but one of an acceptance of the fact that we are members and that as such we should play an active part.

This is nowhere more true than in the area of involving national parliaments. Given the importance of scrutiny within Parliament, this is one area where the UK could and should be taking the lead. The scrutiny system as it stands in the UK is more comprehensive and developed than any other within the Union. However, this is not a reason for complacency. Post Maastricht there are still many important scrutiny issues to be resolved, yet Member States are already considering further developments at the current IGC. At the heart of these issues is the concept of accountability.

Today, it is the co-decision procedure which operates independently of scrutiny arrangements in the House of Commons, that causes most difficulties for the Select Committee Though at first sight it may appear that under co-decision Parliament faces similar problems to those previously created by the cooperation procedure, there is one important difference. Under the cooperation procedure it is the Council of Ministers who have the final say about the proposal and it is for them to collectively decide whether the European Parliament amendments are to be accepted.

Under co-decision however, the rules change somewhat. Here it is not readily apparent which institution has had the final word when the Conciliation Committee is convened. It is difficult to ascertain which institution was the motivating force behind the joint text agreed. From a scrutiny perspective this is undesirable. The Select Committee can only exert control over the minister in the Council and not over the actions of the European Parliament. Furthermore, if the UK minister is outvoted when the Council approves the joint text by qualified majority, the House of Commons cannot hold him accountable for a document which he did not vote for because it was fundamentally different from that originally scrutinised by the Commons (and based on the original common position) some months previously.

The co-decision procedure does not fit in with the scrutiny arrangements in the House of Commons for two reasons. Firstly, from a practical point of view, though it is a lengthy and resource consuming process, it is also one that can come to a rapid conclusion once a joint text is agreed. This makes it difficult to monitor. Secondly from a political point of view, it means power is taken away from ministers and given to the European Parliament, which is not subject to House of Commons control.

Co-decision together with the introduction of the Inter-Governmental Pillars has eroded further the ability of the House of Commons to hold accountable ministers who make legislation at a European level. This balance needs to be redressed and the Procedure Committee review will be a positive start to this process. Similarly the House of Lords with its unique *modus operandi* has a valuable contribution to make and this is examined in more detail in Chapter 10. However, whatever the final result it can be said with certainty that with the present institutional arrangements in the EU, full democracy can only be attained if national parliaments are encouraged to take their role of scrutiny seriously. This would be no more than is required by the Maastricht Treaty Declaration.

PART III:

THE HOUSE OF LORDS

CHAPTER 7

THE HOUSE OF LORDS AND THE EUROPEAN UNION

INTRODUCTION

In chapters 7 to 11, the focus is upon the work of the House of Lords which flows from the UK's membership of the European Union. The starting point in this chapter will be a brief historical background into the scrutiny process in the House of Lords. This is then followed in chapter 8 by an assessment of the work of the Select Committee on the European Communities and in chapter 9 its various Sub-Committees. Throughout the course of chapter 9, a number of comparisons with the scrutiny arrangements in the House of Commons will be made. However, such a comparison, though important, is not the main consideration. The aim is to produce a comprehensive analysis of the work of the Select Committee itself, and illustrate that at present it plays a vital and arguably irreplaceable role in the scrutiny process.

This latter point, will be illustrated when consideration is given as to how the scrutiny arrangements in the House of Lords would endure any reform of the second chamber (chapter 11). The central question of this discussion will be whether a reformed second chamber could continue its valuable role of scrutiny? This discussion is essential given the present political climate. In 1997, constitutional reform is at the heart of the government's agenda. Therefore, in these circumstances, the role the House of Lords plays today in the scrutiny process and what any reform could mean for this process, must be fully evaluated.

The final aspect of this analysis (chapter 10) will concentrate on how the House of Lords has coped with the developments post Maastricht. The primary focus will be an evaluation of the arrangements for the scrutiny of legislation under the Inter-Governmental Pillars. This discussion will highlight the difference in approach taken towards this issue by the Lords and the House of Commons and will attempt to rationalise this difference.

HISTORICAL BACKGROUND

The Maybray-King Report [1]

On the 20 December 1972, the House of Lords appointed a Select Committee under the Chairmanship of Lord Maybray-King (referred to as the Maybray-King Committee) to consider the most appropriate methods to introduce into the House of Lords for the scrutiny of European legislative proposals. The Select Committee on Procedure for Scrutiny of Proposals for

---

1   See HL 194 (Session 1972-73) Second Report by the Select Committee on Procedures for Scrutiny of Proposals for European Instruments.

European Instruments, as it was officially known, needed to work with some urgency as the United Kingdom's accession to the European Community occurred on 1 January 1973. In their Report,[2] they noted that it was essential to set up effective procedures to scrutinise Community proposals and to do so as quickly as possible.

The Maybray-King Committee had the following Terms of Reference:

> "To consider procedures for scrutiny proposals for European Community Instruments."

In the production of its Report the Committee adopted a broad interpretation of its Terms of Reference. They took the stance that their final recommendations should contain proposals for scrutinising all Community proposals while they are still at a formative stage and before they are considered by the Council of Ministers. The point was not lost on Maybray-King that the only real influence the House of Lords could have was prior to a final decision being taken in the Council of Ministers. This is an identical conclusion to the Foster Committee in the House of Commons.[3]

The Maybray-King Report identified the following documents as being the prime objectives for scrutiny by the new Select Committee:[4]

(a) regulations, whether by the Council or Commission;
(b) directives, whether by the Council or Commission;
(c) decisions whether by the Council or Commission;
(d) the Community budget;
(c) Community Treaties to be made by the Council with third parties;
(d) recommendations and opinions by the Council or the Commission; and
(e) Commission memoranda concerning Community matters.

The interesting point, mentioned only briefly at this juncture, is that though the Terms of Reference for both Maybray-King and the Foster Committee were similar, the final recommendations for what type of Select Committees were to be established could not have been different. This in fact is a difference which has grown wider over the last twenty-three years.

In forming their conclusions and recommendations, the Committee held 24 evidence sessions both in the House itself and in Brussels and Strasbourg and other European Community capitals.[5] The reason for this wide consultation lies in the fact the Committee tried to draw upon the experiences of

---

2   *Ibid.* p. ix.
3   See HC 143 (Session 1972-73).
4   See 316 above.
5   All oral evidence together with any written memoranda may be found in HL 194 (1972-73) pp. 1 - 251.

other Member States and their approach to scrutiny. This wide consultation appears today to have borne fruit. It is readily accepted by both the Commission and European Parliament and the national parliaments of other Member States, that the House of Lords Select Committee on the European Communities makes an outstanding contribution to the debate of European legislative proposals and European issues generally. The author has even received anecdotal evidence in the course of an interview with a Clerk to the European Communities Select Committee, that the former President of the Commission, Monsieur Jacques Delors, read Reports produced by the House of Lords Select Committee in bed!

The aims of the Maybray-King Committee

In coming to its final conclusions as to what type of Select Committee should be established in the House of Lords, the Maybray-King Committee considered the following issues:[6]

(a) how and by whom proposals are made;
(b) the number and degree of their importance;
(c) who has the power of decision on them; and
(d) at what point Parliamentary influence can best be brought to bear.

Implicit in these questions is an acceptance by the Committee that the final proposals will at best be a compromise. Question (d) above addresses the issue which twenty-three years on still troubles both the Lords and Commons Select Committees. Trying to influence a process over which you have very little effective control is an impracticable notion. The fact that the Committee posed the question as how influence can *best* be brought to bear suggests that the final proposals will be a compromise. The best option is not necessarily the most desirable option. This is apparent today even more so than in 1973. With the rapid increase in the use of Qualified Majority Voting by the Council of Ministers and the extension of the role of the European Parliament via the Co-decision procedure it can be strongly argued that Parliamentary influence of the minster is in decline. A decline which many have suggested is in fact terminal.

The Maybray-King Committee like its Commons counterpart, the Foster Committee, recommended that the most appropriate form of influence will be to inform the minister of Parliament's opinion *prior* to him or her giving final approval in the Council of Ministers. However, of dismay to the Committee was the fact that the House of Lords would have no formal control over the Commission, the institution whose function it is to make legislative proposals. There is no relationship between any national parliament and the Commission. The only parliament to which the Commission responds is the European Parliament. This was a difficult point to accept by the Committee,

---

6   See HL 194 (session 1972-73) p. xii, para. 9.

coming as it did from a parliamentary tradition where accountability and scrutiny are the cornerstones of its work. The fact that this was not the case in European affairs, especially when at that time an unelected Parliament "controlled" an unelected Commission, caused consternation among peers.[7] Sir Nicholas Soames who was Vice-President of the Commission at the time gave the following justification of this position to the Maybray-King Committee:[8]

> "...as far as the Commission is concerned, it has one Parliament to be served and that is the European Parliament. We cannot have nine Parliamentary masters."

Over the years, informal links have developed between the House of Lords and the Commission. However, this arrangement, though a positive step forward, is still regarded as unsatisfactory. The influence of the Commission has certainly grown in the intervening twenty-three year period since the UK joined what was then known as the European Economic Community (EEC). Today it acts as external negotiator in areas such as trade and environmental matters as well as having powers of delegated legislation from the Council. The author therefore shares the view of many peers and MPs who believe that the Commission should be subject to direct scrutiny by national parliaments in each Member State. This would significantly reduce the democratic deficit still prevalent within the EU today.

PROPOSALS FOR THE SELECT COMMITTEE

Appointing a Select Committee

Having concluded a very wide and informative investigation into the issues, the Maybray-King Committee made a number of recommendations which they thought would be essential to the establishment of an effective scrutiny procedure in the House of Lords. In fact, what they recommended in 1973 has stood the test of time remarkably well.

The initial and perhaps most important recommendation was that European Community affairs would be scrutinised via a Select Committee and not a Standing Committee. They came to this conclusion because they saw this as being the most appropriate vehicle for preparing in-depth and comprehensive reports which could then be debated by the House generally. Furthermore, this Select Committee would fit into the overall structure of the Lords which regularly appointed Select Committees to carry out a variety of inquiries.

During its investigation and deliberations, the Maybray-King Committee was extremely mindful of the fact that the one thing it did not want to recommend was a mirror image of the House of Commons Select Committee. In an

---

7   See HL 194 (Session 1972-73) pp. 121-125.
8   *Ibid.* p.121, Q.428.

interview with MR Michael Pownall, a former Clerk to the Select Committee on the European Committees, he stressed the importance of avoiding duplication between the two Select Committees.[9] He in fact described the duplication of work in a calamitous manner by referring to it as "disastrous". The purpose of these two different Committees, he believes, is to create a "complementary scrutiny system" with an exchange of information between them.

The most apparent way of avoiding this problem was to adopt a completely different internal structure for the Select Committee. With this in mind, they concluded that the most suitable proposal would be for the establishment of a number of Sub-Committees within the Select Committee itself. The justification for this is rooted in one of the most persuasive arguments for not reforming the House of Lords. That is that the House of Lords contains many experts who have the time to meticulously examine legislative proposals in detail. The Maybray-King Committee made the observation, that these Sub-Committees could be staffed by peers who have expertise and wide experience of:[10]

(a) a wide number of subjects;
(b) the parts and regions of the UK; and
(c) Community affairs and UK law.

The House of Lords set its stall out right from the start. Scrutiny of legislative proposals was the main task of this new Select Committee. But, this would be done in the context of examining the wider issues of policy and the merits of that policy. This recommendation goes to the heart of the difference between the Commons and Lords Select Committees. The proposal of these Sub-Committees (which was accepted by the government) explicitly illustrates that the House of Lords Committee was intending to work to a much longer horizon than its House of Commons counterpart. The recommendation of six Sub-Committees covering all the major policy areas of the EEC meant that the House of Lords Select Committee on the European Communities would have much more of an inquisitorial function.

Finally, Maybray-King recommended that the Select Committee was to have the usual powers to send for persons and papers, which would allow it to examine ministers, officials and experts in the manner of the House of Commons Committee. They also proposed that specialist advisers should become an integral part of the Sub-Committees. This was logical given the narrow policy areas they would consider and with which they may need assistance. All these issues will be considered in more detail in the next chapter.

SELECT COMMITTEES IN THE HOUSE OF LORDS

Before considering the detailed work of the Select Committee on European Legislation it is necessary to examine the context within which scrutiny takes

---

9   The interview took place in the House of Lords on the 28 April 1995.
10   See HL 194 (Session 1972-73) p. xli.

place in the House of Lords. Most important is the fact that there is no system of Departmental Select Committees as are found in the House of Commons. Thus, all European issues are considered by the European Communities Select Committee. This places a large burden upon the Committee because unlike the Commons there is no division between the scrutiny of European Legislation (the Scrutiny Committee) and the consideration of European policy generally (the Foreign Affairs Select Committee).

Furthermore, Select Committees in the House of Lords are predominantly appointed on an *ad hoc* basis. Along with the European Communities Select Committee, the only other permanent Committee is the Science and Technology Select Committee. Therefore, the House of Lords is more flexible in its review of government activity. These investigative Committees conduct more wide ranging and in depth inquiries which are often not based on any specific government policy or legislative proposal.

Thus it is within this context that the European Communities Committee operates. It is the most active Committee in the House of Lords, producing on average 20-25 reports per year. These reports on the whole have proved influential both at a national and European level.

CHAPTER 8

THE WORK OF THE SELECT COMMITTEE ON THE EUROPEAN COMMUNITIES[1]

INTRODUCTION

In this chapter, the analysis focuses on the work and working methods of the Select Committee on the European Communities. At this juncture, however, the specific concern is with the Select Committee itself and not with the five Sub-Committees which are appointed by it. These will be the subject of a closer analysis in the next chapter.

Chapter 7, outlined the historical background to the establishment of a Select Committee in the House of Lords and the difficult task the Maybray-King Committee faced in devising a scrutiny system that will be both relevant and effective. In particular, this meant that the Select Committee would fulfil the essential function of scrutiny and, perhaps just as important, act as an advisory body that would consider future trends in the European development. In short, the Lords Committee had to fill a gap which the House of Commons Committee for a variety of reasons simply could not.

To examine its success or otherwise in performing these functions it is desirable to start with an appraisal of the task which the Select Committee has been asked to carry out on behalf of the whole House. Inevitably, this means an analysis of the Standing Orders of the Committee which set out its Terms of Reference.

THE TERMS OF REFERENCE

In the Second Report from the Select Committee on Procedures for Scrutiny of Proposals for European Instruments,[2] the Committee recommended that the new European Communities Select Committee should have the following Terms of Reference:

> "To consider Community proposals whether in draft or otherwise, to obtain all necessary information about them, and to make reports on those which in the opinion of the Committee, raise important questions of policy or principle, and on other questions to which the Committee consider that the special attention of the House should be drawn."

---

1   For the work of the Select Committee generally, see Erskine May *Parliamentary Practice* (twenty-first edition 1989). However, this is somewhat out of date now. See also Drewry (ed.) *The New Select Committees* (1985), Chapter 2 "Select Committees in the House of Lords". However, this is also out of date as both works were written prior to the Report from the Select Committee on the Committee Work of the House (The Jelicoe Report) in 1992. See HL 35-I (Session 1991-92).

2   See HL 194 (Session 1972-73).

The first comment on these Terms of Reference is that they are extremely wide and thus give the Select Committee great scope for conducting enquiries.[3] This is facilitated by the appointment of the aforementioned sub-committees. Out of this arrangement, the Committee produces on average 25 reports each year, many of which are extremely lengthy and highly detailed. The reports are regularly based on obtaining evidence from a wide variety of interested parties as well as government officials and ministers.

At first sight, the Terms of Reference of the Select Committee on the European Communities may appear similar to those of its House of Commons counterpart. However, on closer analysis this is most definitely not the case. Firstly, the names of the Select Committees illustrates clearly the difference between the two. As stated, in the Lords it is referred to as the "Select Committee on the European Communities". This gives the impression that it is not merely a Select Committee whose sole task it is to scrutinise European legislative proposals. However, that is not to say that this scrutiny role is not an important function of the Committee, and this issue will be examined further in subsequent paragraphs.

Remit of the Select Committee

The most significant aspect of the Terms of Reference is in the words "other questions to which the Committee consider that the special attention of the House should be drawn". This remit of the Committee opens the doors for it to conduct wide ranging enquiries into issues that are not related to any specific legislative proposal. These freestanding enquiries are often into Green and White Papers published by the Commission. For example, in 1992, the Select Committee produced a comprehensive and thought provoking report on the complex issue of Enlargement of the EU.[4] Another example of this can be seen in the highly influential report on Fraud and Financial Mismanagement in the European Community.[5] Most recently the Select Committee has completed an inquiry into the 1996 Inter-Governmental Conference.

What the production of this type of report illustrates is that the Select Committee on the European Communities has a much greater freedom to investigate wider issues, that are not related to legislative proposals. These Reports, are an in-depth evaluation of government or Community policy in a particular area, or an investigation into the merits of a legislative proposal.

---

3   This very point was made by Mr. Michael Pownall, a former Clerk to the Select Committee, in a lecture delivered to the European Institute of Public Administration (EIPA), in Maastricht on 6-7 June 1994. This lecture entitled "Parliamentary Scrutiny of European Union Affairs: The case of the United Kingdom House of Lords" (pp. 143-149) was part of a wider conference examining the role of National Parliaments in the EU. All the lectures are contained in a book published by the EIPA called *The Changing Role of Parliaments in the European Union* (1994).
4   See HL 5 (Session 1992-93).
5   See HL 34 (Session 193-94).

In his lecture to the European Institute of Public Administration,[6] Mr Michael Pownall illustrated quite succinctly how wide these Terms of Reference really are. He made two crucial observations.[7] His first point was that the Terms of Reference permitted the Committee to consider draft texts under the two new Inter-governmental Pillars, without the need for any amendments. This is important because the passage of legislation under the Pillars created a new legal process which is technically outside the competence of the EC.

Therefore, by having this wide interpretation, the House of Lords Committee has avoided the problem encountered by the Commons Select Committee. Because the Commons Committee is charged with the scrutiny of "European Community Documents",[8] proposals under the Pillars are not presently within their remit. Thus, the Lords Committee being able to consider "other questions" has removed the complication faced by the House of Commons. The Lords have already conducted major Pillars inquiries e.g. EUROPOL.,[9] whereas the House of Commons is still trying to develop a comprehensive scrutiny procedure.

The second point made by Mr Pownall was that the Select Committee on the European Communities could consider proposals made by the Agreement of the Eleven (now Fourteen). This is legislation coming forward under the Social Chapter of the Maastricht Treaty, to which the United Kingdom has secured a controversial "opt-out". Though these are legislative proposals which at present have no legal impact in the United Kingdom, the Committee can still consider them as part of a wider inquiry.

In either of the two cases above, he said that if the government were uncooperative in the provision of a text, so that they could not pursue their inquiry, he as the Clerk would simply obtain the proposals from the Official Journal, and scrutiny would proceed on this basis.

Are the Terms of Reference too wide?

As can be see from the discussion above, the role of the Select Committee on the European Communities covers more than just the procedural task of scrutiny of legislative proposals. This "free" role it has, is considered by many commentators[10] (including this author) as the strongest aspect of the entire scrutiny system in both Houses. Professor St J.N. Bates, identified the Committee as providing "an interesting example of the development of approach and influence of a Select Committee over a ten year period."

6　See 327 above.
7　*Ibid.* See p.144.
8　See Standing Order 127 (1) (c) for a definition of European Community Document.
9　See HL 51-I (Session 1994-95).
10　See Drewry (ed.) *The New Select Committees* (1985) Chapter 2 "Select Committees in the House of Lords" pp. 38-39.

Perhaps the most telling observation about the Committee and the one which most illustrates its value can be seen in a comment made by Donald Shell in his chapter on the work of the European Communities Committee published in *The New Select Committees.*[11] He describes the Committee as:[12]

> "...specifically proactive rather than simply reactive in its approach"

This summarises succinctly the main difference between the respective Committees in the House of Commons and House of Lords. In Chapter Three on the work of the Select Committee on European Legislation the Commons Committee was described as being essentially 'reactive' (see p.62 above). That is, it responds to the agenda which is set by the Council of Ministers. However, in the Lords, the Select Committee can initiate its own inquiries on a topic of its own choosing. Most significantly, this allows the Committee to anticipate future European Community developments.

One further point which the above observation illustrates relates to the enduring applicability of the Terms of Reference of the Lords Select Committee. Since its inception, the Terms of Reference of the Lords Committee have undergone *no* change. They have been flexible enough to adapt to any developments. However, this has not been the case for the Commons Committee which since 1973 has tried to secure an amendment to its Standing Order on at least five occasions, and only with limited success.[13]

Let us now turn to the issue which is central to this part of the discussion. That of whether the Select Committee on the European Communities has Terms of Reference which are too wide? The argument behind this assertion is based on the proposition that by having such a wider remit, the Select Committee is distracted from its task of scrutiny and concentrates too much on wider policy investigations, which though interesting may not be directly applicable to the present European agenda.

In the most recent review of the work of the Select Committees in the House of Lords, The Select Committee on the Committee Work of The House[14] (commonly referred to as The Jelicoe Committee) investigated how the role of the European Communities Committee could be further developed. Central to this was the question of whether the Terms of Reference required further modification. The general view was that no amendment was required. Some witnesses though suggested that the present remit was too wide.

---

11 *Ibid.* p. 246-281.

12 *Ibid.* p. 248.

13 Most recently an amendment was made after the Procedure Committee Report in 1989. The government put forward a proposal to allow the Committee to consider consultative documents which contain important proposals for the future development of the Community. This however, is not the same as the Lords which can initiate an inquiry based on a much wider subject.

14 See HL 35-I (Session 1991-92).

In his evidence to the Jelicoe Committee,[15] the Clerk of the Parliaments drew the Committee's attention to what he described as "the fundamental uncertainty" about what the precise role of the European Communities Committee was. He emphasised the point that for him this uncertainty stemmed from the fact the Terms of Reference of the Committee were too wide. He illustrated this point by claiming that the Select Committee itself was on occasion confused about how it should approach inquiries. He identified a variety of different approaches which the Committee adopted depending on the subject before them.

During his evidence he said[16] that sometimes the Committee assessed the desirability of proposals from a Community perspective; sometimes it scrutinised the impact of European Community proposals on the United Kingdom; and sometimes it conducted inquiries directed largely towards domestic matters in the United Kingdom using Community proposals as a "peg" for the inquiry.

Similar criticisms were echoed by other witnesses. They felt that the Committee would be best served by concentrating more on in-depth inquiries and leaving the detailed scrutiny of legislative developments to the House of Commons Committee. The former Minister of State at the Foreign Office, The Right Honourable Tristan Garel-Jones MP, felt that the Committee could move "upstream" concentrating on early drafts of Commission papers on major issues. He gave the example of Commission consultative documents or "Green Papers" as being ideal for early in-depth study. He said:[17]

> "...I can see advantages in the Committee taking a more forward looking approach..."

Mr Garel-Jones makes a valid point. His concern is not so much with the Terms of Reference being too wide, but with the actual tasks performed by the Committee. In essence he is suggesting a more limited role for the Committee which concentrates on the sort of in-depth inquiries suggested above. This was a point echoed by other witnesses. Most notably, the Trades Union Congress, in written evidence it submitted,[18] made the point that there was a tendency to "miss the boat" on the part of the Lords Committee. There was no point in carrying out an in-depth inquiry if it was too late to influence or form part of the debate. By leaving routine scrutiny to the Commons Committee, the Lords Committee could have more time to ensure its major reports were produced at the appropriate time to have the maximum impact and influence.

Along similar lines, Sir Christopher Prout MEP, leader of the Conservative group in the European Parliament, pointed to the need for greater focus by

---

15   *Ibid.* p. 104.
16   *Ibid.*
17   *Ibid.* p. 125, Q.254.
18   *Ibid,* p. 257.

the Select Committee. In his oral evidence, he warmly welcomed the Select Committee's reports into wider Community issues by describing them as "most useful". However, he felt that this was achieved at the expense of scrutiny of legislative proposals, and perhaps more importantly in the influence the Committee exerted over the government in the Council of Ministers.[19] This he identified as the main weakness of the Committee and an argument for it being more selective in its work. He saw the key to this selectivity lying in a more flexible approach to scrutiny by the Committee (See QQ 491-493, pp. 193-194).

However, the above opinions were not shared by every witness. Perhaps the most respected and influential witness on this subject was the then Chairman of the Select Committee on the European Communities, Baroness Serota. She believed that the Committee had struck a good balance between the need for scrutiny and the benefit of undertaking more in-depth wide-ranging inquiries.

She described the Terms of Reference in the following manner:[20]

"The Terms of Reference which are extremely broad have served us well. They have enabled the Select Committee to operate extremely flexibly and adapt to the changing situation within the Community."

Baroness Serota identifies the point which was made earlier. Her response is directed at the fact that the Select Committee is not inhibited in its work, unlike its House of Commons counterpart. Though wide, the Terms of Reference are viewed by her as being "specific". They direct the Committee into the procedures it is to use when carrying out an inquiry. Furthermore, implicit in her evidence is the fact that the Committee is fully aware that it must make its inquiries relevant for them to be influential. By influential she means aimed specifically at our own government.[21]

How influential is the Select Committee?

The issue of influence and how effective the Committee is, needs to be judged in the light of the central aim of the Committee. The Terms of Reference direct the Committee to look at "...important questions of policy or principle...". This means, at the core of their function is to examine the merits of the legislative proposal or policy. No Committee which does this can be ignored and the government accept this. The fact that the Resolution of the

---

19   *Ibid.* p. 197, Q.506.
20   *Ibid.* p. 39, Q.45.
21   Baroness Serota also gave evidence to the Select Committee on Procedure in the House of Commons in 1989. She made the point that the primary aim of the Select Committee is to influence the Government. See HC 622-II (Session 1988-89) pp. 122-131 and Appendix 21 pp. 145-146.

House of 30 October 1990 extends equally to the House of Lords,[22] indicates that the government takes seriously *all* the functions of the Select Committee on the European Communities.

The contrasting views and opinions outlined above illustrate the complex nature of the scrutiny process. Each party, whether from the government, a European Institution or the Committee itself take a different view of how the scrutiny task can be best performed. At the heart of this dispute lies the issue of what is the most effective and productive manner in which to influence the government prior to the Council of Ministers. From this author's perspective, the House of Lords performs a task that is unique not only in the United Kingdom but the European Union as a whole. The high esteem in which the Committee and its Reports are held throughout the Community is almost legendary. Their reports are also said to influence the Commission. This undoubtedly, is an extremely positive characteristic.

However, can this multi-task approach be sustained in a European Union which is continually growing? The crucial question to be asked today is whether there needs to be a complete overhaul of the scrutiny process, starting with an evaluation of how and where the mechanics of scrutiny will take place. Critics of the present arrangements point to the fact that there is duplication of work by the two Select Committees, i.e. each look at every document put before them. Would it not therefore make sense to divide this task and give it exclusively to one institution (probably the House of Commons) with the other (the House of Lords) considering itself with more wide-ranging policy issues?

Such a division is attractive as it would give both Committees the necessary time to effectively perform their respective tasks. This is a powerful argument, as members of both Committees have commented to the author upon the lack of time available to complete all their tasks. On this basis, the Terms of Reference of the House of Lords (and House of Commons) need to be reviewed. It would then be up to each House, after full consultation with the other to devise a scrutiny system that meets the needs of all parties and maintains and strengthens the central pillar of the scrutiny process, that of influencing the government in the Council of Ministers.

However, this is an unlikely proposition in the foreseeable future. There is at present little cooperation between the Houses on business matters generally[23] and each Committee desires as wide a role as possible. The main argument against this division is that it would be very difficult for each Committee to do this exclusive task. Thus, the Lords felt they could not consider policy and its merits without a constant referral to legislative proposals and vice versa. In this context therefore, scrutiny in the Lords will continue in its present multi-faceted form.

---

22   For more detail on the operation of the Resolution of the House see also the chapter
     3, "The work of the Select Committee of European Legislation."
23   The main exception to this is the Joint Committee on Statutory Instruments.

THE SCRUTINY FUNCTION OF THE HOUSE OF LORDS

The discussion has up to now focussed on the wider role of the Select Committee, concentrating primarily on the Select Committee's ability to consider the merits of both a policy and a legislative proposal. What the above discussion illustrates is the fact that the Select Committee in the House of Lords has a much wider brief than its Commons counterpart.

However, the above discussion is only half the picture. The wider investigative powers are essential if the Lords is to fulfil the requirements of its Terms of Reference, but the key aspect of its work must be the scrutiny of each legislative proposal that is submitted from the Council of Ministers.

Let's consider the Terms of Reference again. They require the Select Committee to:

> "Consider Community proposals whether in draft or otherwise, to obtain all necessary information about them and to make reports on those which in the opinion of the Committee *raise important questions of policy or principle*...(my italics)"

The key phrase is in italics. This demonstrates that the Committee is concerned with only those proposals that will have some impact on UK law. Thus in essence, their selection criteria for the production of detailed reports is not too dissimilar from that in the House of Commons where the Committee will recommend further debate in one of the two Standing Committees if the proposals raises "questions of legal or political importance".

However, there is one substantial difference between the two. This lies in the fact that even though both Committees are charged with doing a similar task of scrutiny, the criteria for conducting a more detailed inquiry are different. Thus, in the House of Lords, the Committee does have a greater discretion to recommend debate in one of the Sub-Committees because the concept of questions of policy or principle is much wider than that of legal or political importance. That is to say, a legislative proposal may raise important questions of policy but have minimal legal impact on the UK.

What is the aim of the scrutiny function?

It is possible to separate the scrutiny function into two separate tasks. The primary task is to influence the minister prior to final approval being given to a legislative proposal in the Council of Ministers. In an interview with a former Clerk to the Select Committee he said that "scrutiny is the priority" of the Select Committee.[24] This assertion is undoubtedly correct and it is important that in the context of producing lengthy reports this vital function is not neglected.

---

24   Interview in the House of Lords 28 April 1995.

The reason so much emphasis is placed upon the scrutiny function is that as already stated, it is the only way in which the minister may be influenced.[25] This has been an enduring concern for the Committee, which stretches back to the days of the Maybray-King Report. In a debate on the Maybray-King Report, Lord Shepherd saw three prime objectives of the Select Committee:[26]

> "acquiring information and knowledge;
> securing a full appreciation of the consequences of any decisions and proposals; and
> *influencing Ministers.* (my italics)"

What the above extract from Hansard illustrates is that accession to the European Community marked a shift in balance between the Executive and Parliament. Thus, it would no longer be Parliament which had the final say on a legislative proposal but an institution over which Parliament had no direct control except in so far as it could ensure the minister would follow Parliament's wishes.

Thus the establishment of the scrutiny procedures in *both* Houses was an attempt to shift the balance back in favour of Parliament. For the House of Lords however, this attempt to influence has become more pronounced. It recognises that influence may be exercised through other Community institutions. Therefore, reports are regularly sent to the Council Secratariat, to the current Presidency, to the Chairman or Rapporteur of the relevant Committee in the European Parliament, to the Cabinet of the Commissioner in charge of the legislation and to all other national parliaments scrutiny committees.

What the above illustrates is that the Lords has developed its scrutiny process to reflect the fact that the United Kingdom minister is just one small, but important, part of the legislative process. The growth of Qualified Majority Voting means that influence must now be sought in other corners of the European Union. For the interests of the United Kingdom to be preserved and even enhanced the support of other Member States is needed. The Lords by producing such high quality reports are both stimulating debate within the Community and influencing other Member States.[27] For example, the Select Committees recent Report on Fraud and Mismanagement in the Community's Finances[28] was acknowledged as a highly valued inquiry amongst the Commission and the other Member States. It articulated in a non-partisan way the concerns which the government had held for many years, but which the government had not been successful in putting across, primarily because it was viewed by other Member States as another complaint by a "Eurosceptic" government.

---

25 See HL 35-I (Session 1991-92).

26 See Hansard Cols 759-839 (Session 1973-74).

27 For another discussion of these issues see G. Drewry (ed.) *The New Select Committees* (1985), Chapter 2 by Professor T. St. J. N Bates "Select Committees in the House of Lords" pp. 49-52.

28 See HL 34 (Session 1993-94).

Another example of the Committees influence over the final agreed directive was given by the former Clerk during the course of an interview.[29] He pointed out that recent legislation on Product Safety and Unfair Contract Terms[30] reflected many of the recommendations made by the Select Committee in its Report. Likewise other recommendations made in the 1980s on wider powers for the Court of Auditors and clearer duties on Member States to fight fraud all found their way into the Maastricht Treaty.

The influence therefore is clear. The Select Committee through its detailed investigation and debate does have a measurable degree of influence. The challenge facing the Committee today is to ensure that this influence is maintained, especially in the light of the growth of Qualified Majority Voting. The other concern relating to the scrutiny function and the ability to influence ministers is one which was discussed earlier in this chapter. That is whether the wider more investigative functions of the Select Committee detract from the scrutiny function. The evidence given to the Jelicoe Committee was mixed, with a split forming between Members of the Select Committee on the one hand who valued the present role and others including government ministers and MEPs who favoured a narrowing of the Select Committee's functions. As stated above, the Committee performs its tasks with the primary aim of influencing the minister. The use of wider investigations into policy issues, is viewed as a very helpful part of this process.

Similarly, the Select Committee maintains a high degree of influence by having a substantial political momentum to their inquiries. Thus, a greater impact and therefore influence is attained if an inquiry is conducted into a politically relevant issue. This has two benefits. Firstly, an inquiry will give the Select Committee an opportunity to question the government on its policy without the political partisanship witnessed during Question Time in the Chamber. Secondly, it affords the Committee the possibility to raise its own profile by carrying out such an enquiry. This is important for the Committee as it wants to be seen to be effective.

However, one important criticism should be noted of the Committee. The evidence suggests that the Select Committee may, because of its working methods, be caught out by either the quick moving nature of decisions in the Council of Ministers or a significant change in policy during the course of a detailed inquiry. In either of these two instances it will lose its influence. It must ensure that reports are ready in good time to be debated by the House and digested by the minister. Thus, timing is a key element of maintaining influence. If there was to be any significant difficulty in completing a report so that it can have maximum impact, then the Committee may need to reconsider its working methods and most importantly be more selective in conducting an inquiry.

---

29   See n. 24, at p. 142.
30   See HL 57 (Session 1989-90).

The Committee as an information point

At the start of the previous section, the observation was made that the scrutiny function can be separated into two exclusive tasks. The principal task of influencing the minister has already been identified and discussed. The second task is not too dissimilar, but has a wider target audience. That is, during the course of its scrutiny function, the Select Committee seeks to act as an information point both for the House of Lords and the wider public.

This aim to inform is based upon an important idea. Namely that scrutiny of European legislative proposals and policy should not be viewed as a specialist separate area which is completely distinct from the other work of the House. Though the scrutiny task is to a large degree removed from the Chamber and dealt with by specialist Sub-Committees, it is essential that all members are aware of important developments.

What the discussion of the Terms of Reference of the Select Committee clearly illustrates is the fact that the Committee plays a pivotal role in the entire scrutiny process. It has been put to the author on many occasions by both Peers and MPs, that the extensive role of the Committee is one which could not readily be removed. The next section concentrates on the actual mechanics of the scrutiny process and how the Select Committee gets to grips with the difficult task of analysing each document to decide whether it requires for further inquiry. This will include examining the role of the major characters in the scrutiny process, analyse the use of specialist advisers, and consider how effective the working methods of the Committee are to cope with the task in hand.

THE MECHANICS OF THE SCRUTINY PROCESS

Before beginning the detailed analysis of the scrutiny process one important point needs to be reiterated. That is, that both the House of Lords and the House of Commons examine each and every document. There is *no* division between them. However, as has already been seen, and will become even more apparent from the following discussion, the House of Lords adopts an entirely different approach to scrutiny. The main difference lies in the choice of document which will be considered further by the Committee. The Committee has developed a preference for proposals which will have a long gestation period and are of a much wider Community significance. This contrasts starkly with the Commons where the Standing Committee only has, at most, three hours to consider the document and decide upon its merits.[31]

---

31   See Chapter 4 "Debating European legislative proposals in the European Standing Committees and on the Floor of the House".

The sift

There are 800-1000 documents deposited in the House of Lords every year for the Committee to consider. The appropriate government department will then produce the Explanatory Memorandum (EM) which summarises the proposal by indicating its legal, financial and policy implications, the procedure that will be followed in negotiations, and the likely timetable for consideration by the Council of Ministers. Once completed, and signed by the minister concerned, the EM is submitted to Parliament within a fortnight.[32] Thus, from this perspective, both Houses start their scrutiny procedure from the same basis. Most importantly, however, as in the House of Commons, the Resolution of the House of 24 October 1990 applies *equally* to the Lords. This means the government is subject to the same limitations of not giving final approval to a proposal in Council, until the scrutiny process is completed.

The trigger for the sift is the deposit of the EM. The sift in the Lords take place every Monday at 9.30 a.m. and therefore everything received up to this time will be included. However, the former Clerk stated in his interview[33] that the Committee will not be prepared to accept an unsigned EM or a document by fax.

The actual sift is carried out by the Chairman of the Committee with the assistance of the Clerk.[34] They aim is to have the sift completed by the end of business on Monday. It is worth noting at this juncture that the government does not deposit all documents on the grounds of confidentiality. Most commonly these are documents submitted to the Inter-Governmental Conference convened under Article 236 TEU (See Chapter Ten).

However if a document is submitted and has been sifted by the Chairman, it then begins the next stage of the scrutiny process. In the House of Lords, a document is then placed in one of seven categories which determine what the next step will be. These are as follows:[35]

(i)   List A, of documents recently transmitted to the Committee, though not to require special attention;
(ii)   List B, of documents which have been remitted to the Committee or Sub-Committees for further consideration;
(iii)   List C, of documents which have been remitted to the Committee or Sub-Committee, are not to be reported to the House;
(iv)   List D, of documents reported since January 1992 for the information of the House;
(v)   List E, of reports to the House on European Communities docu-

---

32   A more detailed discussion of this process can be found in Chapter 3 The Work of the Select Committee on European Legislation.
33   See n. 24, at p. 142.
34   This was a recommendation made by the Maybray-King Committee. See HL 194, p. xlii, para. 118.
35   The results of the sift are published in a regular *Progress of Scrutiny* Report by the Select Committee.

ments for debate including Reports since January 1992 and those to
be debated;

(vi) List F, of documents which have been the subject of Correspondence
with Ministers since July 1994, which will be published in a Report
to the House;

(vii) List G, of outstanding government responses.

Of most importance are Lists A and B. These contain a majority of the documents which are considered during the course of the Chairman's sift. The crit-
ical factor which determines whether a document is placed in List A or B,
depends upon whether it is considered that the proposal raises important
questions of policy or principle (as per the Terms of Reference). However,
there are no formal criteria which the Chairman follows in coming to his
decision that the document raises questions of policy or principle. They make
the judgment as to what needs to be looked at with advice from the legal
adviser. The only variable which may affect the Chairman's judgement is
whether there is enough time to complete a detailed inquiry. It is the function
of the Clerk to ensure that the timetable is both manageable and can be met.
This he will do with the consultation of Clerks from the various Sub-Committees, where the detailed scrutiny and investigation will take place.

If the Clerk confirms that the time is available, the Sub-Committee will be
informed immediately and they will receive all the necessary documents. This
decision will then be confirmed at the next meeting of the whole Select Committee. The main Committee meets only every two to three weeks. It is therefore different from its House of Commons counterpart which meets on a
weekly basis when the House is sitting. This fact confirms the different working methods of the two Committees in the respective Houses. In the Lords
the majority of the scrutiny takes place in smaller specialised Sub-Committees
which indulge in longer more detailed inquiry.

Does the weekly sift ensure scrutiny is effective?

If during the sift the Chairman and his advisers recommend that the proposals are remitted to one or more of the Sub-Committees, this does not automatically mean that the Sub-Committee will conduct a detailed inquiry. This
would not be possible, as nearly half of all proposals are deposited in this way.

It is the case more often than not that the Sub-Committee will not consider the proposal as meriting further consideration. This means that the proposal has "cleared" the scrutiny hurdle and so the scrutiny reserve may be lifted
and the minister can give his agreement or otherwise in the Council. Approximately one tenth of proposals are the subject of full reports to the House. The
following statistics will show the workload of the Committee and the sift statistics for each calendar year:[36]

---

36 These statistics come from the six monthly government publications "Developments
in the EC". The references are as follows: 1990: Cm 1234, Cm 1457; 1991: Cm
1657, Cm 1857; 1992: Cm 2065, Cm 2168; 1993: Cm 2309, Cm 2525; 1994:
Cm 2675, Cm 2798.

Workload of the Committee and its Sub-Committees
Sift Statistics (By Calendar Year)

	'90	'91	'92	'93	'94	'95
Documents in Sift "A"	586	605	645	670	667	778
Documents in Sift "B"	283	208	203	191	229	193
Total number of documents	**869**	**813**	**848**	**861**	**896**	**971**
% documents in Sift "B"	32.5	25.5	24	22	25.5	20

Sift "A" – Documents not requiring further scrutiny by Sub-Committee.
Sift "B" – Documents referred to Sub-Committee for further consideration.

The above figures make interesting reading especially in the light of the view of the Maybray-King Committee. In 1973 it was of the opinion that only about 5 percent of documents would be referred to one of the Sub-Committees. As the figures above show however, in recent years the figure has been on average at least **five** times that amount. This therefore raises the question of whether the Select Committee is recommending too many documents for further debate?

From the earliest days of the scrutiny process, the Select Committee has regularly referred more than the envisaged five per cent of documents. Furthermore, the referral number may on occasion be as high as 33 per cent, for example when a new Member State joins the Community or when Commission activity is particularly high.

The present sift system is probably the most effective way of ensuring that the Select Committee carries out the function that it has been charged with. This was the opinion of the Jelicoe Committee in 1992,[37] and one which the author readily shares. It recommended no amendment to the way it works. If we examine the aim of the sift for a moment, then it will become more readily apparent why it is considered so effective.

The sift aims to be objective. This means that the Select Committee refers legislative proposals to the Sub-Committee which raise questions of legal, financial or policy importance. The referral is made irrespective of what the Sub-Committee's actual workload is. This is based on the premise that it is up to the actual Sub-Committee to determine whether further inquiry is required. In effect, there is a double sift. This is completely different to the procedure in the House of Commons. When the Select Committee recommends further debate in one of the two Standing Committees, the Standing Committee has absolutely no discretion as to whether it conducts the debate. However, in the Lords the matter is purely one of discretion for the Sub-Committee. They take the final decision, about what type of report will be produced, i.e whether it is a full inquiry followed by a debate in the Chamber, or one produced merely for information purposes.

The one negative aspect of this may be that the Sub-Committee have too great a workload. What this "secondary sift" means in practical terms for the

---

37   See HL 35-I, (Session 1991-92) p. 27, para. 41.

Sub-Committee is that it has to give time at the beginning or end of an evidence taking session to consider whether they should undertake an inquiry at some future time and what mode this inquiry will take. More often than not, however, they will decide not to pursue an inquiry, primarily due to lack of time. An alternative will be to conduct the inquiry after it has concluded the current one, but this may lead to scrutiny which is too late to catch the Council deliberations and therefore have no influence. This prospect is not desirable. This means the Committee may conduct a limited inquiry based on Correspondence with Ministers, in which the final report is only produced for "Information Purposes".

This is a problem which the former Clerk discussed with the author. He felt that it may be possible for the full Select Committee to take a more considered approach during the sift and make judgments about the importance of a proposal more frequently. However, such increased activity would inevitably mean more meetings and work for the Select Committee. This difficulty with the Sub-Committees workload is a problem which the Select Committee feels must be addressed, especially in the light of recent developments in the European Union's decision making process. The practical effect of this development is that inquiries will be conducted more rapidly, Council decisions may intervene before the Committee concludes its deliberations or the Conciliation Committee proposes far reaching amendments to the original legislative proposal. Thus, there needs to be a less rigid approach to the conduct of inquiries. This may be more readily achieved, if the initial sift was more selective and the Sub-Committees would therefore concentrate primarily on legislative proposals that affect major policy considerations. Whether such a change could occur without an amendment to the Terms of Reference is unclear. However, given the recent developments outlined above and the increasingly large workload, the time may have arrived for this to be considered.

The use of Correspondence with Ministers

In the course of the interview with the former Clerk of the Committee he stated that the role of the actual Select Committee is predominantly a formal one. Its primary task is one of endorsing the work of the five Sub-Committees. In addition, it also considers all correspondence between the Sub-Committee and ministers. This use of Correspondence with Ministers by the Committee and Sub-Committee has developed substantially in recent years and will now be considered in more detail.

It is often the case that the initial Explanatory Memorandum provided by the minister will not be sufficient. This may be due to a number of reasons including the fact that the proposal has changed and therefore a new EM may be required, or that the initial EM was just too brief. Either way the Sub-Committee will require more information if scrutiny is to be completed on time and thus be effective.

If Correspondence needs to be sent, then it is established practice that it is sent in the name of the Chairman of the whole Select Committee (at present this is Lord Tordoff). He will draft a letter which will then be placed before the entire Committee for approval before being sent to the minister for a reply. However, given that the scrutiny process can be a fast moving one and that the Committee meets only every two weeks there may not be time to obtain the approval of the entire Committee. In such circumstances, the Chairman of the Sub-Committee will write direct to the minister and inform the Chairman of the Select Committee immediately of his action.

However, if the Chairman of the Sub-Committee is pursuing an issue of *policy* with the minister concerned, then he must inform the Select Committee first. This will be dispatched to both the Clerk and the Chairman. In most cases a draft copy of the letter will be sent. But, there will be some rare occasions where only a note that the letter has been dispatched will be sent to the Clerk and Chairman, because of the urgency of the Correspondence. The practice for Correspondence with Ministers is set out at the beginning of each Report that contains all recent correspondence. It reads as follows:

CORRESPONDENCE WITH MINISTERS

"As part of their work on Community proposals the Select Committee send letters to Ministers to express their views on proposals under scrutiny. The procedure of sending a letter may be adopted when the timetable of the Council of Ministers is too short for the Select Committee to publish a report, or if the enquiry indicates that the points at issue do not warrant a full report. Such letters pass the same stages of approval as a Report, and are normally signed by the Chairman. Occasionally, the Chairman delegates authority to a Sub-Committee chairman. Letters on complex legal issues are sent by the Chairman of Sub-Committee E (Law and Institutions). Chairmen of other Sub-Committees may be authorised to write where the timing of discussions in the Council of Ministers does not permit consideration by the Select Committee. In such cases the Select Committee consider the letter at their next meeting."

The former Clerk informed the author that he actively encouraged the Clerks of the Sub-Committees to utilise Correspondence with Ministers as frequently as possible. His reasoning for this centred on the fact that it is more effective and less time consuming than trying to arrange an oral evidence session when the minister will attend the Sub-Committee in person. Often such a meeting may not be possible for a number of weeks. Furthermore, he stated that such Correspondence with the Minister allows the Select Committee to obtain a brief summary of the document, or any amendment. Given the large number of documents coming before the Sub-Committee, this is an efficient way of conducting an inquiry.

The Correspondence with Ministers is published every six months.[38] It sets out all letters that have been sent to the Committee and any reply which was given. Such a report is produced for the Information of the House. The

---

38   For an example of Correspondence with Ministers See HL 74 (Session 1995-96).

Correspondence with Ministers has been an extremely successful development in the House of Lords scrutiny procedure. Ministers have welcomed the development as being particularly time efficient and the correspondence has attracted some public interest as well.

MEMBERSHIP OF THE SELECT COMMITTEE

Permanent Members

The actual Select Committee today has a membership of 20 Peers. This was reduced from 24 following the report by the Jelicoe Committee in 1992. However, that Committee recommended that the total number of members on the main Select Committee be cut even more radically to just 12 members. In addition, the Jelicoe Committee recommended most controversially that members of the main Select Committee would not be members of one of the five Sub-Committees.

This proposal was however rejected as being unworkable, a sentiment echoed by the former Clerk of the Select Committee who was also Clerk to the Jelicoe inquiry. In his interview, he stressed the point that such an arrangement would lead to an inevitable duplication of work by the Sub-Committee. The Sub-Committee would need to consider the issues before beginning its inquiry, thereby inevitably doing all the preparatory work which the main Committee had already carried out. Thus, the benefit of having Peers as members on both the main and one or more of the Sub-Committees is clear. It ensures a familiarity with the issues, and a continuity that leads to more efficient and effective scrutiny.

Selection of Members

In total there are approximately 60 Peers who are involved in the work of the European Communities Committee. On the whole, recruitment to the Committee is easy, with many Peers having some particular interest in European affairs. There is a Committee of Selection in the House of Lords, which is charged with the task of selecting members for the Committees and ensuring that the rotation rule is observed (see below). Likewise, attendance is also very good. This is primarily due to the fact that the specialist Sub-Committees are composed of Peers with a keen interest in the subject. This ensures that they are more likely to attend. Furthermore, a majority of the Peers involved in the Committee are Life Peers. These are the Peers who are often referred to as the "Working Peers", that is they take an active role in the work of the House. Life Peers are usually those who have had a political career in the House of Commons and are thus familiar with the working and methods of Select Committees.

When the Select Committee was first established in 1973, the membership rotated every 3 years. This was subsequently raised to 5 years. However, the Jelicoe Committee viewed this as being too long and recommended a return to the original 3 year period.[39] However, this was rejected and a compromise of a 4 session rotation rule is now in place. A Peer can only rejoin the Committee after he has been absent for one full Parliamentary session.

The reason for this was that the Jelicoe Committee saw this rotation rule as a way of ensuring the maintenance of the high standard of scrutiny by the Committee. They saw this 3 year rotation period as achieving a balance between ensuring that there is continuity on the Committee, but also as a means of guaranteeing the appointment of new Members. In particular those who may have been admitted to the Lords in the last two or three sessions. e.g after a General Election. However, the above rule only relates to each individual Sub-Committee. Thus there is nothing preventing a Peer from joining another Sub-Committee after 4 years have passed. This is a point which the Jelicoe Committee strongly disagreed with.

The final point worth noting about the membership of the Lords Select Committee is the existence of the dual mandate. This is the situation that Members of the Lords are also Members of the European Parliament. Though this also exists in the Commons (most notably among the Ulster MPs) the Lords made a more positive usage of this arrangement, by using it as an strong informal link with the European Parliament. However, following the 1994 European Parliament Elections this dual mandate came to an end in the Lords and it looks unlikely to be resurrected. The former Clerk, regretted this to some extent because he viewed the dual mandate as a positive step that allowed the United Kingdom Parliament to exert its influence within the European Parliament.

The use of Co-opted Members

One of the main differences between the membership of the Commons Committee and the Lords Committee, is that the Lords makes greater use of Peers who have a particular specialist knowledge. It does this by co-opting Peers on to the relevant Sub-Committee for the duration of that particular inquiry. This is an effective way of utilising the variety of specialist knowledge available in the Lords. The Jelicoe Committee went one stage further by recommending that a if a co-opted Member is sought for a particular inquiry then a Member with less expertise should stand down to for the duration of that inquiry.[40] This will ensure that membership of the Sub-Committees is kept to the 12 that has been in place since 1973.

Though this procedure outlined is somewhat akin to the permitting of attendance and speaking of MPs at Standing Committee meetings, where an MP who has a particular constituency interest may attend, there is one main difference. Unlike the MP who does not form part of the quorum nor can he vote, the co-opted Peer is a full Member of the Committee with all the voting and attendance rights of the full time Members. This undoubtedly encourages participation in the Sub-Committee.

---

39   See HL 35-I (Session 1991-92) p. 48, paras. 155-156.
40   *Ibid.*

The Chairman of the Select Committee

The Chairman of the Select Committee, at present Lord Tordoff, is an office holder in the House of Lords. His full title is the Principal Deputy Chairman of Committees. Though his role is not limited to the European Communities Select Committee, this is his primary function. Uniquely amongst Peers he receives a salary for his duties. It is worth pointing out that all other Peers are not paid for their membership of the Select Committee. As stated above, the most important function of the Committee Chairman is to carry out the sift every Monday morning and be responsible for all Correspondence with Ministers.

Like all members of the Committee, the Chairman is also subject to the rotation rule and will not usually hold the position for more than three Parliamentary sessions. The Chairman is elected by the main Select Committee with nominations usually being unopposed.

THE STAFFING OF THE SELECT COMMITTEE[41]

Clerks and Support Staff

The Clerk can best be described as the secretary of the Committee. The main task is to plan the agenda of the Committee. This requires a great deal of forward planning to ensure that inquiries are both current and relevant. Thus the Clerk must always have one eye on the Commission and the proposals it makes, as well as being aware of the Council of Minsters who may reject a proposal leading to the convening of the Conciliation Committee. Thus under these circumstances, it is essential that the Clerk and Chairman have a very good working relationship. The Chairman and therefore the whole Committee are reliant on the Clerk for procedural guidance and administrative back-up. Most notably, the Clerk should have an intimate knowledge of previous inquiries carried out by the Committee.

The Clerks are composed of a career staff who work exclusively in the House of Lords. There are approximately 20 Clerks in the Lords, and 8 of these are devoted to European Community business. The Clerks are rotated on a 3 yearly basis. In evidence given to the Jelicoe Committee, the Clerk of the Parliaments indicated that the staff levels are on occasion too low, especially when there are a large number of Sub-Committee inquiries. The most relevant criticism was that of a Clerk not being able to be involved in two simultaneous inquiries without experiencing great difficulty. Despite this, there were no changes made to the staffing levels following the Jelicoe inquiry.

Legal Advisers

The Select Committee has its own staff of full time legal advisers whose primary task is to advise the Committee on the impact of European legislative

---

41   For more information on this See HL 35-I (Session 1991-92) p. 34 paras. 105-110.

proposals on UK law. The majority of the work for the legal advisers is concerned with Sub-Committee E, the Law and Institutions Sub-Committee. Here the legal advisers take over the function of the Clerk and co-ordinate the work and timetable of the Committee. Their role will be looked at more closely when examining the work of Sub-Committee E in the next chapter.

Specialist Advisers

The use of specialist advisers by the Select Committee and the various Sub-Committees is a very positive aspect of the Lords scrutiny process. In evidence to the House of Commons Procedure Committee the use of specialist advisers in the Lords was described as "flexible, economical, effective and should be retained at more or less its present level."[42] This was a view that was fully endorsed by the Jelicoe Committee.

Quite correctly, they viewed specialist advisers as being integral to effective scrutiny. Not only can they provide the necessary background knowledge needed to carry out an inquiry, they can also contribute to the greater understanding of European issues in the House as a whole. For this reason, the Jelicoe Committee saw advantage in the establishment of a panel or pool of specialists to whom the Committee could turn whenever they needed the appropriate advice. Today there is no formal panel in existence and specialists are appointed as and when they are needed.

CONCLUDING REMARKS

What the above discussion illustrates is the fact the primary concern of this Select Committee, as is the case with its House of Commons counterpart, is to influence the government in the Council. The influence comes via the scrutiny process and is entrenched through the Scrutiny Reserve in the Resolution of the House of 30 October 1990.

However, this is perhaps where any substantial similarity between the two Committees ends. As the next chapter will illustrate more starkly, the Lords Committee gives more autonomy to the Sub-Committees to decide whether or not to conduct a more in-depth inquiry. The main Committee itself merely rubber stamps any decision they come to.

Whilst considering the influence of the Committee, it is important to note once again that the Lords Committee has a much wider audience than merely the government. They also target the European Institutions, most notably the Commission and Parliament. The lack of any formal links means that the development of strong informal links is important. To influence and be aware as early as possible of legislative developments means the Lords is in a strong position. The fact that House of Lords Reports are regularly cited by the Commission, e.g. the inquiry into Fraud and Mismanagement in the Com-

---

42   See HC 19 (Session 1989-90) para. 19.

munity is a testimony to this influence. In the authors opinion, this is an influence that needs to be nurtured. The Committee's primary value lies in its ability to synthesize and distil a mass of information for both the House and the wider general public.

However, despite all these successful wide ranging inquiries, it would be wrong to overstate the Committees influence. The point cannot be forgotten that the House of Lords is just one Chamber in Parliament out of fifteen in the European Union and there is always the risk that both it and the House of Commons may become isolated if governments continue to adopt a negative approach to European Community affairs. The risk is that all the good work of the last twenty-three years and the cultivating of relationships around the Community may be for nothing.

CHAPTER 9

THE WORK OF THE SUB-COMMITTEES IN THE HOUSE OF LORDS

This chapter is concerned with the methods and process by which the House of Lords conducts the rigorous scrutiny of European legislative proposals. The analysis will centre on the work of the five Sub-Committees which are permanently appointed and charged to undertake this task. In addition, the contribution made by *ad hoc* Sub-Committees to the scrutiny process will be assessed and evaluated. In both cases, the appraisal will concentrate on how effective these Committees are in fulfilling the primary task of the Committees identified in the last chapter – that of influencing the minister in the Council via scrutiny of European Community legislative proposals.

INTRODUCTION

The first point to make at the outset is that the scrutiny work undertaken by the Sub-Committees in the House of Lords is, in the author's opinion, probably the most developed and productive part of the entire scrutiny process in *both* Houses of Parliament. This premise is based on several grounds. The first lies in the quality of personnel who are involved in one or more of the Sub-Committees. If one examines the membership list of the Sub-Committees,[1] it becomes readily apparent that a majority of the members are former MPs with a history of involvement in European affairs, peers who have some specialist knowledge about a particular area of European policy, or Lords of Appeal whose expertise in legal matters concerning the European Union is second to none.

The second reason is rooted in the quality of reports which are produced by the Sub-Committees. This proposition will be examined in more detail later on in this chapter, but at this point the argument will be only briefly outlined. The members of the Sub-Committees have the valuable commodity of time on their side. Thus, when carrying out an inquiry in to a legislative proposal they do not work to such a narrow deadline as the Standing Committees in the House of Commons. This permits a wide consultation of a variety of witnesses, all of whom have a contribution to make to the inquiry. It is this extensive consultation which in the authors opinion is the foundation of an influential report.

It is the primary task of the Sub-Committees to carry out an investigation into the merits of a legislative proposal. Following the main sift by the Chairman of the Select Committee, who decides whether the proposal "raises important questions of policy or principle", the document is then passed on

---

1   For an up to date list of members, see *The House of Lords and the European Union*, Information Sheet No.4 published by the Journal and Information Office in the House of Lords.

to the appropriate Sub-Committee, which are divided on subject grounds. It is then up to the Sub-Committee to decide whether or not to conduct an in-depth inquiry in to the legislative proposal. The alternative for the Committee is to only produce a brief report for information purposes, or to just note the document and conduct no further scrutiny. The fact is that out of approximately 1000 documents before the Select Committee every year, only 25 reports are on average produced. The overwhelming majority of documents do not raise "important questions of policy or principle" and are predominantly procedural in their nature.

The use of Sub-Committees by the House of Lords to do the essential scrutiny work is what differentiates the process there from its House of Commons counterpart. Though the Select Committee and the five Sub-Committees are required to draw such important questions of policy or principle to the House, the Chamber itself plays *no* part in this part of the process. This is in stark comparison to the House of Commons where up until 1991, all debates on European Community documents took place in the Chamber. Even since 1991, some proposals are still debated in this way, notably the Community's draft Budget. Today, the Standing Committees only having the power to debate for two and a half hours – a major difference to the House of Lords.

However, from its inception in 1973, the House of Lords has delegated European Community matters exclusively to these specialised Committees. This has on occasion led to the criticism being levelled that the scrutiny process in the Lords is conducted in isolation from the remainder of the House's work. This is somewhat unfair especially if the comparison with the Commons is being made. It must therefore be stressed that unlike the Commons there is no system of Departmental Select Committees which will consider European policy of their relevant department. In the Lords, all scrutiny of European matters is conducted by the Select Committee and its Sub-Committees.

Therefore, given the voluminous nature of this task, delegation of the task is probably the most effective way for European affairs to be considered. However, as the Standing Orders state, the Committees carry out this task on behalf of the House. They must place all reports before the House and there will often be a vigorous debate of the reports findings giving all peers an opportunity to contribute. In addition, all peers have the opportunity to raise European issues at Departmental Question Time in the Lords. What therefore the Lords have achieved over the last twenty-three years is a balance of effective scrutiny within a limited time frame in Committees and ensuring the participation of the whole the House in the final debate.

HISTORICAL BACKGROUND

The Maybray-King Recommendations

The proposal of Sub-Committees was put forward initially by the Maybray-King Committee in 1973.[2] The Committee was of the opinion that only via a system of Sub-Committees could the necessary scrutiny of legislative proposals take place. Thus, the use of small specialist Sub-Committees has become the key feature of the scrutiny system in the Lords. The Maybray-King Committee left the initial decision as to the number of Sub-Committees and their subject areas up to the Select Committee itself. However, it made the following suggestions as to possible Sub-Committees:[3]

Finance, Economics and Regional Policy.
Agriculture.
External Trade and Treaties.
Environment, Social Health and Education.
Energy and Transport.
Law.

What the Maybray-King Committee did was to identify the dominant areas of European Community activity and those which would have a major impact on UK policy and legislation. Thus in 1973, the House of Lords had taken a more considered approach to scrutiny than the House of Commons. In the Commons, debate of European Community documents took place on the floor of the House and only in Standing Committee in exceptional circumstances. The effect of this was that, unlike the Lords, the Commons did not build up any body of expertise in European Community issues. In fact, the Commons did not move over to using Standing Committees more until 1991.[4] However, these are not comparable to the Sub-Committees in the Lords. Even though the Standing Committees are split into subjects, their primary function is different, namely the detailed scrutiny of the merits of a legislative proposal. Unlike the Lords Sub-Committees, they are not investigative and therefore do not hold witness sessions or receive written evidence except from the minister concerned.

The Maybray-King Committee further recommended that the Membership of each Sub-Committee should be minimal. Three to six members was seen as being the most appropriate. The rationale behind this was that only in such small Committees could the detailed inquiry take place. Too many members and the Sub-Committee would in effect be a Select Committee. Furthermore, the larger the membership, the greater the potential for disagreement. This does not mean that the Sub-Committees were not intended

---

2   See HL 194 (Session 1972-73) pp. xli-xlii, paras. 113-116.
3   *Ibid.*
4   For more discussion on the Standing Committees see Chapter 4.

to be a forum for debate. In fact quite the reverse. The debate was intended to lead to a consensual decision that reflected the views of the *entire* Sub-Committee. By recommending a small membership, the Maybray-King Committee was encouraging consensus, and most importantly avoiding the production of minority reports.

Over the intervening twenty-three year period, this consensual approach has grown into one of the major strengths of the Sub-Committees. It has ensured that debate always concentrates on the fundamental issues before the Sub-Committee and the production of high quality reports.

The Law and Institutions Sub-Committee

At this juncture it is appropriate to point out that during the course of this chapter, the work of the Law and Institutions Sub-Committee as it has become known, will be the subject of "special treatment". The reason for this is twofold. Firstly, in the authors opinion this Sub-Committee carries out the most important work of any of the Sub-Committees. Its concentration on the legal implications of legislative proposals goes to the heart of the scrutiny function. Secondly, as this investigation has been approached from a lawyers standpoint, a Sub-Committee that concentrates on matters legal holds more interest for the author, especially in the light of the Sub-Committees Terms of Reference. However, all other Sub-Committees will undergo a rigorous analysis but the emphasis there will be on how these remaining Sub-Committees concentrate on issues of policy as well as the mechanics of scrutiny.

From the outset of the scrutiny procedures in the House of Lords, there have been special arrangements for the consideration of the legal implications of European legislative proposals. The Maybray-King Committee made the following suggestions as to issues a Law Sub-Committee might wish to consider:[5]

(a) whether Regulations impliedly repeal existing UK legislation;
(b) whether any Regulation may make it desirable to amend other UK legislation, even where this is not obligatory, in order to comply with that Regulation;
(c) the most appropriate means (whether by statute law or by delegated legislation) for bringing draft Directives into operation in the United Kingdom in those cases where they cannot be brought into operation by administrative action.

The Report then continued by confirming a recommendation made in the First Report by the House of Commons Committee that considered that Houses arrangements for the scrutiny of European issues.[6] They agreed with the view that the government should be under an obligation to inform Parlia-

---

5   See HL 194 (Session 1972-73) p. xli, para. 114.
6   See HC 143 (Session 1972-73) para. 7 (c).

ment of the effect which any Community legislation would have on the United Kingdom law and what additional legislation would be introduced, if the instrument were made. It would then be up to the Law Sub-Committee to examine the government's views when considering points (a) to (c) above.

Today, the above arrangements have been condensed into one task for the Sub-Committee, that of considering the *vires* of a legislative proposal. Most importantly, the Committee will consider whether a particular proposal does impliedly repeal existing UK legislation (as per (a) above). This is important because the Sub-Committee is guarding one of the most important Constitutional principles in English Law – that of implied repeal.

STRUCTURE OF THE SUB-COMMITTEES

Subject orientated Sub-Committees

The Sub-Committee arrangement in the House of Lords has evolved over the last twenty-three years. The major changes have centred on the actual subject brief of each of the Sub-Committees. Originally, there were five Sub-Committees, covering the subject areas recommended by the Maybray-King Committee. This was increased to seven in the 1975-76 session but reduced to six in the 1986-87 session, primarily to allow for the staffing of *ad-hoc* Sub-Committees. The six Committees appointed were as follows:

List of Sub-Committees 1986-1993

Sub-Committee A	Finance, Trade and Industry and External Relations
Sub-Committee B	Energy, Transport and Technology
Sub-Committee C	Social and Consumer Affairs
Sub-Committee D	Agriculture and Food
Sub-Committee E	Law and Institutions
Sub-Committee F	Environment

The Sub-Committees appointed during this period reflected the dominant areas of Community activity. For example, originally in 1973, there was no separate Environment Committee, but this changed in 1975 and was kept until 1993. During this eighteen year period, environmental matters came to the fore, with many legislative proposals being developed by the Commission and the Council of Ministers. However, following the Report for the Select Committee on the Committee Work of The House,[7] the Sub-Committees were rearranged once more to reflect more accurately the main areas of Community legislative activity. Thus since 1993 they have had the following structure:

---

7   See HL 35-I (Session 1991-92).

Sub-Committees 1993-1996

Sub-Committee A   Economic and Financial Affairs, Trade and External
                   Relations
Sub-Committee B   Energy, Industry, Transport and the Working
                   Environment
Sub-Committee C   Environment, Public Health and Education
Sub-Committee D   Agriculture, Fisheries and Consumer Protection
Sub-Committee E   Law and Institutions
(Sub-Committee F   Home Affairs and Social Policy – see p. 163 below)

Two points are readily apparent on examination of the above Sub-Committee list. First is the reduction to five Sub-Committees, as was the case when the Sub-Committees were originally established in 1973. The primary reason for this was to address the staffing problems that had become more regular with an increase in the use of *ad hoc* Sub-Committees by the House of Lords generally.

The second point, relates to the organisation of the subjects among the Sub-Committees. The area of social affairs previously dealt with by Sub-Committee C is now no longer specifically mentioned. This reflects the fact since the signing of the Maastricht Treaty, the United Kingdom has retained autonomy in social affairs via its "opt-out". Thus, consumer affairs which was previously coupled with social affairs is now scrutinised along with Agriculture and Fisheries. A strange combination!

Similarly, the emphasis on environmental issues is no longer as great and thus it too does not warrant its own Sub-Committee. It will be interesting to see how this particular development works out. Most notably, it is the question of whether environmental affairs and legislation are receiving the detailed scrutiny that is required for the many complex proposals still coming forward?

Over the last Parliamentary session, Sub-Committee C has conducted two major inquiries, both of which relate exclusively to environmental affairs. The first inquiry was in to a proposed directive on Drinking Water (7208/95) and the second in to Access to Information on the Environment. It is apparent that environmental issues are still dominant within the Community and therefore, the evidence suggests there is still a need for a specialised Sub-Committee to investigate and scrutinise them.

In their report, the Select Committee on the Committee of the Work of the House (the Jelicoe Committee) criticised the Sub-Committee structure for being too rigid (this important issue will be returned to after a detailed consideration of the work of each of the Sub-Committees in the next section). The Jelicoe Committee were of the opinion that in particular:[8]

"there is a need for a Sub-Committee structure which has a degree of flexibility and is capable of adjustment in line with priorities and in response to the requirements of the House."

8   *Ibid.* p. 46, para. 145.

This view was behind their recommendation for a decrease in the actual number of Select Committees and an increase in the use of *ad hoc* Sub-Committees. In fact, the Jelicoe Committee even flirted with the idea of recommending only three subject based Sub-Committees and placing a greater emphasis on the use of *ad hoc* Sub-Committees.

Therefore, if we take a closer look at the Sub-Committees appointed before 1993 and those after 1993 it is evident that they do quite accurately reflect the political priorities of both the government and the European Community. Sub-Committees prior to 1993 reflected the needs and aims of the establishment of the Single European Market. For example, a Sub-Committee on Social and Consumer Affairs reflected accurately much of the legislation coming forward under the Single Market programme. However, post 1993, a Sub-Committee dedicated exclusively to these two areas no longer exists. This is primarily due to the fact that, as already stated, post Maastricht, the UK is not subject to legislative proposals coming forward under the Social Chapter.

However, most important are the changes made by the Maastricht Treaty in the area of Inter-Governmental cooperation. These are important developments which require much detailed scrutiny. In particular, is the fact that the proposals have not, initially at least, been subject to any organised scrutiny by the House of Commons. Thus, the ability of the Lords to be more flexible and meet these new challenges and shoulder the burden of the detailed scrutiny has been extremely important. This has only been possible because of the decrease in the number of permanent Sub-Committees and the ability to appoint more *ad hoc* ones.

Today therefore, the central theme in the Sub-Committee structure is one of flexibility. This aim of flexibility relates to two recent developments. Firstly the legislative changes introduced by the Maastricht Treaty and secondly to the increased role of the Sub-Committees in the areas of policy evaluation. Since 1993, the evidence suggests that the Sub-Committees have become more forward looking by anticipating both legislative and policy developments within the Community. At the forefront of this development is the increase in the use of *ad hoc* Sub-Committees by the Lords.

At the start of the 1996-97 Parliamentary year, the Select Committee appointed a sixth permanent Sub-Committee, Sub-Committee F. It is charged with investigating Social Affairs, Education and Home Affairs. A legal adviser's to the Select Committee informed the author that this decision was taken to fill the gaps which were left in the Sub-Committee structure. It was felt that these policy areas were not receiving the detailed scrutiny they deserved. The area of Home Affairs is designed to scrutinise proposals under the Justice and Home Affairs pillar and has thus relieved some of the pressure on Sub-Committee E.

However, the decision to scrutinise Social Affairs is questionable given the UK opt- out. A Sub-Committee focussing on this area was not deemed necessary in 1993 and it is difficult to justify its inclusion. This said, by January 1997, the Sub-Committee had yet to begin any inquiry and thus any further judgment about its appointment would be premature and needs to be considered in the light of its activity over an entire Parliamentary session.

Ad hoc Sub-Committees in the Lords

The Jelicoe Committee in its investigation saw great advantage in the increased use of *ad hoc* Sub-Committees. This was a view shared by the then Leader of the House, Lord Waddington, in his written and oral evidence to the Jelicoe Committee.[9] In his evidence he argued, quite correctly as it has turned out, that many of the important issues which will confront the Community over the next ten years will not be completely suited to subject related inquiries. This therefore will be the realm of the *ad hoc* Sub-Committees.

Recently, an *ad hoc* Sub-Committee concluded an important inquiry into the 1996 Inter-Governmental Conference. As can be seen from the nature of the inquiry, it did not fit within any of the existing subject Sub-Committees and was not based on any legislative proposal. In fact the inquiry concentrated on specific political issues facing the European Union, for example, the enlargement of the Union and the progress of Economic and Monetary Union (this inquiry is considered in more detail on pp. 180-182 below).

This is the structure of the Sub-Committees today. They are designed to meet the diverse needs of the main Select Committee in its complex scrutiny task. In the forthcoming sections an evaluation of how each of these Sub-Committees addresses this task and how successful they are in achieving it will be made. In the course of this, reference will be made to particular inquiries carried out by the Sub-Committees as examples of the type of inquiry a Sub-Committee may conduct throughout the session.

THE WORK OF THE SUB-COMMITTEES

The Terms of Reference

The most interesting point here is that the five of the current Sub-Committees do not possess individual Terms of Reference. Rather, they are subject to the same Terms of Reference which are given to the main Select Committee (there are exceptions to this rule, most commonly when an inquiry is launched into a matter which has not arisen from an EC directive). Only Sub-Committee E, the Law and Institutions Sub-Committee has its own specific Terms of Reference. This is because of the nature of the work of the Sub-Committee, i.e. its concentration on legal issues raised by European Community proposals.

In the light of what has been said above, it will be of benefit to look at the relevant part of Terms of Reference once again to have a clear view of what the Sub-Committees task actually is:

> "To consider Community proposals whether in draft or otherwise, to obtain all
> necessary information about them, and to make reports on those which, in the

---

9   *Ibid.* p. 104. See also the evidence of Sir Christopher Prout MEP at p. 194, Q 493.

opinion of the Committee, raise important questions of policy or principle, and on other questions to which the Committee consider that the special attention of the House should be drawn"

As can be seen from the opening line above, the primary task is to scrutinise European Community legislative proposals, and also to consider any other important questions of policy. This task carried out by the Sub-Committees is done so on behalf of the House. The Select Committee and each of the Sub-Committees have delegated to them the function of detailed scrutiny. Therefore, either the Chairman of the Select Committee during the weekly sift decides that no further scrutiny is needed, or the document is passed on to the Sub-Committee who decide whether it merits a full investigation. Alternatively, a Sub-Committee may conduct a free standing inquiry into a particular EC policy. In either case, the requirements of the Terms of Reference are met.

Sub-Committee Membership

Since the Jelicoe Report, the membership of each of the Sub-Committees has been reduced to a maximum of twelve. It was felt that if the membership were any larger, then this would inhibit the effectiveness of the Sub-Committees. As mentioned previously, the major strength of the Sub-Committees is their consensual approach and ability to investigate complex issues in a methodical manner. These strengths are undoubtedly reduced if the Sub-Committees are too big.

The use of co-opted Members is a very beneficial step by the Sub-Committees. They add their wide experience and expertise to the inquiry. They sit with two to four Members of the main Select Committee on each of the Sub-Committees. This ensures a degree of continuity amongst the membership, but is flexible enough to allow the Sub-Committee to alter its composition to meet the needs of each particular inquiry. All permanent members of the Sub-Committees are subject to the three year rotation rule as outlined in the previous chapter.

Support staff

Each of the Sub-Committees has a Clerk attached to it, though the Clerks do have other duties to perform, most notably working on other Sub-Committees. The vital function each Clerk performs is to ensure that the Sub-Committee has all the necessary information to conduct an inquiry and that there is sufficient time to complete the inquiry.

Uniquely, Sub-Committee E, the Law and Institutions Sub-Committee has two full time legal advisers who assist the Sub-Committee to carry out its specific task. Most importantly, they ensure that the Sub-Committee has all necessary information before embarking on any inquiry, of the legal background and implications of a particular proposal.

Specialist Advisers

The use of specialist advisers by the Sub-Committees continues to be one of the great assets of the whole scrutiny process in the Lords. Their experience and expertise, which when coupled with that of the co-opted peers makes for a formidable combination. However, the Jelicoe Committee felt their influence could be increased still further if the specialist advisers were retained after the conclusion of an inquiry to give advice and assistance on future inquiries and programmes.[10] It was felt, this would help the Sub-Committees to be more selective in selecting subjects for inquiry.

This proposal is a positive step for the reason that, with the increase in the number of legislative proposals coming forward, the Sub-Committees will be under increased time pressure when it comes to the completion of an inquiry. On this premise, the Sub-Committees will have to be even more selective in the future in deciding which subjects will be inquired into more fully. The advice of specialist advisers under these circumstances will be even more valuable.

In the forthcoming sections, a closer investigation of the work undertaken by each of the five Sub-Committees is presented. Though this will involve an analysis of some of the reports produced over the last two Parliamentary sessions the primary issue will be the working methods and aims of the reports as opposed to evaluating the subject matter of the report. For the analysis, a cross section of reports on a variety of issues which reflect fairly the work of the Sub-Committees in an average Parliamentary year, have been selected. This presents the opportunity to examine the various approaches taken to scrutiny and examination of European issues generally, by the different Sub-Committees.

SUB-COMMITTEE A – ECONOMIC AND FINANCIAL AFFAIRS, TRADE AND EXTERNAL RELATIONS

The subject matter of this Sub-Committee has broadly remained the same for the last twenty-three years. Essentially, the Sub-Committee has been concerned with economic issues. Any changes have revolved primarily around what title is to be given to the Sub-Committee as opposed to amending its role significantly.

In two recent Parliamentary sessions (1994/95 and 1995/96) Sub-Committee A conducted two major inquiries, both of which illustrate in their own way the broad approach to scrutiny which the Sub-Committees have adopted.

---

10   *Ibid.* p.53, para. 168.

The Maghreb inquiry

In the 1994/95 session, this Sub-Committee produced a highly detailed report on the *Relations between the EU and the Maghreb Countries*.[11] This inquiry was initially not based on any EC document. The inquiry was conducted because the Sub-Committee felt that:[12]

"Mediterranean questions were going to be an important part of the European Union's agenda in 1995."

What the above quote illustrates is that firstly, the Sub-Committee sets its own agenda, and secondly, the Sub-Committees adopt a very forward looking perspective in relation to issues of policy. During the course of this inquiry, the Commission published several documents on this very issue, which the Sub-Committee considered in close detail.[13] However, the point is clear. When the Terms of Reference state for the Sub-Committee to consider "other questions to which the Committee consider that the special attention of the House should be drawn", the Sub-Committee interpret this as including future policy developments. It also illustrates that the Select Committee and the six Sub-Committees are not exclusively scrutiny Committees in the mould of their House of Commons counterpart.

If one takes a closer look at the background to the inquiry, the Sub-Committees reasons for conducting it are even more apparent. Furthermore these are reasons which one would not automatically view as being directly connected either with the European Union or with UK Foreign policy. The Sub-Committee pointed out that up until mid 1996, the Presidency of the EU will lie with France, Spain and Italy – all countries with close ties to the Maghreb countries. Thus, it was felt, that during this eighteen month period, policy would be influenced to quite a degree by activity in the Mediterranean. Secondly, the Sub-Committee also state that they felt there was a "widespread lack of knowledge of the Maghreb countries in the United Kingdom".[14] On this basis, they also viewed their role as an informative one, for both the House and the country at large, about the political and economic situation in these countries.

A closer look at the wide variety of evidence received during the course of the inquiry illustrates further the point that the Sub-Committees are not merely scrutiny committees. On the basis of this evidence it can be argued

---

11   See HL 58 (Session 1994-95).
12   *Ibid.* p. 5.
13   The following documents were scrutinised by the Sub-Committee in the course of their inquiry: (i) 10428/94 (COM(94) 427) Commission Communication entitled *Strengthening the Mediterranean Policy of the European Union: Establishing a Euro-Mediterranean Partnership.* (ii) 5766/95 (COM(94) 72) Commission Communication entitled *Strengthening the Mediterranean Policy of the European Union: Implementing a Euro-Mediterranean Partnership.*
14   *Ibid.* p. 6, para. 2.

that scrutiny is no longer the primary task of the Sub-Committees. Reports produced over the last two or three Parliamentary sessions indicate a definite move towards consideration of policy. This will become even more apparent in the forthcoming sections.

In relation to the inquiry concerning the EU and the Maghreb countries, the Sub-Committee took evidence for a period of approximately six months. In terms of a Parliamentary session, almost an entire one. This therefore precluded the Sub-Committee from any other inquiry into legislative proposals, with all other documents coming forward under the sift not being subject to the same detailed scrutiny. There were thirteen evidence sessions in total, which included the Ambassadors of Algeria, Morocco and Tunisia, the European Commission and several academics.[15] Visits to the three countries were also arranged during the course of the inquiry. In the light of this, are not these Sub-Committees now more akin to the Departmental Select Committees in the House of Commons whose brief is to consider the policy, expenditure and administration of the relevant department?

The EMU inquiry

At the start of this chapter when the Terms of Reference were considered it was stated that there were occasions when a Sub-Committee would have specific Terms of Reference that related to the inquiry at hand. This is usually the case if the inquiry is into a subject that has not arisen out of a legislative proposal. The recent EMU inquiry is one such investigation. Once again, as with the Maghreb inquiry, the primary consideration of the Sub-Committee is an issue of policy and not legislation. The Terms of Reference illustrate the point clearly:

> "If EMU goes ahead and a significant number of Member States are not willing to join at the outset, what are the implications for the Single Market, the EU budget, and for relations with other non-participating countries more generally, and what does the UK need to do now to prepare for EMU, irrespective of the eventual decision whether or not to join?"

The reason for this inquiry is to consider future EU and government policy. The primary aim of this inquiry though is to contribute to the controversial EMU debate. This is notwithstanding the fact that the United Kingdom have opted out of automatic Monetary Union. Thus, the Sub-Committees illustrate once again that they work to their own agenda.

Above it was stated that the Sub-Committees are behaving in a similar way to the Departmental Select Committees in the House of Commons. This EMU inquiry adds weight to this assertion. The nature and subject matter of the inquiry is one which could easily have been conducted by the Treasury Select Committee in the House of Commons.

---

15   A full list of witnesses is contained in Appendix 3 of the report, p. 40.

This examination of the work of Sub-Committee A over the two Parliamentary sessions demonstrates the diversity of issues which face the European Union in Economic and Trade matters. Obviously, this Sub-Committee, like all others, has a limited amount of time and must make difficult decisions about how best to use it. However, in this authors opinion, Sub-Committee A has, over the last two Parliamentary sessions at least, veered to far into the realm of policy consideration at the expense of the scrutiny of legislative proposals.

SUB-COMMITTEE B – ENERGY, INDUSTRY, TRANSPORT AND THE WORKING ENVIRONMENT

Sub-Committee B today has a broad remit. Since 1993 it has been concerned with a range of industrial and infrastructure issues. In the last two Parliamentary sessions, it has undertaken two major inquiries, one on European Union Energy Policy[16] and the other investigating Tourism in the European Union.[17] Both of these Reports related to a politically non-controversial subject matter.

The Energy Policy inquiry

The Report on European Union Energy Policy is an example of the House of Lords at its best. That is, the Lords held an inquiry into a complex issue, where opinions varied across the EU, and yet produced a report that has been valuable to the debate. Once again the use of many expert witnesses was at the core of the successful report.

The basis for the inquiry was not a legislative proposal but merely a Commission Green Paper. This is merely a consultative document published by the Commission when it seeks views and opinions on a given subject. Thus, if we return to the Terms of Reference for a moment, it can be seen that such inquiries are permitted because the Sub-Committee can consider Community proposals "whether in draft or otherwise".

The Sub-Committee considered the following Commission papers:

4523/95 COM(94) 659 final	Green Paper "For a European Union energy policy"
11881/94COM(94) 1918 final	Commission Report on the collection of information concerning investments of the interests to the Community in the petroleum, natural gas and electricity sectors

---

16   See HL 87 (Session 1994-95).
17   See HL 39 (Session 1994-95).

The most apparent point from these two documents is that the Sub-Committee in inquiring into them, is engaging in scrutiny of a pre-legislative nature that is different in substance to the scrutiny it undertakes prior to the minister giving agreement in the Council. The aim of such a report is to influence the *actual* legislative proposal put forward by the Commission to the Council of Ministers. The House of Lords has realised the importance of this influence despite the lack of any formal links with the Commission. It is well known that the Commissioners read reports produced by the Lords and it is also common knowledge that the Commission cannot ignore a report, such as this one on European Union energy policy, that is based on the opinions of many leading experts in the field.

SUB-COMMITTEE C – ENVIRONMENT, PUBLIC HEALTH AND EDUCATION

The subject areas of Sub-Committee C changed substantially in 1993. Prior to this date the Sub-Committee was concerned with Social and Consumer Affairs. Today however, though concerned with the Environment, Public Health and Education, it is apparent from the reports produced over the last two Parliamentary sessions that environmental issues dominate the Sub-Committee's agenda.

The Phare Programme inquiry

In the 1994-95 session, the members were concerned with an inquiry entitled "Environmental issues in Eastern Europe: The Phare Programme".[18] The basis for this inquiry was that the House of Lords Select Committee felt more information was needed about countries such as Poland, the Czech Republic and Hungary, who they saw as being full members of the European Union in the near future.

This inquiry was similar in its form to that conducted by Sub-Committee A into the relationship between the EU and the Maghreb countries. Most notably, it was not based on any particular Commission document or legislative proposal but was merely an evaluation of a particular EU environmental programme. Within this context therefore, the Sub-Committee thought it appropriate to have specific Terms of Reference for this inquiry which reflected more accurately the aims of the Sub-Committee and be of more value for information purposes for the entire House. Thus the Sub-Committee had the following Terms of Reference:[19]

> "to consider the adequacy and effectiveness of the EU's Phare programme to prepare the countries of Central and Eastern Europe to meet the environmental obligations on EU membership"

---

18   See HL 86 (Session 1994-95).
19   *Ibid.* p. 6, para. 8.

The Terms of Reference gave the Sub-Committee a very wide brief. It allowed for a wide variety of evidence, both oral and written, to be submitted and involved visits overseas to all the countries concerned. In addition, a specialist adviser was also appointed specifically for the duration of this inquiry.[20] This reflects what is now common practice within the House of Lords when preparing a report.

The most obvious point about this inquiry, is that it was concerned purely with EU policy. To be more specific, it was concerned with the development of an EU policy. It was a forward looking report that was aimed at both the Commission and Council of Ministers and was intended to contribute to the debate on enlargement of the EU.

In the light of what has just been said above, the assertion made earlier in this chapter deserves to be repeated. That is, that the Sub-Committees appear to be shifting towards the consideration of policy as being their primary task. This inquiry lasted approximately five months and occupied all the Sub-Committee's resources. It thus prevented any other inquiry from taking place.

However, on the positive side, the inquiry was another example of what the House of Lords Sub-Committees do best. That is, long, detailed and influential inquisitorial investigations carried out in a consensual manner. This fact alone adds much weight to the argument against reforming the House of Lords. But, it also raises the difficult question of what role the House of Lords should have in the European legislative process. Given the increased concern with policy issues, is the case for a strict division of labour between the two Houses now irresistible? This author's opinion, stated previously, is that a review of the present arrangements in both Houses is long overdue. However, neither House will be willing to restrict its role. Thus in these circumstances, Sub-Committees in the Lords will continue to devote the majority of their time to evaluating policy developments and not concentrating on the detailed scrutiny of legislative proposals.

SUB-COMMITTEE D – AGRICULTURE, FISHERIES AND CONSUMER PROTECTION

The subject matter of this Sub-Committee has not varied much since it was established in 1973. Then as today, it is predominantly concerned with agricultural issues and most notably the Common Agricultural Policy and Common Fisheries Policy. Over the last two Parliamentary years, the Sub-Committee has conducted two major inquiries. The first was based on Commission proposals to "Reform the Sugar Regime"[21] and the most recent one was concerned with the "Veterinary Certification of Animals and Animal Products".[22]

---

20   A full list of witnesses may be found in Appendix 3, p. 34 of the Report and the views of the Specialist Adviser in Appendix 4, p. 38.
21   See HL 28 (Session 1994-95).
22   See HL 46 (Session 1994-95).

The Sugar Regime inquiry

The report into the Reform of the Sugar Regime was one based on a specific Commission proposal. The document, 1141/94, was to form the basis of European Union's response to the decisions taken at the GATT Uruguay Round. The background to this document was that the Commission had intended to issue its proposals in time for adoption by the Council in December 1994. However, as they were only published in late November of that year, the Council was not ready to adopt the measures in December.

In the report the Sub-Committee states that it carried out this inquiry to:[23]

"...enable the Select Committee's opinion on the proposals to be published before decisions are made in the Council."

In essence, the Sub-Committee is performing its primary function. That is to scrutinise a particular legislative proposal and inform the minister of its view so as to influence the minister *prior* final adoption by the Council. Obviously, in scrutinising a particular piece of legislation the Sub-Committee also examines the policy implications of the legislation. However, the difference between this inquiry and say the one carried out by Sub-Committee C in to the Phare programme is that this inquiry has as its focus the Commission legislative proposal. The aim therefore of the two inquiries is quite different. The one by Sub-Committee C is designed to influence at the consultation stage whereas this one by Sub-Committee D is intended to influence at the decision-making stage.

This report also illustrates the main limiting factor of the entire scrutiny process. Above, a brief background to the inquiry was given. As can be seen, the time between the publication of the legislative proposal by the Commission and the date intended for adoption by the Council was particularly short. In this case however because of the late publication of the proposal, the Council meeting was put back, and the Scrutiny Reserve ensured that the Sub-Committee could give proper attention to the proposal. This though will not always be the case. There are occasions where an immediate decision will be needed by the Council and thus the Scrutiny Reserve will be ignored. It will then be up to the minister to come to the dispatch box an explain his or her actions. Similarly, the growth in Qualified Majority Voting will mean that the UK minister may be outvoted by the other Member States. They know that they will not have to observe the UK's Scrutiny Reserve if they can achieve the desired majority without the UK's support. This today is one of the biggest challenges to the scrutiny process both in the House of Lords and the House of Commons.

---

23   *Ibid.* p. 5, para. 1.

SUB-COMMITTEE E – LAW AND INSTITUTIONS

Since 1973, there has been a specialist Sub-Committee whose sole task has been to scrutinise the legal implications of particular legislative proposals as well as examining the Treaty base and to vet questions of *vires*. This multiplicity of these tasks places an extremely heavy burden upon the Sub-Committee, both in man hours and resources. The point must be stressed that Sub-Committee E is the only specialist committee to look exclusively at the legal implications of legislative proposals in both Houses of Parliament.

In addition, this role has recently increased substantially. Since 1994, Sub-Committee E has taken on the difficult and complex task of scrutinising proposals coming forward under the Inter-Governmental Pillars. Following the Select Committee on the European Communities Report into the House of Lords Scrutiny of the Inter-Governmental Pillars of the European Union,[24] it was decided that this additional task would fall to Sub-Committee E with no special arrangements to facilitate this change. The first such inquiry undertaken by the Sub-Committee was in to the EUROPOL[25] proposals for establishing greater co-operation between national police forces.

Structure of Sub-Committee E

Given the nature of work of the Sub-Committee it is no surprise to learn that the membership is predominantly lawyers. It has now become established practice that the Chairmanship of Sub-Committee E is in the hands of a Law Lord. Such an appointment makes sense because it allows some of the most senior lawyers in the United Kingdom to carry out the scrutiny of many technical and complex legislative proposals. In the author's opinion, there is no substitute for the type of experience they can bring to the task and their contribution is arguably one of the strongest aspects of the entire scrutiny system.

The Sub-Committee itself comprises a maximum of twelve members. Like all the other Sub-Committees, it makes effective use of co-opted Members for inquiries, especially lawyers who may have a particular interest in the inquiry. For example, Lord Wilberforce and Lord Lester of Herne Hill are regularly co-opted on to the Sub-Committee.

Specialist Staff

Like all other Sub-Committees, Sub-Committee E has the assistance of a permanent staff to assist it in its weekly task. However, unlike the other Sub-Committees where the Clerk is responsible for organising the agenda and ensuring there is enough time to conduct an inquiry, here it is the function of the legal adviser. At present there are two legal advisers for the Sub-Commit-

---

24   See HL 124 (Session 1992-93)
25   See HL 51 I and II (Session 1994-95).

tee. In the course of an interview, a former legal adviser[26] stressed the importance of having the necessary documents prepared for each meeting as well as making the appropriate decision about which document will actually be the subject of an investigation. Legal issues are always difficult because they have to be viewed in the context of the European Court of Justice which is the final arbiter in any dispute. The Sub-Committee always has to be fully aware of the Court's views as they may affect their own inquiry.

Sub-Committee E – The Terms of Reference

As previously stated, Sub-Committee E is unique amongst its counterparts in that it has always had its own very specific Terms of Reference. These are tailored to meet the requirements of the Sub-Committee in its crucial task of advising the government about the correct legal base for a Commission proposal. In performing this task, Sub-Committee E makes very frequent and effective use of Correspondence with Ministers. This strong reliance on letters as the means for obtaining government views on a proposal reflects the fact that the Sub-Committee usually works to a very tight deadline.

The Terms of Reference which were revised and extended in 1983 are as follows:

> "To consider and report to the Committee on:
> (a) any Community proposal which would lead to significant changes in United Kingdom law, or have far reaching implications for areas of United Kingdom law other than to which it is immediately directed:
> (b) the merits of such proposals as are referred to it by the Select Committee;
> (c) whether any important developments have taken place in Community law; and
> (d) any matters which they consider should be drawn to the attention of the Committee concerning the *vires* of any proposal"

From the Terms of Reference it is immediately apparent that the Sub-Committee has a very wide ranging and important role in the scrutiny process. In (a) above, the Sub-Committee is charged with the task of evaluating the likely impact on existing UK legislation of Community proposals. In particular, the Sub-Committee concentrates on the question of implied repeal. This also extends to an assessment of the impact on legislation which is not specifically targeted by the Community proposal. This is an ideal task for a Sub-Committee whose membership is composed predominantly of lawyers!

The task itself requires the Sub-Committee to make a judgment about the likely impact of the proposal. In (a) above reference is made to proposals

---

26   The Conversation took place with Mrs Eilleen Denza at the House of Lords on Friday 24 February 1995.

which will have either a "significant" effect on UK law, or have "far reaching implications" on other unconnected legislation. Thus in both cases, the Terms of Reference appear to imply that the Sub Committee is concerned only with those proposals that will have a major impact. Each legislative proposal will inevitably have an effect. The question that the Sub-Committee has to address is whether the effect is one that will merit further detailed scrutiny by way of an in-depth inquiry.

In coming to this conclusion, the Terms of Reference themselves offer a degree of guidance. The Sub-Committee should have regards to the "merits of the proposal", whether it is part of a "important development" in Community law, and perhaps most crucially the *vires* of the proposal. The issue of the *vires* of the proposal will now be considered in more detail.

Legal Work of the Sub-Committee

In considering the *vires*, the Sub-Committee are primarily concerned with the question of whether the powers as provided by the Treaty have been used in the appropriate way. This has been particularly important in scrutinising additional powers given to the Commission, both, by the Single European Act and within the Maastricht Treaty. In addition to investigating secondary legislation, Sub-Committee E is also concerned with primary legislation, i.e. the Treaty base and whether secondary legislation is being brought forward under the correct Treaty provision.

A prime example of this aspect of the Sub-Committee's work was seen immediately after the introduction of the Single European Act 1986. Under the SEA Article 100A of the EEC Treaty provided for the Council of Ministers to adopt Single Market measures by qualified majority. All these measures were introduced via proposals originating from the Commission. Sub-Committee E held the opinion that the Commission had given an extremely wide interpretation to Article 100A and argued that some of the proposals should have been introduced through some alternative Treaty provision such as Article 100 or Article 235, both of which require the Council to act in unanimity.

Through the effective use of the Correspondence with Ministers, the Sub-Committee were able to inform the government of their view in time to influence the minister, before the final decision was taken by the Council. In the majority of instances, the government shared the Sub-Committee's concern about the over enthusiastic use of Article 100A. Similarly, in its 1989 Report on the Border Control of Persons,[27] the Sub-Committee concluded that Article 8A of the EEC Treaty did not impose the obligation to remove national border controls. The UK government adopted an identical position.

However, the Sub-Committee and the government are not always in agreement. For example in its 1990 Report on the Rights of Student Residence,[28] the Sub-Committee adopted the Commission's view where they used Article 7

27   See HL 54 (Session 1988-89).
28   See HL 27 (Session 1989-90).

of the EEC Treaty as the legal basis for the Directive. Article 7 contained provisions against discrimination on grounds of nationality and allowed the Council to adopt provisions to this effect by qualified majority. The UK government however, contended that such legislation should have been introduced via Article 235 which required unanimity in decision taking by the Council of Ministers. Thus, the Sub-Committee acts independently of government and puts its duty to scrutinise the UK government and the views its holds above any exclusive national interest. Furthermore, as the above example illustrates, it will criticise the government when it feels that this is appropriate.

What is apparent therefore, is that in consideration of the *vires* of a proposal, the Sub-Committee is particularly directing its attention at the Commission and the use of its powers as given to it by the Treaty. However, the influence can only be exerted over the minister in Council – a wholly different institution. This is perhaps the most pressing argument for establishing direct formal links with the Commission. The Sub-Committee with its great legal experience and knowledge, would be a persuasive force on the Commission in disagreements of the type outlined above. Whereas the minster may be viewed as being obstructive, the Sub-Committee independent of the Executive and with no political agenda may be regarded as being constructive. Their ability to be persuasive in a subtle way is a great strength of the Sub-Committee structure as a whole. The establishment of formal links with the Commission would give this persuasiveness an added impact. Influencing the initiator of legislation would be far more effective than influencing only your own minister who may be outvoted by a qualified majority.

Residual functions of Sub-Committee E

In addition to the primary function of considering legal issues surrounding the Treaty, the Sub-Committee also has an important role to play in the evaluation of policy. As can be seen in the Terms of Reference, the Sub-Committee is required to consider the merits of any documents referred to it ((b) above) and to keep abreast of any important developments in Community Law ((c) above). Most importantly, in the latter task, the Sub-Committee must follow carefully any developments within the European Court of Justice (ECJ). However, this role is restricted to purely one of monitoring the ECJ. Though it is regularly informed of decisions it does not express any opinion or criticism of a decision. It must be remembered that its task is limited to examining *only* Community Proposals that would lead to a significant change in policy. It does not extend to examining ECJ decisions which may clarify a particular existing directive.

From the above discussion it is evident that Sub-Committee E has an extremely heavy burden placed upon its members. Its dual task of inquiring into both legal issues and policy developments is one that no other Sub-Committee will face. In the last two Parliamentary sessions, this task has been made all the more arduous because of the role it now plays in the scrutiny of proposals under the Inter-Governmental pillars. Thus Sub-Committee E always has a full agenda. In the next section, there will be a detailed examination of recent reports produced by the Sub-Committee over the last two Parliamentary sessions which illustrate how it approaches its important role of scrutiny.

Sub-Committee E Reports

Sub-Committee E publishes reports like any other Sub-Committee. The starting point for any inquiry is usually a Commission proposal. In the last two Parliamentary sessions (1994-95 and 1995-96) it has conducted no free standing inquiries into major issues of policy. In fact, this Sub-Committee because of its specific Terms of Reference has a predominantly legislative character to its inquiries. Any inquiry into policy is usually linked to legislative proposal. However, given the role this Sub-Committee now plays in the scrutiny of the Inter-Governmental Pillars, it is adopting a more policy orientated approach to its work.

In the 1994-95 Parliamentary session, the Sub-Committee undertook two major inquiries. One was concerned with a legislative proposal under the European Community and the other under the Third Inter-Governmental Pillar of Justice and Home Affairs.

The Right of Establishment of Lawyers Inquiry

This Sub-Committee E inquiry was an investigation into a draft European Parliament and Council Directive proposal for extending the Right of Establishment of Lawyers within the Community.[29] The proposal read as follows:

| 6293/95 (COM(94) 572) | Draft European Parliament and Council Directive to facilitate practice of the profession of lawyer on a permanent basis in a Member State other than that in which the qualification was obtained. |

If one looks at the Terms of Reference for Sub-Committee E again, it will be seen that this inquiry was carried out because it concerned a "important development in Community law". In the introduction to the report,[30] the point is made that free movement of lawyers has proved to be a controversial issue within the European Community. It took the Council of Bars and Law Societies of the European Community (CCBE) seventeen years to agree a draft proposal. The above proposal departed from a number of principles that were in the CCBE proposal and it was for this reason that Sub-Committee E decided to conduct the inquiry.

The inquiry itself was very specific. This was reflected in the witnesses called by the Sub-Committee to give evidence, predominantly made up of

---

29   See HL 82 (Session 1994-95).
30   *Ibid.* p. 6, para. 3.

lawyers and legal organisations, e.g. The General Council of the Bar and the Law Society of Scotland.[31]

The inquiry itself was a very detailed one. It centred on the practical implications of introducing the directive and the most appropriate manner by which to ensure that standards are maintained. The inquiry looked at the issue from a European perspective and not just from an exclusively UK one. This is a an increasing feature of Sub-Committee inquiries. As stated above, they now aim to influence decision making within the European Institutions and not just at a government level.

The report itself was produced for "information purposes" for the House. It was therefore not the subject of a full scale debate within the chamber. However, following a decision of the Court of Justice in *Gebhard v. Milan Bar Association*,[32] Lord Slynn, the Chairman of the Sub-Committee at the time raised the issue in the Chamber[33] and questioned the government minister on the significance of this decision on the proposed directive. Therefore it can be seen that the report is an important way of raising the profile of an issue and ensures that the government does have to make some response to the Sub-Committee. This is effective scrutiny.

The EUROPOL Inquiry

The Europol inquiry[34] was the first inquiry into a proposal coming forward under the Inter-Governmental Justice and Home Affairs Pillar. It concerned provisions in the Treaty on European Union to establish police cooperation for preventing and combating serious forms of organised international crime and drug trafficking. Though the report was based on two documents, they were not Community proposals. The documents were as follows:

(P) 9757/93	Draft Convention to establish Europol
(P) 12321/1/94 REV 1	Draft Decision on joint action concerning the Europol Drugs Unit.

In the field of inter-governmental cooperation proposals come not from the Commission but from the European Council. Thus the scrutiny which takes place is from a different base. The end result of the proposal will not be a directive, but a Convention which will require enacting legislation in the UK.

However, the aim of the scrutiny process is the same. It is an attempt to influence the minister, in this case the Home Secretary, before he gave his final approval to the Convention in the European Council. The major difference between proposals under the Inter-Governmental Pillars and Community Law is that the proposals are kept confidential until final agreement is

---

31   A full list of witnesses can be found in Appendix 2, p. 20 of the report.
32   Case C-55/94. Judgment was delivered on 30 November 1995.
33   See HL Deb. cols. 243-256 (18 June 1996).
34   See HL 51-I and II (Session 1994-95).

reached among the Member States and there is no requirement to publish the proposals at all. As far as the EUROPOL inquiry was concerned, the draft Convention was made available to Parliament six days before the Home Office gave evidence to Sub-Committee E. From a scrutiny perspective this is undesirable, a point the Select Committee made in its 1993 Report on the scrutiny arrangements for the Inter-Governmental Pillars.[35]

The above point was one also picked up by witnesses who gave evidence to the sub-Committee. "Justice" pointed out that the draft Convention was produced in November 1993 but did not reach the public domain until mid 1994. "Liberty" voiced similar concerns by disagreeing with the practice of placing the draft Convention in the Library of the House but not making it public. These comments are justified. If the Sub-Committee is to produce an influential and effective report, then both the witnesses and the Sub-Committee must have full access to the facts as early as possible. Otherwise any evidence will be pure speculation and hearsay, giving it little or no value. Furthermore, it will not be possible to influence the minister concerned if the report is produced too late. Without these two requirements, scrutiny is ineffective.

The actual EUROPOL inquiry was the usual thorough and precise task which has become the hallmark of the House of Lords Sub-Committees. There were a variety of witnesses called to give evidence from both government and interest groups. The actual inquiry was particularly suited to Sub-Committee E. It concerned many technical and complex legal issues which were tailor made for a committee of lawyers to investigate.

However, this inquiry was the first that dealt with proposals under the Inter-Governmental Pillars. It is thus difficult to assess the impact this inquiry had, and in particular one cannot say with certainty that all future inquiries will be as thorough. Perhaps this inquiry had an element of "novelty value" and future inquiries will be more limited due to lack of time. Whatever the developments, the success of the scrutiny arrangements for the two new Pillars will only be judged in the light of future inquiries and reports.

THE USE OF AD-HOC SUB-COMMITTEES IN THE HOUSE OF LORDS

In addition to the two established Select Committees, the House of Lords has provision to set-up *ad hoc* Committees to conduct inquiries into issues which are viewed as being important. In the Report by the Select Committee on the work of the House,[36] they described the *ad hoc* Committees as having a "very positive" impact on the work of the House. Because there are no Departmental Select Committees in the House of Lords, *ad hoc* Committees are frequently appointed to conduct inquiries into both narrow legislative proposals and broader departmental inquiries.

---

35   See HL 124 (Session 1992-93), pp. 22-23, paras. 52-55.
36   See HL 35-I (Session 1991-92) p. 18 paras. 40-43.

The Select Committee on the European Community itself appoints *ad hoc* Sub-Committees. These are in addition to the now six existing Sub-Committees. An *ad hoc* Sub-Committee will be appointed by the main Select Committee to conduct an inquiry which is concerned with a subject that in the Committee's opinion does not fall within the ambit of any of the existing Sub-Committees. Thus such an ad hoc Sub-Committee will be appointed with specific Terms of Reference for the duration of that particular inquiry only.

Membership of Ad Hoc Sub-Committees

Membership of *ad hoc* Sub-Committees is open to any peer. However, on the whole, a majority of the members are peers who already serve on one or more of the existing Sub-Committees.[37] The advantage of the *ad hoc* Sub-Committees is that it allows those peers who have a special interest in the given subject to be a part of that inquiry. In the last major *ad hoc* Sub-Committee inquiry into the 1996 Inter-Governmental Conference,[38] Lord Tebbit, a former minister with forthright views on the direction of the European Union, was invited to join, and Baronness Serota, a former Chairman of the Lords Select Committee who retired from her post in 1992, was also a member. The make up of the Committee tries to reflect as far as possible all shades of opinion within the House. The Report itself reflects this very fact.

Terms of Reference

Unlike the six permanent Sub-Committees which have either the same Terms of Reference as the main Select Committee or in the case of Sub-Committee E its own Terms of Reference, each *ad hoc* Sub-Committee is given its own particular Terms of Reference that are tailored for the inquiry at hand. This is sensible, in that it allows each *ad hoc* Sub-Committee to focus in on the essential issues at the heart of the inquiry or address the concerns of the Select Committee and House as a whole. Once appointed the *ad hoc* Sub-Committee conducts the inquiry in the usual way and it has all the same powers to call witnesses and papers as the five other Sub-Committees have. In addition, it can, like all other Sub-Committees appoint Specialist Advisers for the duration of the inquiry and travel abroad should the need arise.

Ad Hoc Sub-Committee on the 1996 Inter-Governmental Conference

This was the last major inquiry undertaken by an *ad-hoc* Sub-Committee in the House of Lords. The Sub-Committee was appointed in January 1995 and published its Report in November 1995. The aim of the inquiry was to look forward to the 1996 Inter-Governmental Conference and consider what the

---

37   In the inquiry into the 1996 IGC 9 out of 12 members on the *ad hoc* Sub-Committee were sitting members of one or more of the other Sub-Committees.
38   See HL 105-I (Session 1994-95).

likely developments in the European Union would be. As will be seen from the Terms of Reference below, the inquiry covered such a broad and diverse range of issues that it could not have been undertaken by any one Sub-Committee on its own. The Terms of Reference are as follows:[39]

> "To consider the matters which are to be reviewed at the Inter Governmental Conference which will be convened in 1996, in particular
> (a) The policies and forms of cooperation introduced by the Maastricht Treaty and whether they need to be revised in order to ensure the effectiveness of the mechanisms and institutions of the Community; and the relationship of the institutions with the Member States.
> (b) The need for and scope of co-decision between the Council and the European Parliament.
> (c) The budgetary provisions of the Treaty, including the arrangements for compulsory and non-compulsory expenditure.
> (d) The functioning of the Community institutions, given the prospect of future enlargement of the Community, including such questions as the composition of the Commission and the system of Qualified Majority Voting.
> (e) Review of the classification of Community acts."

The most evident point from the Standing Orders is that this *ad hoc* Sub-Committee was concerned exclusively with policy and not legislative proposals. The inquiry focussed on the burning issues within the European Union today, notably co-decision and enlargement. However, the aim of the inquiry was no different from any other conducted by a permanent Sub-Committee. The inquiry was designed to coincide with the government preparations for the IGC and most importantly to *influence and advise* the government. Partly due to reports published by both the House of Lords and House of Commons, the government published its own White Paper in response in March 1996.[40] In fact, this White Paper is testimony that the government *does* listen to the views of the Select Committees in both Houses.

Nature of the Inquiry

As stated above, the subject matter of the inquiry was very broad and many witnesses were called to give evidence. Because the inquiry covered a variety of policy areas, the *ad hoc* Sub-Committee consulted with the other established Sub-Committees for their advice and opinions on some of the more complex or controversial issues.[41]

---

39   *Ibid.* p. 6, para. 3.
40   See Cm 3181 (Session 1995-96) *A Partnership of Nations: The British Approach to the European Union Inter-Governmental Conference 1996.*
41   For an example of such a Memorandum, see HL 105 (Session 1994-95) Appendix 5, p.85. This Memorandum came from Lord Middleton, Chairman of Sub-Committee D (Agriculture and Food) to Lord Tordoff Chairman of the *ad hoc* Sub-Committee.

Essentially therefore, the *ad hoc* Sub-Committee works no differently to any of the other permanent Sub-Committees. However, an *ad hoc* Sub-Committee is primarily concerned with policy and does not engage in the routine scrutiny of legislative proposals. Thus, they are an effective means of addressing the important issues within European Union, whilst permitting the permanent Sub-Committees to scrutinise the important legislative developments which continue to come forward. In essence, the House of Lords European Communities Committee has devised a division of Labour that ensures the limited Parliamentary time is used more effectively.

CONCLUDING REMARKS

At the outset of this chapter, the point was made that the primary aim of the Sub-Committees is to influence the minister through the scrutiny activities of the sub-Committee. From the analysis above, it is evident that the House of Lords arrangements for doing this are on the whole effective. Both the quality and nature of the reports has made them influential with the government and with the European Community institutions. However, the question that must be considered is whether the arrangements could be improved?

Reforming the Sub-Committees

One of the most common criticisms levelled at the present arrangements is that the Sub-Committee structure is too rigid. To be more precise, the criticism is that there are too many permanent Sub-Committees. In the Jelicoe Report,[42] both the then Leader of the House of Lords, the Right Honourable Lord Waddington, and the former Foreign Office Minister Tristan Garel-Jones (amongst others) made the point that the a reduction in the number of Sub-Committees would lead to greater flexibility within the system, and thus to more active effective scrutiny.[43] In effect, what they were arguing for was an increase in the use of *ad hoc* Sub-Committees. This would, in their opinion, allow for inquiries to be more specific and remove the rather artificial nature of the subject based Sub-Committees. The point was quite correctly made, and is probably even more true today, that many important general issues facing the Community now fall within the remit of more than one subject-related Committee. Furthermore, this authors research has also indicated that the Sub-Committees on occasion had a difficulty in finding a suitable subject for inquiry an would on occasion be inactive.

Though the Sub-Committees are a great asset to the scrutiny process, there is an increasing need to review the work of the Sub-Committees, especially in the light of the increasing pressures coming as a result of the developments of the Inter-Governmental procedures. One possibility would be a Sub-Com-

---

42   See HL 35-I (Session 1992-93).
43   *Ibid.* p. 104.

mittee that is dedicated to the exclusive scrutiny of Inter-Governmental proposals with its own Terms of Reference. This would permit it to carry out the necessary detailed inquiries that are essential for effective scrutiny. The argument for this development is strengthened by the fact that proposals coming forward under the Inter-Governmental Pillars are not legislative proposals along the lines of those agreed within the Council of Ministers of the European Community. As the discussion of the EUROPOL inquiry above illustrates, a whole new process of law making based on confidential negotiations, which can be concluded very rapidly, has been created. The introduction of Sub-Committee F to examine Home Affairs is therefore given a cautious welcome by this author. For the House of Lords to assert its influence, there must be the appropriate machinery that will permit it to execute this task – possibly outside of Sub-Committee E's remit.

The reforms outlined above reflect only the author's opinions which have developed during the course of his research. In addition to this though, there is still is a positive role for subject based Sub-Committees within the scrutiny process. However, this should be streamlined to three Sub-Committees at most, with a greater reliance being placed on *ad hoc* Sub-Committees to carry out the inquiries which do not fall within one of the Sub-Committees. Most importantly, this would allow for inquiries to be carried out more quickly as an *ad hoc* Sub-Committee could be established for each inquiry. Such a development would be an improvement on the present arrangements where an inquiry will be delayed until the current one is concluded, or not held at all due to lack of time. This would be a more balanced scrutiny arrangement because it would go a long way to meeting the diverse requirements of the House of Lords European Communities Committee which focuses on both legislation and policy.

The work and working methods of the Sub-Committees

Essentially, the Sub-Committees are investigative in their nature. Indeed, their working methods of conducting detailed and long inquiries leads to the conclusion that they could best be described as "working parties". What is most apparent about the way they conduct an inquiry is the consensual approach they adopt.[44] All inquiries reflect the views and opinions of all Sub-Committee members and evidence sessions are public and always published in full. This consensual approach means there is never a minority report produced. This is undoubtedly a strength of the Sub-committees. The fact that reports concentrate on contributing to the debate of the issue at hand and not on questions concerning the UK's continued membership of the European Union has made the reports as respected as they are throughout the entire European Union.

However, within this role, it is essential that the Sub-Committees do not lose sight of the central pillar of their work – that of influencing the minister.

---

44   For more on this issue see Eileen Denza *Parliamentary Scrutiny of European Legislation* Statute Law Review (1993) p. 63.

Though a report produced by any of the Sub-Committees is not binding upon a minister, he will find it difficult to ignore. The high level of expertise on the Sub-Committees, which is continually being increased by the addition of new life peers with direct experience of European institutions such as the Commission, Council of Ministers and Court of Justice, will mean that any report will be both comprehensive and of a very high standard.

Furthermore, scrutiny is only effective if the minister listens to what the Sub-Committee has to say. At present there are no constitutional arrangements to make the minister listen, as is the case in the Danish Parliament where the Danish Folketing Market Committee issue the minister with a mandate from which he can only derogate if prior approval is received from the Committee. However, it is apparent that reports produced by the Sub-Committees are almost indispensable, leading to ministers taking account of the views within them automatically.

This chapter has concentrated on the backbone of the scrutiny arrangements in the House of Lords. What has become apparent is that there is a system in existence which is beginning to struggle to meet the ever increasing demands placed upon it. Therefore, in the next chapter the evaluation will move on to how the recent developments within Inter-Governmental cooperation have been addressed by the House of Lords and how successful they have been in ensuring that government remains accountable for decisions taken under the Pillars.

CHAPTER 10

ARRANGEMENTS IN THE HOUSE OF LORDS FOR SCRUTINY OF THE INTER-GOVERNMENTAL PILLARS

INTRODUCTION

In this chapter, the focus is exclusively on the arrangements in the House of Lords for scrutinising proposals that are being brought forward under the Inter-Governmental Pillars. This considers the developments introduced since the Maastricht Treaty which are primarily concerned with extending political cooperation between the Member States. It is the very fact that because under this process a new and unique system of law-making has been established, that both the House of Lords and House of Commons have had difficulty in developing effective scrutiny mechanisms to meet the new challenge. As will be illustrated, the present arrangements for scrutiny of the pillars in the House of Lords are not ideal. In particular, the restricted availability of information (specifically draft documents) because of confidentiality severely limits the Committee's ability to conduct effective scrutiny.

In the Treaty of European Union signed by all Member States in Maastricht on 7 February 1992, the Union created consists of three distinct pillars. The first and central pillar is the European Community which will continue to operate as before and issue legislation in the form of directives, regulations and decisions. The second pillar[1] is intended to establish a "common foreign and security policy including the eventual establishment of a common defence policy".[2] The final pillar is intended to increase co-operation between the Member States in the field of "justice and home affairs".[3] Once again the cooperation between the Member States is of a political nature and thus totally distinct from the central pillar.

OBJECTIVES OF THE INTER-GOVERNMENTAL PILLARS

The Second Pillar: Common Foreign and Security Policy (CFSP)

The objectives of the CFSP are:[4]

> "– to safeguard the common values, fundamental interests and independence of the Union;
> – to strengthen the security of the Union and its Member States in all ways;

---

1 See Title V, Article J of the Treaty on European Union.
2 As stated in the Preamble to the Maastricht Treaty.
3 See Title VI, Article K of the Treaty on European Union.
4 See Article J.1.2. of the TEU.

    – to preserve peace and strengthen international security, in accordance with the principles of the United Nations Charter as well as the principles of the Helsinki Final Act and the objectives of the Paris Charter;

    – to promote international cooperation;

    – to develop and consolidate democracy and the rule of law and respect for human rights and fundamental freedoms."

The Treaty on European Union provides that these two objectives are to be pursued in two ways:[5]

> *First* by establishing systematic cooperation with Member States in the conduct of policy. This is achieved by consultation and exchange of information, but may be formalised whenever the Council deems it necessary by defining *common positions*. It is the responsibility of the Member States to support and uphold a common position, including ensuring that their national policies conform to it; and
>
> *Second*, by the Member States gradually implementing *joint action* in the areas in which they have important common interests. It is for the Council to decide that a matter should be the subject of joint action; and a joint action, once adopted, shall commit the Member States in the positions they adopt and in the conduct of their activity.

The Third Pillar: Justice and Home Affairs

The objectives under this pillar are two promote cooperation in matters of "common interest". Article K.1 of the Treaty defines these as including *inter alia* asylum policy, external border controls, immigration policy, cooperation against terrorism and drug trafficking and other serious international crime. The Member States exchange information and then:[6]

    – adopt *joint positions* and promote...any cooperation contributing to the pursuit of the objectives of the Union;

    – adopt *joint action* (subject to the test of subsidiarity); and

    – draw up conventions for adoption by the Member States under their national constitutional requirements.

As is evident from the above extracts from the Treaty on European Union the primary objectives of both pillars is to increase political cooperation between the Member States in policy areas which under the central pillar of the European Community were traditionally viewed as being the exclusive domain of each individual Member State. Cooperation on policy of this kind is based on political agreement and not on a system of directives and regulations. Therefore, it is the manner in which the two new pillars function that is the vital

---

5   See Article J.3.4 TEU.

6   See Article K.3.2 TEU.

factor which influences the scrutiny arrangements in the House of Lords. This will now be examined in more detail.

FUNCTIONING OF THE INTER-GOVERNMENTAL PILLARS

Though the two flanking pillars, as they are called, have quite different objectives, they have in common the fact that work undertaken within them will not lead to the adoption of Community legislation under the procedures which are familiar to the Select Committee on the European Communities. As stated above, the policy areas covered by the pillars are legally outside Community competence. In fact, the procedures used are closer to classical diplomacy rather than the more formal law making procedures used in the central pillar of the European Community.

Role of the European Institutions

Under the two flanking pillars the role of the European institutions is wholly different to that seen under central pillar. Most notably, it is the role of the European Parliament that is diminished and the Council of Ministers and Commission who take the lead roles. Under the CFSP the European Parliament is consulted on "the main aspects and the basic choices" of the CSFP and its views "duly taken into consideration". It is also regularly kept informed of the development of the CFSP.[7]

Under the Justice and Home Affairs pillar, the European Parliament is "regularly informed of discussions" and consulted on "the principal aspects of activities". Its views are then taken into consideration. However, in neither pillar, the European Parliament does not have the right to be consulted on the detail of the proposed actions. Furthermore, the European Parliament cannot insist on its views being taken into account. Contrast this with its role under the central pillar, where the co-decision procedure requires close consultation with the European Parliament.

The other major significant difference lies in the role of the Court of Justice. Because the procedures used are technically outside the European Community, the Court will not be the arbiter of any disputes except where the Member States agree beforehand. The results of any negotiation will instead be binding under international law.

As far as the Commission is concerned, the development of the two new pillars marks a new departure for it. For the first time the Commission is "fully associated" with inter-governmental work and will be able to put forward proposals. However, the Commission does not have exclusivity on making proposals with most in fact coming from the Member States and the Presidency of the Council in particular.

---

7   See Article J.7 TEU.

Decision making under the Inter-Governmental Pillars

It is within the realm of decision making that the biggest difference lies between procedures used within the inter-governmental sphere and the procedures used to make Community law under the Community Treaties. Under the new inter-governmental procedures, the discussions may be completely confidential until final agreement has been reached among the Members States. Furthermore, there is no requirement that proposals are published and if as is likely, this tradition continues, they will not be published. The argument behind this confidentiality is that Member States could not negotiate effectively if their views were in the public domain. Also, it is considered a courtesy to other Member States, of not divulging confidential information that is the subject of negotiations.

However, there is one obvious drawback with this position. From a scrutiny perspective it makes the job of the House of Lords Select Committee very difficult. Most importantly, if the Select Committee is only given details of a proposal once negotiations are concluded, then it can have little effective influence.

Within the scrutiny context lies another important issue, that of the impact of the proposals under the pillars on domestic law. The largest impact will come from proposals under the Justice and Home Affairs pillar, where changes may be needed in areas such as asylum and immigration law. The proposals *may* come forward as a treaty which will then require ratification by every Member State including the United Kingdom. In such circumstances, Parliament will be informed and could object. However, this could only be done *if* domestic legislation was required. Only in such circumstances could Parliament have a veto. However, the text of the treaty could not be amended, unless the government wished to re-open negotiations. This is an unlikely prospect given that the original negotiations would already have been a very lengthy exercise, and other Member States would be reluctant to re-negotiate.

In other situations, work under the inter-governmental pillars may not lead to a treaty that requires ratification or any amendment in domestic law. However, the common positions adopted as a result of these negotiations could place significant constraints on the UK's ability of individual action. This potentially causes major problems for Parliament. There are no existing constitutional procedures that require Parliament to be consulted in such circumstances. Thus, in either of the above instances, major developments in UK law may take place and Parliament is only a bystander. The Executive has in effect taken on the role of law maker. How has the Lords tried to redress this balance?

PROPOSALS TO SCRUTINISE THE INTER-GOVERNMENTAL PILLARS

In the 1993 report *House of Lords Scrutiny of the Inter-Governmental Pillars of the European Union*,[8] the Select Committee on European Legislation made the following observation:[9]

---

8   See HL 124 (Session 1992-93).
9   *Ibid.* p. 22, para. 48.

"We think that it is essential that work under the inter-governmental pillars of the European Union should be supervised by national parliaments."

This observation was in line with the Declaration attached to the Maastricht Treaty which stated:

"The Conference considers that it is important to encourage greater involvement of national Parliaments in the activities of the European Union".

As far as the British government are concerned, it is Parliament and not any other institution which should perform this important task of scrutiny. In evidence given to the Select Committee both the Home Secretary and Foreign Secretary at the time were strongly of the opinion that this should be the case. In particular, they both argued against any delegation of the scrutiny function to the European Parliament, which only has a peripheral role in the Inter-Governmental Pillars. The Right Honourable Michael Howard MP, the Home Secretary, articulated this view in his typically robust manner:[10]

"On accountability, it is clearly extremely important. I think that the appropriate way of establishing Parliamentary accountability in relation to the third pillar is to national parliaments. The European Parliament has to be informed of activity in this area but accountability is to be to national parliaments."

Michael Howard went on to justify this statement by stressing the main difference between decision making under the two flanking pillars and that of the central pillars. Under the flanking pillars, there is no Qualified Majority Voting, all decisions are taken by unanimity. The European Parliament itself has no input into the proposal with there being no equivalent to the co-decision procedure under the pillars. Therefore, under these circumstances the minister can *always* be held accountable to Parliament for any decision taken in the Council.

In addition to the above reason, he also stressed the importance of maintaining a productive dialogue with the Select Committees in both the House of Lords and House of Commons. This he viewed as an integral aspect of the scrutiny function of the Select Committees. In essence, what Michael Howard is accepting is the assertion that only by influencing the minister can effective scrutiny be exercised by the Select Committees.

In his evidence to the Select Committee inquiry, the then Foreign Secretary, the Right Honourable Douglas Hurd MP, made a similar observation recognising the importance of the work of the Select Committees. He said:[11]

"Our aim would be to let you as soon as the negotiating mandate has been approved and to keep you informed as much as possible about how it progresses,

---

10   *Ibid.* Minutes of Evidence, p. 7, Q.2.
11   *Ibid.* Minutes of Evidence, p. 41, Q.113.

the negotiations that go on and their scope, *and always to seek your views before conclusion of an agreement* (my italics)".

The Foreign Secretary like the Home Secretary has appreciated the constitutional significance of ministerial accountability at the despatch box and to the respective Select Committees. In a Parliamentary democracy such as the United Kingdom, ministerial accountability for decisions taken by government must be at the core of Parliamentary activity. In its response to the Select Committee Report, the government accepted this important constitutional proposition:[12]

> "The Government fully support the Committee's conclusion that accountability for work under the inter-governmental pillars of the European Union should be to national parliaments....The Government believe that it is an important feature of the inter-governmental process that national governments of member states should be accountable to national parliaments, not to the European Parliament, on business under these pillars. The Government have consistently defended the role of national parliaments in this respect and will continue to do so."

From the above discussion it would seem that scrutiny of proposals under the inter-governmental pillars is an easier task for the Select Committee. All decisions are taken by unanimous approval and the government appear to be enthusiastic on the role of Parliament in the process. However, a closer examination of the detailed proposals under which the Select Committee work will dispel this view.

ARRANGEMENTS FOR SCRUTINY UNDER THE INTER-GOVERNMENTAL PILLARS

Provision of documents to Parliament

In the course of their inquiry[13] the Select Committee on European Legislation suggested three possible (though not exhaustive) criteria on which a document should be supplied to Parliament for further investigation to take place. These are:[14]

(i)   significance – particularly where the rights or duties of individuals may be affected;
(ii) the eventual need for United Kingdom legislation;
(iii) the imposition of legally binding commitments on the United Kingdom.

---

12   See Cm 2471 (Session 1992-93), p. 3, para. 2 (i).
13   See n. 8, at p. 188.
14   See HL 124 (Session 1992-93) p. 23, para. 53.

These criteria went further than what the Home Secretary offered in his evidence to the Select Committee. Mr Howard agreed to provide Parliament with a full text of any proposals or convention only if it necessitated subsequent primary legislation. The Select Committee, in the criteria outlined above, suggests that documents which require *secondary* legislation or impose legal commitments should also be deposited in Parliament.

In their reply, the government in principle agreed to the Select Committees proposals but with one important proviso. The government stressed that if a document was of a confidential nature, or that its disclosure could weaken the governments negotiating position, then it would not release such a document in to the public domain. This confidentiality exception is one which both the Home and Foreign Secretary stressed in their oral evidence to the Select Committee and which the government also emphasised in its response to the Select Committees report. In the light of this, the question which must be asked is whether this confidentiality will always be justified, especially with regards to the effect this will have on effective scrutiny.

In their report, the Select Committee argued quite strongly that the three criteria outlined above, should be applied equally to both the second and third pillar.[15] Though they accepted that each pillar would produce different results in terms of the action to be taken by Parliament at the end of negotiations, they argued that the process of the Council reaching a common position through the negotiations, would be the same in either case. However, the government did not share this view and its response to the Select Committee put forward the proposals for scrutiny of the pillars. In particular, the government felt that under the Justice and Home Affairs pillar there would be a greater need for primary domestic legislation to implement the results of any negotiations. In their response to the Select Committee the government pointed out that proposals under the Justice and Home Affairs pillar will lead to:[16]

> "...conventions joint positions and guidelines which are of a longer-term and legislative character and may need to be implemented by primary legislation in the United Kingdom. The Government envisage that CFSP documents, on the other hand, will usually be non-legislative and short-term, and that a need for UK implementing legislation is very unlikely to arise. The vast majority will also have to remain confidential until agreed and published, for diplomatic and security reasons."

This reply does, in this author's opinion, call into question the governments commitment to the role of Parliament in the scrutiny of inter-governmental affairs. The actual proposals put forward by the government and now practised in the House of Lords place the government's negotiating position above any other consideration. The confidentiality argument appears to be put forward at every opportunity by the government and may be viewed as being more important than effective scrutiny by Parliament. This inevitably leads

---

15   *Ibid.* p. 23, para. 55 and p. 26, para. 66.
16   See Cm 2471 (Session 1992-93) p. 3, para. (ii).

one to question the value of the Declaration in the Maastricht Treaty which was supposed to strengthen the role of national parliaments in the European Union. This Declaration can only carry weight if the government which insisted on its inclusion is totally committed to both the principle and spirit of it. Otherwise the Declaration is merely empty words. The next point to consider is how effective the arrangements in the House of Lords are in meeting the "requirements" of the Maastricht Treaty Declaration.

Scrutiny of the Common Foreign and Security Pillar

As stated above, the Select Committee were of the opinion that documents which fell within one of three criteria should automatically be provided to Parliament.[17] However, the actual position today is considerably more limited than this. In particular, the government's argument of the need for confidentiality in these negotiations dominates the scrutiny arrangements.

The scrutiny arrangements are built upon the existing procedures in the House of Lords. The government provide the Lords with texts of CFSP statements, declarations, common positions and joint actions *only once they have been agreed.* The government refuse to provide the Lords with any drafts of CFSP documents. This position is in keeping with other areas of foreign policy and covers the vast majority of texts. However, the government do provide Parliament with certain CFSP documents if they fall within existing scrutiny guidelines or if the documents are not subject to confidentiality requirements and meet one of the three criteria put forward by the Select Committee. In practice both these situations are extremely rare.

Thus, it is immediately apparent that scrutiny of the CFSP pillar is an extremely difficult task, made all the more difficult by the government's commitment to confidentiality. Scrutiny is for all purposes pointless once the common position has been agreed. If we accept that the purpose of scrutiny is to influence the government, then under these arrangements this is not possible. There needs to be a clear commitment by the government to providing texts in good time to allow for scrutiny. In essence, similar (if not exactly the same) procedures should apply as they do under the central pillar of the European Community. However, given the government's position, this is extremely unlikely to happen.

Why is there a need for confidentiality?

The CFSP is a development of European Political Cooperation (EPC) which like CFSP was always outside structures of the European Community. These procedures have always been of a confidential nature. This is primarily for three reasons. First, because of the need by the government to keep its own negotiating position secret from other Member States. Second, because of the delicate and sensitive nature of matters under discussion. And third, to respect

---

17   See n. 15, at p. 191.

the position of other Member States who also require secrecy for similar reasons. The Select Committee recognised these important points and was prepared to adjust its scrutiny procedures to accommodate the government. They stated in their report that the early provision of documents was essential for effective scrutiny but that they also recognised the special requirements of the Inter-Governmental pillars and the CFSP pillar in particular:[18]

> "It is a corollary of our requests for extensive information that we should exercise our scrutiny function actively and with some degree of sensitivity."

The government rejected this compromise in its response to the Select Committee. As stated above, it was not prepared to provide draft texts except in very limited circumstances. The reasoning is not made clear in the government response but one may speculate (perhaps cynically) that it is probably connected with a concern of confidential information being leaked to the media or perhaps more significantly to sceptical backbenchers.

Therefore, from the above discussion it is plainly evident that different procedures and different objectives apply to the CFSP pillar than to the European Community. To that extent a comparison between the two is not always appropriate. However, both have one crucial aspect in common, that of the executive (i.e. ministers) taking decisions outside of the UK's Parliament. There must be effective control of this by Parliament. In the author's view, it is not enough for a minister to justify his position once it is too late to influence.

Scrutiny of the Justice and Home Affairs Pillar

In a memorandum to the Select Committee, the Home Secretary proposed the arrangements for scrutiny of the Justice and Home Affairs pillar.[19] Under this pillar the Council of Ministers adopt common positions in the same way as under the CFSP pillar. They do not adopt Community legislation. The Home Secretary pledged to provide the following information:[20]

- the first full text that is tabled of any Convention or proposals which will, if agreed, require later primary legislation in the United Kingdom, except where the proposal relates to security arrangements or operational matters and publication could prejudice the effectiveness of the intended action; and
- substantial changes which subsequently occur during the negotiation of the final text.

There is a definite distinction between the arrangements under these two pillars. In particular the secrecy aspect is not as prominent under the third pillar.

---

18   See HL 124 (Session 1992-93) p. 24, para. 28.
19   *Ibid.* Minutes of Evidence, pp. 1- 6.
20   *Ibid.* p. 5, para. 26.

As is plainly evident from the Home Secretary's own memorandum, he will issue the "first full text of any Convention". Thus scrutiny for the Select Committee is a much easier task. They have the opportunity to discuss the proposals before the final text is agreed. Furthermore, if following this scrutiny there are "substantial changes" to the final text, the minister will provide the relevant documents to Parliament. There is a secrecy exception, but it is not central to the governments approach.

There are essentially two reasons for this. Firstly, the subject matter under discussion is not as sensitive as under the CFSP pillar. e.g. immigration and asylum policy or judicial cooperation. Secondly, and perhaps most importantly, proposals under the Justice and Home Affairs pillar will almost always require primary legislation to implement the Convention or Treaty subsequently agreed. Thus, Parliament must know as early as possible what effect any Convention or Treaty will have on existing domestic legislation and be allowed to debate it fully.

The first House of Lords Select Committee Report[21] on a Justice and Home Affairs proposal came in 1995 and concerned the EUROPOL Convention to establish closer police cooperation within the European Union. The inquiry itself took the form of any other Select Committee inquiry and was carried out by Sub-Committee E, the Law and Institutions Sub-Committee. The Home Secretary himself gave evidence to the inquiry and talked about the progress in setting up EUROPOL. This evidence was in fact given prior to the final approval of the Convention in the Council of Ministers. Thus, the minister will under this pillar keep Parliament informed as far as possible where security concerns are not compromised.

However, the Home Secretary's proposals for disclosure of documents are short of what the Select Committee wanted. In his memorandum, the Home Secretary was only prepared to release documents where primary legislation was required. Thus, he apparently excluded from the Justice and Home Affairs arrangements documents that would need to be implemented by secondary legislation. This is disappointing and it is a little difficult to understand the reasoning behind this decision. Surely, *any* document requiring domestic legislation would be of interest to Parliament and not merely those which require primary legislation. Once again therefore, the commitment of the government to the Declaration in the Maastricht Treaty intended to enhance the role of national parliaments in the European Union must be questioned.

The primary criticism of the government concerns its rather indifferent approach to scrutiny. At the European level, it champions vociferously the national parliaments of the Union. In practice however, the situation is different. Obviously, there are legitimate concerns of security and confidentiality and these are respected. But the development of the pillars has made formal a procedure for inter-governmental negotiation, where previously they were conducted on an *ad hoc* basis. In the past if two or more governments shared a

---

21   See HL 51-I (Session 1994-95).

common policy they would meet to discuss their approach or simply tele-phone each other and adopt a common stance. Now under the pillars, fifteen Member States are involved, leading to a much more concerted action. It is the introduction of this formal procedure under the pillars, as a forum for inter-governmental negotiation that makes scrutiny essential. In essence it is not just the subject matter that needs to be scrutinised, but also the proce-dures involved in making the decisions.

THE USE OF EXPLANATORY MEMORANDUM

If we cast our minds back to chapter 3 detailing the work of the Scrutiny Committee in the Commons and chapter 8 on the Select Committee on the European Communities in the Lords, we will remember that central to those scrutiny arrangements was the provision of an Explanatory Memorandum (EM) by the lead government department. The aim of this EM is to provide both Select Committees with the government's opinion on the document under scrutiny.

The Common Foreign and Security Pillar

However, from the discussion above, it is clearly evident that the provision of EM's by the government is not entirely appropriate when either Select Com-mittee is considering a document under the CFSP pillar. The primary reason for this relates to the issues of confidentiality which dominate negotiations under this pillar. The more limited disclosure requirements that the Select Committee was prepared to accept have already been outlined, but these were turned down by the government. Thus, the Select Committee has no prior knowledge of what proposals a particular document may contain. All the Select Committee can hope for is that the minister will come to the House and explain the need for secrecy once the matter is in the public domain – a classic case of closing the stable door once the horse has bolted.

The Justice and Home Affairs Pillar

The position here with regard to the provision of EM's is slightly different because under this pillar, there is not such a dependency upon confidentiality. In their reply to the Select Committees report, the government[22] intimated that it would in principle be prepared to supply an EM to Parliament provid-ed that it came within one of the three established criteria. Thus the govern-ment went part of the way in meeting the Select Committees proposals.[23]

In their response to the Select Committee the government proposed that provision of EM's would be on the same timescale as for EC documents – ten

---

22   See Cm 2471 (Session 1992-93) p. 4, para. (iv) (b).
23   See HL 124 (Session 1992-93) pp. 22-23, paras. 52-55.

working days. This may be subject to delay if the government needs to consider more closely whether the EM should be issued, for example if there are issues of confidentiality. Thus, the Select Committee itself has no input in this decision. It is left purely to the government to make a value judgment about the nature of the subject matter in the proposal.

THE SCRUTINY RESERVE

The scrutiny reserve is embodied in the Resolution of The House of 24 October 1990.[24] As mentioned in previous chapters, this Resolution is the cornerstone of the scrutiny process by preventing the minister from giving final agreement to a proposal in Council before scrutiny has been concluded by the Select Committees. The Select Committee in their 1993 report argued very forcefully (and quite correctly) for the extension of the scrutiny reserve to cover proposals coming forward under the pillars. The following extract from this report illustrates both the Committee's arguments for extending the scrutiny reserve and its concern about a failure to do this:[25]

> "We believe that the objective should be a system under which the Government undertake, wherever possible, not to agree to a proposal in the Council until Parliamentary scrutiny has been completed. Since the Single European Act opened the way for greater use of majority voting in the Council and thus speeded up generally the process of reaching agreement, it has been necessary for this Committee to work more flexibly, and there have also been occasions when the Government was outvoted or found it necessary to override the scrutiny reserve. We are not convinced that the speed or pressures are any greater at least under the Justice and Home Affairs pillar. The scrutiny reserve has been of great value in concentrating minds both of those in Government and those in Parliament on the need for timely expression of views, and while we accept that there may be a higher proportion of cases where Ministers – in particular the Foreign Secretary – will find it necessary to override the scrutiny reserve, we are not persuaded that it should not apply at all to decision making on justice and home affairs and foreign affairs."

The government flatly rejected any extension of the scrutiny reserve. Their reasoning was based upon the fact that they will provide all documents to theCommittee in good time to allow for effective scrutiny and that decision making in the Council will often be a quick process and therefore there will be no time for a reserve. The government concluded its reply by stating that:[26]

> "...the Government do not think it appropriate that outstanding scrutiny requirements should prevent the United Kingdoms agreement."

---

24   See C.J. 1989-90, p. 646.
25   See HL 124 (Session 1992-93) pp. 24-25, para. 62.
26   See Cm (Session 1992-93) p. 5, para. (vii) (b).

The above statement raises many questions. Most important is the one which has been referred to a number of times previously. This relates to the governments commitment to the role of national parliaments in the EU. The Declaration in the Maastricht Treaty safeguarding the role of national parliaments is meaningless in the light of this statement. Parliament must in the absence of any other effective scrutiny continue to have some control over the activities of the minister in the Council. Statements such as the one above do nothing except undermine this need.

Given the above scenario, one is naturally led to ask the question why the government has committed itself to provide EM's on proposals under the Justice and Home Affairs pillar? It seems logical that once you accept that EM's will be provided then you must accept the limitations of the Scrutiny Reserve. The scrutiny reserve is designed to allow the Committee to investigate the proposal, and the EM is the starting point of this investigation. There is no point in the Committee spending valuable time and resources on conducting an inquiry only for the government to approve the document prior to the conclusion of the Committee's deliberation. Thus unless the reserve is incorporated into the scrutiny procedure, the present arrangements are not fully effective.

Furthermore, the scrutiny reserve as presently worded would in fact meet the concerns of the government. Firstly, as far as confidential matters are concerned, the 1990 Resolution states unequivocally, that confidential matters are not subject to the scrutiny reserve.[27] Secondly, when a quick decision is needed, the Resolution allows the minister to give approval and then report to the House as to why this was done.[28] Both of these cases are already common under the EC pillar and work reasonably well. There is no reason why the Reserve should not apply to documents which do not come within either of the two exceptions above. Therefore, if the requirements of speed or confidentiality are genuine they will be covered by the 1990 Resolution.

In the light of what has been said above, there is strong evidence for the extension of the scrutiny reserve to at least the Justice and Home Affairs pillar. In fact the Home Secretary himself has imposed something akin to a reserve in the Council of Ministers. On 23 November 1995, Michael Howard stopped negotiations on the draft corruption protocol to the fraud convention and the draft joint action on racism and xenophobia proposal, to allow Parliament to conclude its inquiry. These proposals were seen as important enough to warrant this action. Surely, once the government has accepted that some proposals need further inquiry, the case for a formal extension of the scrutiny reserve is irresistible. This change is now long overdue.

---

27   See C.J. 1989-90, p. 646, para. 3(a).

28   *Ibid.* para. 4.

THE ROLE OF THE SUB-COMMITTEES IN THE SCRUTINY OF THE PILLARS

The House of Lords developed no new procedures or vehicle for scrutiny of the Inter-Governmental pillars. In its 1993 Report, the Select Committee on European Legislation recognised that scrutiny of the pillars would place increased burdens on the already busy Sub-Committees. However, in 1993, the Select Committee were not in a position to say what the exact effect of this increased workload would be and that the matter would need to be reviewed after an initial period of operation.

However, the Select Committee made the observation that the activity of the Sub-Committees in scrutinising proposals under the Inter-Governmental pillars will be dependant upon the extent with which ministers supply Parliament with documents and give them the time engage in a meaningful debate.[29] Thus it is not appropriate to make any assessment of this given that many of the documents will be of a confidential nature and will not therefore be provided to Parliament in time to allow for an in-depth inquiry. Thus each document will be taken on its own merits.

The burden of scrutiny initially fell on Sub-Committee E, the Law and Institutions Sub-Committee. In an interview a former Clerk to the Select Committee on the European Communities,[30] stated that the Inter-Governmental pillars had placed a "quite substantially increased burden on Sub-Committee E". However, he continued by stressing that as Sub-Committee E was chaired by a Law Lord, the scrutiny work of the Inter-Governmental pillars was "tailor made" for it.

A closer look at the EUROPOL inquiry will illustrate this very point. In particular, it is the very complex nature of this inquiry, focussing as it does on the legal consequences of the Convention, and how it will be implemented into UK law which demonstrates that a Committee of lawyers have the necessary expertise to execute this task. Though there has only been the one inquiry to date, the former Clerk suggested that these arrangements would work well, primarily because of the personnel involved.

However, at the start of the 1996-97 Parliamentary session, the Select Committee on the European Communities appointed a sixth Sub-Committee (Sub-Committee F) which is charged with scrutinising Social Affairs, Education and Home Affairs. It is the Home Affairs aspect of the Sub-Committees work which covers proposals under the third pillar. In conversation with a legal adviser to the Select Committee, he pointed out the importance of this task as being the primary motive for establishing this Sub-Committee. Furthermore, it will also relieve much of the pressure on Sub-Committee E which has an ever increasing workload.

By December 1997, Sub-Committee F had undertaken only three inquiries and thus it is not possible to assess accurately what impact it will have on the scrutiny process. There are mixed views to be taken about the creation of

---

29   See HL 124 (Session 1992-93) p. 25, para. 63.
30   Interview with Mr Michael Pownall, House of Lords, 28 April 1995.

this Sub-Committee. On a positive note it is undoubtedly beneficial that a Sub-Committee now focuses on the third pillar. It should quickly develop an expertise which will be beneficial. It may eventually lead to similar arrangements being established for the CFSP pillar.

However, on the debit side, the appointment of another Sub-Committee reinforces the already over rigid structure of scrutiny in the Lords. In particular it goes against the recommendations of the Jelicoe Committee in 1991 which envisaged fewer permanent Sub-Committees and more *ad hoc* ones. Until the Sub-Committee has been active for several sessions no final judgment can be made on this point. Although it is worth bearing in mind that given the limited number of documents coming forward even under the third pillar, it is questionable as to how much of the Sub-Committees time will be taken with examining proposals under the JHA pillar.

THE SELECT COMMITTEE'S TERMS OF REFERENCE

In its report "The House of Lord's Scrutiny of the Inter-Governmental Pillar of the European Union", the Select Committee reviewed its Terms of Reference in the light of the new role it would take on in scrutinising proposals coming forward under the Inter-Governmental pillars. It concluded that the Terms of Reference as they stood permitted the Committee to carry out such inquiries.

The Terms of Reference themselves order the Select Committee to consider "Community proposals". In 1973, this could only have meant for the Committee to consider proposals for Community legislation. However, the Committee rightly felt that the phrase "Community proposals" is capable of:[31]

"bering a wider construction, and proposals for the Community to participate in or negotiate international agreements have been considered in several enquiries"

Furthermore, the Terms of Reference also permit the Select Committee to consider "other questions". As has already been seen in the preceding chapters, this gives the Committee licence to inquire into more general issues, such as policy developments, consultative documents and non-legislative Council acts (eg. Recommendations and Opinions).[32]

Notwithstanding the flexibility of these Terms of Reference and in particular their wide applicability, the Select Committee feel that because of their increased role, their Terms of Reference, should reflect more accurately the task they now perform. This is sensible as it will set in stone the activities of the Select Committee and remove any lingering doubt as to whether the

---

31   See HL 124 (Session 1992-93) p. 25, para. 64.
32   For more discussion on this aspect of the Select Committee's work, see the Second Special Report from the Select Committee on the European Communities, HL 251 Session 1974-75).

Select Committee is competent to carry out such inquiries. For the Committee itself, the change is viewed as being necessary to bring its role into line with the Declaration in the Maastricht Treaty which encourages the participation of national parliaments in the activities of the European Union. The Select Committee proposed the following new Terms of Reference:[33]

> "to consider Community proposals, whether in draft or otherwise, to obtain all necessary information about them and to make reports on those which, in the opinion of the Committee, raise important questions of policy or principle and on other questions, *including the development of other elements of the European Union, namely inter-governmental work on foreign and security policy and on justice and home affairs* (my italics) to which the Committee consider that the special attention of the House should be drawn"

The obvious amendment relates specifically to the work of scrutinising proposals under the pillars. However, it is unlikely that an explicit statement allowing the Committee to carry out such inquiries will make the government more generous in its supply of documents and other information. Any change to the Terms of Reference will be purely of benefit to the Select Committee itself. This was a view held by the government who in their response to the Select Committee report stated that any amendment to the Terms of Reference was purely a matter for the Select Committee and the House of Lords.[34]

CONCLUDING REMARKS

The introduction of the inter-governmental pillars has provided a new challenge for the Select Committee. In particular the need to scrutinise legislative proposals which are decided upon in secret will continue to prove probematical. In fact it is the whole confidentiality issue which undermines the vork of the Select Committee in this area. The reluctance by the government o provide draft texts to Parliament is not in keeping with the spirit of the Declaration in the Maastricht Treaty. The government must realise that Parlament can only carry out its scrutiny function if the government itself displys the necessary goodwill.

Above, the need for confidentiality in this area was discussed. n the authors opinion, it appears that the government is a little preoccupie with this argument. The Select Committee put forward constructive and wckable solutions to deal with these problems. In particular their pledge to ac in a "sensitive" manner underlines their seriousness. The Committee are prpared to conduct evidence sessions in private and not publish their findingsuntil the actual text itself is published. This solution would allow both sides tcfulfil

---

33   See n. 31, at p. 199.
34   See Cm 2471 (Session 1992-93) p. 5, para. (viii).

their commitments. Unfortunately, the government rejected it. This now means that proposals will be brought forward that have not been subject to adequate democratic accountability. Under these circumstances, Parliament is without any effective influence in this important area.

CHAPTER 11

THE SCRUTINY OF EUROPEAN LEGISLATION BY A REFORMED SECOND CHAMBER – SOME VIEWS AND EVALUATIONS OF A REFORMED HOUSE OF LORDS

INTRODUCTION

The 1997 General Election saw the Labour Party elected with an overwhelming majority. Central to their programme is reforming the House of Lords. The question which this chapter will be concerned with is, how these, and other proposed changes could affect the scrutiny function of the House of Lords. Specifically, the evaluation will focus on how these proposals will affect the daily activities of the House of Lords e.g. the meeting of the Select Committee and the Sub-Committees as well as considering whether any proposed reforms would actually be workable in terms of preserving the scrutiny function.

At far as this author is concerned, the scrutiny process in the House of Lords is the most effective, comprehensive and developed machinery of any in the European Union. This includes the House of Commons procedures. This argument is based on three primary reasons:

1. The personnel involved in the scrutiny procedures;
2. The inquisitorial nature of the scrutiny process; and
3. The fact that the House of Lords is unelected.

These factors will now be examined in more detail.

THE PERSONNEL INVOLVED IN THE SCRUTINY PROCESS

At the end of the 1995-96 Session, the membership of the Select Committee on the European Communities was 20. Out of the 20 members 14 were Life Peers and 6 Hereditary Peers.[1] Included in the 14 Life Peers was one Life Peer created under the Appellate Jurisdiction Act 1876 – Lord Slynn. As well as being a member of the full Select Committee, each Peer also sits on one or more of the five Sub-Committees. As the main Select Committee meets only every two weeks, the majority of a Peers time is taken up with attending Sub-Committee meetings.

---

[1]   See House of Lords Information Sheet No.2, *The House of Lords at Work.* March 1996.

Party Affiliation

Though there is party affiliation amongst the Peers on the Select Committee, it also is true to say that party political influences are less pronounced in the House of Lords. In particular, the significant presence of Cross-Benchers dilutes the influence of party pressure. The following figures show the current party make-up of the Select Committee on the European Communities:[2]

Conservative Members	7
Labour Members	4
Lib.Dem Members	3
Cross-Benchers	6

As can be seen from the above figures, the government has no inbuilt majority, unlike Select Committees in the House of Commons which are composed in proportion to the number of MPs elected. Thus, the balance of power on this Select Committee lies to a great extent with the Cross-Benchers.

However, one important point must be stressed. Evidence obtained by the author, especially through conversations with Peers and Officials in the House of Lords, suggests strongly that the Select Committee and indeed the Sub-Committees do not work on party lines. There are no minority reports produced and the Committee always speaks with one voice (This issue is returned to in the next section). This is one of the strengths of the scrutiny process in the Lords. The non-confrontational approach and concentration on the issues before it. This is in contrast to the Commons where debate of any European issues regularly leads to a discussion of tired old arguments relating to our continued membership of the European Union. In 1982, a Report of a Study Group of the Commonwealth Parliamentary Association on *The Role of Second Chambers* made the following observation about scrutiny of European legislation in the House of Lords:

> "...the only really deep analysis of the issues that is available for the parliamentary representatives of the ten countries in the Community. The Lords reports are far more informative and comprehensive than those produced by the Commons committee on European legislation. That is because the Lords Committee Members are more objective and often have close knowledge of the subject under scrutiny. In the Commons party allegiances can come to the fore."

Thus the quality of the debate in the Lords is undoubtedly superior to that in the Commons. However, there is some evidence which shows that over the last five years there has been some drift towards a more politically charged atmosphere in the Select Committee. The reason for this is based upon the intake of Peers following the 1992 general election. This included many

---

2   See House of Lords Information Sheet No.13, *House of Lords Attendance and Membership Statistics Session 1995-1996.*

members of Margaret Thatcher's administration during the 1980s, some of
whom have very strong opinions on the European Union. For example, the
ad-hoc Sub-Committee on the 1996 Inter-Governmental Conference included Lord Tebbit, whose Eurosceptic views are well known. A former Clerk to
the Select Committee said during the course of an interview[3] that the questioning debate and discussion during the course of this inquiry was more political than he had previously witnessed.

It would be a great loss if the scrutiny process in the Lords were to take on
a more political character. As already said, its strength lies in the conciliatory
approach taken by the peers and the concentration on the issues at hand. The
ad hoc Sub-Committee on the 1996 Inter-Governmental Conference was primarily concerned with future policy of the European Union which provokes
emotive reactions from all sides of the debate. As yet, this has not been translated to the everyday scrutiny work of the other Sub-Committees. One hopes
it remains this way.

Attendance of Peers

Peers are not paid any salary for the work they do. They merely receive a small
allowance for attending the House. This suggests very strongly, that the peers
who take a regular active part in the scrutiny process do so because they have
something to offer and not for any financial reward. This point is not regularly appreciated by those who criticise the House of Lords. If nothing else, the
so called "working peers" who carry out extremely important functions at a
very high standard represent good value for money for the taxpayer.[4] Any
increase in pay would have to be accompanied with an appropriate increase in
activity. The net result being that scrutiny would no longer be as prominent
in a reformed chamber as it is today.

However, the benefit of having these peers involved in the scrutiny process
is more than just mere cost-effectiveness. The single most valuable contribution they make to the scrutiny process is the knowledge and expertise that
they can bring to it. Many of the members of the Committee have former
experience either in government, working for the European Community or in
some other field such as trade unions or business. This makes them invaluable
members of the five varied subject related Sub-Committees. In his article
Leave us Lords well alone, The Times 17 January 1995 Woodrow Wyatt gave
the following example of how effective the Select Committee is:

---

3   The interview was with the former Clerk Mr Michael Pownall at the House of Lords
     on the 28 April 1996.
4   The Institute for Public Policy Research in its 1993 document *Reforming the Lords*,
     made an assessment of the cost of the Lords and its replacement with an elected
     chamber. For the 1992-93 session the House of Lords cost £36.3m. They estimated
     that an elected chamber would cost £69m for the same period. This is against the
     House of Commons which cost £166.6m.

"The Lords European Communities Committee (to which there is no plausible Commons equivalent) led the whole EC in exposing fraud, providing our government with irrefutable evidence with which to force our partners to curtail or extinguish colossal frauds on European taxpayers."

Thus together with co-opted members who are brought in to a particular inquiry because of their specialist knowledge, a Committee of vast resources is assembled. This is unparalleled in either House. Any plans for reconstitution of the Lords such as those in the Labour Party's manifesto which will affect the make-up of the Lords may well serve as operating to the detriment of the Parliamentary process.

Let's return to the attendance of peers again. In the 1994-95 Session[5] there were 142 sitting days in the session. Unfortunately there are no separate figures for attendance of the Select Committee. However, it is not unreasonable to assume that if a peer is in attendance on the day of a Select Committee meeting, he or she will attend that meeting. Of the 142 sitting days, the average attendance of all peers of the Select Committee is 76 – over 50%. Some peers such as Lord Bruce of Donnington attended 140 days and Lord Barnett 126 days. Others such as Lord Slynn of Hadley attended only 29 days, but he was also an active member of the judiciary at the time. However, as Chairman of Sub-Committee E – the Law and Institutions Sub-Committee – the 29 days he did attend were primarily taken up with attending meetings involved with his position as Chairman.

Therefore attendance by members of the Select Committee is very good. They take their work seriously and make a worthwhile contribution in the area of scrutiny of European legislation and policy. The working peers must therefore be commended for the work they do. This section will be concluded by illustrating that peers who do attend the House regularly, are making a positive contribution. The recent House of Lords inquiry into Fraud and Mismanagement in the Community[6] is better than anything mounted in the Commons. The inquiry was based on an in-depth investigation into all aspects of Community administration and its conclusions gave both the government and Commission much important evidence to combat this problem. In fact the issue is on the agenda at the 1996-97 IGC. The House of Lords Select Committee on the European Communities was undoubtedly pivotal in this development.

Judicial participation in the scrutiny process and the Separation of Powers

As members of the House of Lords, the judiciary can and do play an active part in the daily functioning of the Lords. No more so is this seen than in the European Communities Select Committee and in particular Sub-Committee E – the Law and Institutions Sub- Committee. This Sub-Committee is always

---

5   This is the last session for which figures are available. See 3 above.
6   See HL 44 (Session 1992-93).

chaired by a Lord of Appeal, e.g. Lord Slynn of Hadley who was Chairman up to the end of the 1995-96 session. His suitability for the task was that he had previously been Advocate-General to the European Court of Justice.

Sub-Committee E could not function as effectively as it does unless it was staffed primarily by lawyers. Its Terms of Reference require it to consider, *inter alia*, the impact EC legislative proposals have on existing UK law and the *vires* of any legislative proposal. Both these activities involve a highly complex process of evaluating proposed legal developments. Who better to do this than a Committee of lawyers chaired by a highly experienced Lord of Appeal? If these people are the best individuals to do the job why should their membership of the judiciary prevent them from doing it?

One argument put against their participation is that there is potential for a conflict of interest. That is to say a judge is scrutinising legislation which he can in the future be asked to be the arbiter of. However, the author has found no evidence of this at all. In conversation with Lord Slynn,[7] he argued that there is no reason to suggest this. A judge in the House of Lords sits with four others, and their approach is objective and based on the facts before them and not based on deliberations taken in a Select Committee years before. Furthermore, he pointed out that the actual chances of this happening are very remote and research undertaken confirms this.

One aspect of this arrangement that has caused more concern is the point that the judiciary being involved in the legislative process is in conflict with the doctrine of the Separation of Powers. This is quite true. According to this doctrine, judiciary and legislature should be separate to prevent a concentration of power.

However, on closer examination it is quite clear that any infringement of this doctrine is minor. The judiciary, as Lord Slynn pointed out, are careful not to become too involved in the politics of the legislative proposal. They limit their role to scrutiny and are objective in their operation. Though still at the heart of democratic government in this country, the Separation of Powers has undoubtedly been redefined in recent years. One only needs to look at the way in which the Executive has dominated the legislature in recent times as evidence of this fact. A minor infringement by a Sub-Committee in the House of Lords is not sufficient to justify a change in its composition. The fact that there is a mere *potential* for conflict is a small price to pay for the undoubtedly positive contribution this Sub-Committee makes.

THE INQUISITORIAL NATURE OF THE SCRUTINY PROCESS IN THE LORDS

Based upon the fact that party politics do not play such a major part in the House of Lords generally, it is possible to identify this as the primary reason for the more inquisitorial approach adopted by the Select Committee on the European Communities. Together with the fact that the House of Lords has

---

7   The interview took place at the House of Lords on the 18 January 1995.

more time to consider the issues than its House of Commons counterpart, there is the basis for a very influential Select Committee. The Committee can readily move between conducting a broad ranging and highly focussed inquiry with relative ease.

At the heart of this inquisitorial approach is the Sub-Committee structure. They are subject related and have the relevant documents delegated to them, which they are to consider. The Sub-Committee size is particularly suited to conducting inquiries in a more inquisitorial fashion. They are small, with usually no more than six permanent members and five co-opted members. This makes them ideal for discussion. In fact it could be more appropriate to describe the Sub-Committees as working parties. Furthermore, with the assistance of specialist advisers or legal staff they have the potential to get to the core of the issues before them.

Hearing of evidence

Whenever a Sub-Committee conducts a detailed inquiry it will obtain evidence from as many sources as possible. Thus evidence taking may last up to three months. Together with any further deliberation and the inquiry has taken a full six months by its conclusion. Such an inquiry cannot be ignored by government. The evidence as presented[8] suggests strongly that such inquiries have the desired effect – namely to influence the minister before giving agreement in the Council. In addition, and perhaps more significantly, it was stated during the course of an interview with a former Clerk[9] of the Select Committee, that the House of Lords reports are read by the Commission with great interest. He cited the undoubted quality of the reports as the primary reason for their being read by the Commission. The Hansard Society Commission in its 1992 document *Making the Law* made similar observations. In this respect the House of Lords is unparalleled by any other Chamber in the European Union. Perhaps most importantly, these reports give the United Kingdom Parliament a degree of influence in the Commission. This should not be sacrificed.

Sub-Committee reports

Following evidence taking and deliberation, the Sub-Committee publishes its report. This report speaks for the whole Select Committee. There is *no* minority report. This is one of the main distinguishing features of the Select Committee in the Lords.[10] The fact that there is no minority report is a testament to this inquisitorial approach and the lack of any significant party political influence on the Select Committee.

---

8   See Chapters 8 and 9.
9   See n. 7, at p. 207.
10   This is in stark comparison to the House of Commons where Select Committees will often produce a minority report based exclusively on party affiliation. This has most recently been seen in the Home Affairs Select Committee report on gun control where the Conservative members published their own findings and recommendations.

In its deliberations the Select Committee has debated the issues raised by the witnesses and used the evidence it has received to fulfil the task its Terms of Reference require – to produce a report which influences the minister prior to giving agreement in the Council. A report behind which the whole Select Committee can unite is a report that cannot be ignored.

The inquisitorial approach of the Select Committee is the key factor to its unrivalled success. It gives the Committee the influence and respect which is essential for it to be effective. This however can only be continued within the present Parliamentary framework. In the next section the unelected character of the House of Lords will be evaluated and how it strengthens the scrutiny function.

THE UNELECTED HOUSE OF LORDS AND THE SCRUTINY FUNCTION

When critics of the House of Lords call for reform of this institution, they focus their argument on the fact that the Lords is unelected. In particular, they contend that the Lords is both undemocratic and unaccountable. This argument is central in the labour government's plans for reform. These proposals will be examined in the next section to assess their potential impact on the scrutiny process. At this stage however, the focus is on examining and explaining the argument that effective scrutiny, of the type we see today in the Lords, can only be carried out by an unelected second chamber.

The lack of constituency duties

At the heart of this argument is the fact that peers are not burdened by the requirements of representing a particular constituency. This relieves them of a vast amount of work. In turn this permits them the opportunity to devote the necessary time required to carry out their scrutiny task as effectively as they do. If the second chamber was to be fully or even partially elected those members who were subject to the electorate would not have the time to be involved in scrutiny. Constituency and related business would inevitably and understandably take priority. This would be damaging for scrutiny as perhaps some of the more experienced and able representatives could not take as active a part as they do under the present system. In addition this pre-supposes that any elected chamber would continue to have existing peers sitting in it. A point that will be subsequently returned to.

Questions of democratic legitimacy

The second argument relates to the fact that any elected body will always claim a democratic legitimacy. An elected second chamber would undoubtedly have a change of horizons. It would view itself an equal to the House of Commons and would wish to play a more active role in daily Parliamentary activity. The focus would shift from the present one of being primarily a subordinate revising chamber, with the time to review legislation both European, and domestic, to a chamber which takes a greater initiative in legislative activity. Thus the unique function the Lords has today, and one no better illustrated than by the work of the Select Committee, would be lost and replaced by a Chamber whose activity was influenced primarily by the Commons. In particular, if elected it may wish to challenge the Commons more so than it does today.

The lack of party political influence

Electing the second chamber would inevitably make this second chamber more political. In the previous section it was argued that party politics is at a minimum in the Select Committee and this is a great plus. For a candidate to have a chance of being elected, he would have to stand under a party banner. Translate this to any Select Committee charged with reviewing European legislation in this new second chamber and it will undoubtedly be influenced by party politics. To what degree it is difficult to say, and experience in the Commons does suggest that the Select Committee there is not overtly divided on political lines. However, the risk of this is greater and is already witnessed in other Commons Select Committees. Any movement to a more party political approach in a second chamber will be to the detriment of scrutiny and should be avoided.

The informal nature of the Lords

The final aspect of this argument relates to the more informal procedures prevalent in the Lords. The unelected nature of it means that there are no career minded professional politicians who are interested in scaling the party ladder. In fact it is quite the reverse. It consists primarily of retired MPs and individuals who have made a variety of contributions to public life. This valuable skill and expertise is harnessed by the Select Committee and put to excellent use in the scrutiny process. The peers are involved because they want to be involved and not because of some financial or other reward.

   This in fact leads to a related issue. If we elected our second chamber we would expect it to carry out more than its present functions. There would now be professional politicians who would expect to be paid. In return the electorate would expect more than merely continuing with the current tasks. These two factors together would mean an end to scrutiny in its present form. Other considerations, namely constituency and party affairs, would take precedent. At best a scrutiny system similar to the Commons would survive. This is undesirable.

Is the House of Lords undemocratic?

The answer to this question depends to a great extent of how one views democracy. Though this issue will not be examined here, as time and space do not permit, one assertion needs to be made. Democracy is often linked with accountability. Indeed this very point has been articulated at a number of stages in the course of this work. But does accountability necessary mean being elected? For example the Council of Ministers is not elected as a body but each minister is accountable to his Parliament. Similarly, the Commission is appointed but is subject to some accountability by the European Parliament. Though desirable and preferable, being elected is not central to an organisation such as the European Union. In many cases, such as that of the Commission, appointment is the only viable option. This however needs to be counter-balanced by effective accountability and this issue requires further consideration.

If we take the unelected House of Lords, it fails the test of democratic legitimacy because it is not subject to popular control. Also, under criticism is the fact that its members consist of peers who take their place because of their birthright. In the authors opinion, this is focusing on the issue from the wrong perspective. If a hereditary peer is making a valuable contribution to the scrutiny process (as indeed the six current ones do) is it justified to remove them merely because they are not elected? The House of Lords in its present form, and in particular the working peers as seen on the Select Committee, are making a vital contribution to democracy through their involvement in the scrutiny of European legislation. What in fact is being argued, is that democracy stems from the functions an institution performs as well as the personnel involved in it. This is illustrated no better than by the composition of the House of Commons itself. Despite universal suffrage for over seventy years, the Commons has never reflected the make-up of the United Kingdom in terms of the ethnic population or the number of women who make up the electorate. Yet we would not question its democratic legitimacy. Thus concentrating ones criticism on personnel and using this as the central pillar for arguing the Lords is unrepresentative and therefore undemocratic misses the point and is a mistake.

Today the Parliament Acts of 1911 and 1949 limit the power of the Lords. Most significantly this deals with the Lords ability to delay legislation from the Commons. These Acts set the parameters for the Lords activity today. Most importantly they prevent the Lords being a rival to the Commons, leaving it to concentrate on important reviewing tasks such as scrutiny of European Union legislation. In this situation one is left with two Chambers that compliment each other and scrutiny is an example of one such activity where this occurs. This could be even more effective if, as already suggested, the scrutiny procedures in both Houses were reviewed to have a formal division of labour between them.

SOME RECENT PROPOSALS FOR REFORMING THE HOUSE OF LORDS

In this section there will be a brief evaluation of some of the more recent proposals that have been put forward to reform the Lords. The primary objective of this analysis will be to evaluate how these proposals may, if implemented, affect the specific task of scrutiny. Time and space will therefore not permit any other observations about these proposals.

The Institute for Public Policy Research (IPPR)

The IPPR was established in 1988 and describes itself as "an alternative to the free market think tanks".[11] In essence it is a centre-left research organisation which has put forward a variety of proposals for reforming the United Kingdom constitution. Its proposals for reforming the House of Lords were presented in its 1993 document *Reforming the Lords.*[12]

The basic elements of the proposals in this document have at their core an elected second chamber, which they call the Senate. Its elected members would represent regional rather than local constituencies and be elected by Proportional Representation.[13] As far as scrutiny is concerned the document addressed this issue specifically. It recognised the value and quality of this work and realised that this should be preserved. In fact it viewed this Select Committee as a model for other Committees which would be prominent in the Senate.

It recommended a "smaller and more sharply focussed committee".[14] However, no further detail is given. The present Committee consists of twenty members who also sit on one or more of the Sub-Committees. Given the workload of the Committee today, and one which is rapidly increasing, it would be difficult to reduce the size of the Committee significantly without any comparable loss in performance. As to the new committee being more sharply focussed, it is difficult to imagine how this could be so. The present arrangement of six subject related Sub-Committees, each one representing a major policy area of the EU could not be more focussed. The reduction of Sub-Committees from six to five post the Jelicoe Report[15] illustrates this fact (even with the new Sub-Committee F the focus still remains). Furthermore, that Committee's recommendation to make greater use of *ad hoc* Sub-Committees allows the Select Committee to focus on important issues as and when they arise. The *ad hoc* Sub-Committee report on the 1996 Inter-Governmental Conference[16] illustrates this point clearly.

Another recommendation of the IPPR is that the Select Committee should not engage in detailed scrutiny of Community legislation. The authors contend its time could be best served by monitoring major developments in the structure of the Community and Community strategy. This is a little perplexing because a closer examination of the work of the Committee reveals that this is exactly what is done. The report in to the 1996 IGC is one such case. Each of the Sub-Committees itself considers legislative developments and will often carry out an inquiry in anticipation of a Community proposal. In effect the Committee moves up stream and tries to influence the Commis-

---

11   See IPPR *The Constitution of the United Kingdom* 1991.
12   IPPR (1993) Jeremy Mitchell and Anne Davies.
13   *Ibid.* p. 37.
14   *Ibid.* p. 57.
15   See HL 35-I (Session 1991-92).
16   See HL 105 (Session 1994-95).

sion e.g. the inquiry into Relations between the EU and the Maghreb Countries.[17] The authors of this document have missed the point. They make no mention of the work of the Sub-Committees specifically in this context. It is unclear therefore whether this would continue. The present quality of scrutiny could not be maintained unless it was.

One concrete proposal of the document is to remove the presence of the Law Lords in the Senate.[18] The impact of this would be devastating upon the quality of work in Sub-Committee E. In fact it is difficult to see it continuing this work without their presence. This would be a great loss. It is the presence and experience of the Law Lords, such as Lord Slynn, which have made Sub-Committee E the undoubted success it is. They do propose a Sub-Committee which could co-opt legal expertise but it is unclear how this would work and whether Law Lords could be involved. Clarity on this point is needed.

The authors conclude the section on scrutiny of European legislation with the following passage:[19]

> "A reformed committee needs to be concerned more with fundamental issues, for example an examination of the treaty base of proposed legislation. Detailed scrutiny would be best carried out in a sub-committee which would co-opt any necessary legal expertise."

With respect to the authors it appears as if they are devising some new scrutiny function. This plainly is not the case. For the last twenty three years Sub-Committee E has been engaged in this very activity. Its specific Terms of Reference require it to do this. In particular its consideration of the "*vires*" of a proposal and to consider and report on "any important developments that take place in Community law" illustrate this. This inevitably requires consideration of the treaty base, the very thing the authors call for.

The proposals for scrutiny in a reformed second chamber outlined above do not address adequately the issues that have been highlighted in the previous chapters. In particular they do not appreciate the fact that many of the functions they propose are already carried out very effectively.

To the authors credit, they do however recognise the experience and expertise many peers contribute to the scrutiny process and, to the only other permanent Select Committee – the Science and Technology Select Committee. They also recognise this must be protected. In the event of reform they suggest that this expertise should be maintained by the continuation of co-opting members on to the Select Committees. However, the strength of the present scrutiny system is that co-opted members work together as a partnership with already highly experienced peers. For the reasons outlined above it is difficult to see this continuing in an elected chamber because the elected members will potentially not posses the same level of experience as the peers or necessarily

---

17 See HL 58 (Session 1994-95).
18 See IPPR *Reforming the Lords* 1993 p. 38.
19 *Ibid.* p.57.

be as interested in scrutiny to the same degree. They will have other priorities. Under these circumstances the burden will fall on the co-opted members leading to less effective scrutiny.

The Labour Party

Traditionally, the Labour Party has been antagonistic to the House of Lords and outright abolition has been its policy for most of the Labour Party's existence.[20] In 1968, it proposed the Parliament (No.2) Bill which was intended to substantially reduce the powers of the Lords. The Bill failed, primarily due to the fact that the House of Commons did not have the political will to reform the Lords which could then challenge the political authority of the Commons. Since 1968, the Labour Party has spent most of this time in opposition and despite being consistently opposed to the Lords in its present form never was given the opportunity to implement its proposals.

The 1997 General Election brought with it a change of government. Labour has changed into New Labour and with it so has its policy with regard to the Lords. At the core of the present policy is the removal of the hereditary element in the Lords. In its policy document *New Labour New Life for Britain*[21] it makes the following observation:

> "We will remove the right hereditary peers to sit and vote in the House of Lords as a first step towards a more democratic and representative chamber...One proposal we can consider is that the House of Lords has some places reserved by appointment for those who have an outstanding contribution to make. The legislative powers of the House of Lords will remain unaltered. Its function will remain that of a revising chamber."

So, what does this mean for scrutiny? At first sight the proposals do not appear to radical. Initially at least there will not be any significant reforms. However, the removal of hereditary peers may have some effect. The hereditary peers on the Select Committee make an extremely positive contribution. If they are the best people for the job, and undoubtedly they are because they have been appointed to the Committee, why should their experience be discarded because they have inherited their position? Today there are six hereditary peers, all of whom had a very good attendance record during the 1994-95 Session. The average attendance was 62.5 days (slightly lower than the average 76 for all peers on the Committee) but some such as Lord Geddes attended 105 days and Lord Bridges 77 days. Hereditary peers are not traditionally viewed as working peers and thus it is fair to assume that when these peers did attend it was primarily to attend the Select Committee (as stated above, there are no separate statistics for Committee attendance). Any deci-

---

20   In 1908 the Labour Party Conference considered a resolution pledging the party to the abolition of the Lords.
21   Published by the Labour Party in 1996 as the basis of its election manifesto.

sion to remove hereditary peers needs careful consideration especially if the high quality scrutiny wants to be maintained as the document indicates.

People may point to the fact that the document also states (and this is in the quote above) that the proposal for reform will reserve places for the appointment of those individuals who have an outstanding contribution to make. Will this include hereditary peers? The document is unclear on this point. If it does then all the Labour government would have done is to merely change the titles of individuals from hereditary peers to life peers and not addressed the issue of composition in any significant way. This is not an effective use of Parliamentary time.

Thus the policy requires clarification as to how these changes will affect the scrutiny process. In particular, it can be criticised for concentrating on personnel in the Lords rather than its functions. At no stage is the work of the Select Committee on the European Communities mentioned, giving the impression that this crucial task of scrutiny carried out by the Select Committee has not been fully considered. Though the document does state that the House will remain a revising Chamber it is difficult to see how this would continue as effectively when over one quarter of the present membership of the Select Committee on the European Communities will be prevented from participating. There is no guarantee that their replacements would be as competent.

The policy document suggests that the eventual aim of New Labour is to have an elected second chamber. The arguments as to why this will not be to the benefit of scrutiny have already been given and will not be repeated again. However, this analysis will be concluded with one further observation. History suggests that reform of the Lords is a difficult task. The experience of the Parliament (No.2) Bill shows this. Between 1974 and 1979 the Labour government made no attempt to reform the Lords. This Labour government, with many legislative priorities, is to have more success in reform, it needs to have workable proposals. The starting point should therefore be preserving and enhancing the present functions of the Lords. In particular this means developing scrutiny. This is too important an issue to be marginalised by unconvincing arguments that only by reforming the membership can the House of Lords be democratic and representative. Democracy is seen in the Lords when peers hold the minister to account for actions taken in Council and arguably it is done more effectively than in the Commons.

The Liberal Democrats

Ever since the days of the SDP/Liberal Alliance, reform of the House of Lords has been a major part of their policy for constitutional reform. Present Liberal Democrat policy, which they outlined in their alternative Queen's Speech in November 1995, is based on introducing an elected Senate whose primary function would be to provide regional representation and to act as a sort of guardian of the constitution and upholder of civil liberties.

In an interview with James Cornford,[22] a former director of the Institute for Public Policy Research (IPPR) he expressed similar views. He justified these arguments in the following way. He viewed the role of the second chamber as being essentially a revising chamber which kept an effective check on the House of Commons. He felt that on balance these functions were more important than preserving the scrutiny process in its current form. Though he accepted the value of the Lords work in this area and also on the Science and Technology Select Committee, these were probably the only two areas where the Lords made an effective contribution:

> "...when it comes to balancing the two things up, using the second chamber as a control over the House of Commons and probably using it as a means of regional representation are more important things to do than preserving its present character and virtues."

These views along with the policies of the Liberal Democrats do cause a number of difficulties for the scrutiny process. In particular, the argument must be made that scrutiny in its present form could not continue. An elected Senate focussed on constitutional and regional issues would simply not have the time to continue with the in-depth scrutiny that is presently carried out by the Lords. Its horizon will change and be more concerned with the work of the Commons.

Thus the question must be asked. Which body will do the detailed scrutiny that is presently the domain of the Lords? The House of Commons? Very unlikely because it will continue to have an ever increasing workload. Perhaps the European Parliament? This is almost unthinkable in the sense that such a development would mean that the UK Parliament has lost all its influence in the European legislative process. Political opinion on all sides of the House of Commons would not countenance such a development. This leaves only one option – the detailed investigative scrutiny now seen in the House of Lords will be sacrificed to introduce an elected chamber whose functions though they are to include acting as a revising chamber, will not be placing as strong an emphasis on the scrutiny of European issues.

CONCLUDING REMARKS

Scrutiny in the House of Lords works because this institution follows its own agenda. It recognises the limitations of the scrutiny process in the Commons and acts accordingly in a complimentary fashion. Together both Houses have undoubtedly created the most effective and influential scrutiny process in the European Union. This is notwithstanding the many limitations that been have identified in the course of this work.

In nearing the twenty-first century, principles of hereditary entitlement and unelected Parliaments are rapidly becoming unacceptable. Even Lord

---

22   The interview took place on the 6 February 1995.

Hailsham in *The Dilemma of Democracy* accepts that the Lords in its present form will not survive. If it is to be reformed, the reform should have as its starting point an acceptance that *some* of the features of todays House of Lords are worth preserving. This is a prime case of not throwing the baby out with the bath water!

This is what has been attempted in this chapter. It is as an exercise in evaluating and explaining that change does not always have to be revolutionary. In particular, the concentration on personnel in the Lords is looking at the issue from the wrong perspective. This is a criticism that can also be levelled at the recent report by the Constitution Unit[23] entitled *Reform of the House of Lords.* Though this report conceded that in an elected second chamber the current functions of the Lords will persist, it also states that the principal additional function will be to provide "an additional voice for the regions at the centre of the political system". As already stated, in an elected environment, these two functions are not readily compatible. The opinion of this author is that scrutiny will be the loser because the elected second chamber will create its own agenda, and one based predominantly on shadowing closely the work of the Commons.

To conclude, in this chapter the main thrust of the argument has been that only by preserving many of the features of the House of Lords can scrutiny of the current high standard be preserved. One must accept that in this chapter, the scrutiny function has been somewhat isolated from the rest of the Lords functions and that there are other aspects to the Lords work. However this has been done to emphasise the arguments and stress the importance of scrutiny which has been marginalised or overlooked by political parties and organisations who propose reform of the Lords. In this chapter the aim has been to redress the balance by placing scrutiny at the heart of any proposals for reform and increasing awareness of the undoubted high quality work carried out by the Lord's Select Committee on the European Communities.

---

23   The unit is based at the Faculty of Laws University College London.

PART IV:

ARE THE SCRUTINY ARRANGEMENTS EFFECTIVE?

CHAPTER 12

CONCLUSIONS AND EVALUATIONS

INTRODUCTION

The aim of this book has been to follow the legislative process of the European Union, beginning with the consultation and lobbying of the Commission and concluding with approval of the legislative proposals by the Council of Ministers. The endeavour has been to explain and analyse each stage of this process and evaluate its constitutional significance as far as the UK Parliament is concerned. In addition, the intention has been to produce a comprehensive study of an extremely important yet relatively unknown part of the UK legislative process. In this final chapter, the evaluation will begin by assessing the role of the UK Parliament in the legislative process of the European Union and how it could be improved.

PARLIAMENT AND THE EUROPEAN UNION

No constitutional relationship

The primary point to note is the lack of any formal constitutional relationship between both Houses and the Institutions of the EU. In Chapter 2 an explanation for this position was given. Essentially it is based on the threat as perceived by many Parliamentarians (predominantly in the Commons) that the aim of the European Institutions, and in particular the European Parliament, is to supplant Westminster as the sovereign legislative body.

The absence of any established contact is undoubtedly detrimental to the scrutiny process. In particular, it means that Parliament has no effective influence over the Commission and the European Parliament. The latter now being central to the legislative process through its input via the co-decision procedure. In an atmosphere of increasing European integration developing such contacts is essential. MPs cannot argue that European Institutions are marginalising Westminster but yet sit back and not redress the balance by developing such contacts.

The House of Lords on the other hand has long since seen the benefit of such contacts and, though only informal, they are undoubtedly constructive. MPs therefore should take notice of this. In particular, the acceptance by the Lords that the only way to effectively influence is to be at the centre of the debate and policy formulation process would be a good starting point for many MPs. In 1997, twenty-four years after joining the Community it is time to move the debate on from irrelevant arguments of our continued membership of the Community. Practical politics, as all the major parties realise, dictates that the UK should be a member of the EU. As this is the case, it is therefore essential to ensure that their is effective scrutiny.

Scrutiny arrangements within Parliament

In Chapters 3 and 8 above, the work and impact of the Select Committees in
both Houses was explained and analysed. In this chapter, the aim is to briefly
examine whether these two independent procedures provide the most effective use of valuable Parliamentary time. More specifically, the concern lies
with both the duplication of certain tasks and the lack of any formal cooperation between the two Houses on scrutiny generally.

As far as the duplication of tasks is concerned, the central point is that
both Houses examine every document. That is to say, both Committees sift
through each legislative proposal broadly on the same basis. Though the
Terms of Reference are different (with the Lords having a wider brief) this
initial sift has the same net result in both Houses. It determines which documents will require in-depth scrutiny. With approximately 1000 documents
per year, this is a time consuming process. The inevitable question is whether
both Houses need to do this task? For example, could it not be done by the
Commons with their results being used by both Houses?

Under present arrangements, the answer is obviously no. The primary reason is that though both Commons and Lords sift through documents to
decide which require further scrutiny, the reports they produce rarely focus on
the same legislative proposals. Each Committee has its own agenda which is
essentially decided by its Terms of Reference. Furthermore, subjects chosen
for scrutiny in the Lords will often reflect the personal interest and expertise
of members of the subject related Sub-Committees, whereas, scrutiny by
Standing Committee in the Commons reflects the political and policy considerations of the government.

A Joint Select Committee

One possible solution to the above difficulty is to establish a Joint Select
Committee of both Houses. There is precedent for this within Parliament. In
particular, there is an active Statutory Instruments Joint Committee, a Consolidation Bills Joint Committee and the Ecclesiastical Committee.

As far as the Statutory Instruments Committee is concerned, it is a Joint
Committee because it is a resource saving exercise. The ever increasing number of Statutory Instruments means this is a more effective way of conducting
scrutiny of them. A similar principle could apply to the scrutiny of European
legislative proposals. A Joint Committee would remove the problem of duplication and promote co-ordination of inquiries.

However, establishing a Joint Committee would not necessarily mean the
end of the present arrangements whereby both Houses contribute their own
unique qualities to the scrutiny process. Each House could then scrutinise the
documents it wishes within its current arrangements (i.e. Standing or Sub-
Committee). It is just the initial sift which could be performed jointly. This
would also have the added advantage of there being co-ordination of inquiries
between the Committees. Thus greater use could be made of reports completed by the other House.

Currently there are no plans to establish a Joint Committee. In fact the evidence presented suggests that both Committees wish to have as wide Terms of Reference as possible to maximise their input into the legislative process. A strict division of labour between them is unfortunately not welcomed by either Committee (see Chapter 8). In particular the suggestion that the Commons carries out the Sift and the Lords the in-depth investigation is a proposal that has been rejected by both Houses. In short the scrutiny process will remain fundamentally unchanged for the next Parliamentary term. This however must be kept under review especially if the Inter-Governmental conference produces significant constitutional developments.

The House of Lords

Given the fact that any significant change is unlikely to the scrutiny process, the need to preserve the current arrangements is all the more important. In particular this means the positive contribution made by the Lords. The quality of scrutiny that takes place within the Lords raises important questions for the present government which proposes a reconstitution of Parliament and should be considered carefully before making any changes. That is to say, changes to the Lords will not be in isolation. More specifically removing the current scrutiny function from the Lords without any corresponding amendments to other parts of the process will have a detrimental effect on ministerial accountability to Parliament.

   The most important issue here is that in any reform of the Lords the current scrutiny function must be preserved. As was highlighted in chapter 11, reform of the Lords should begin with an acceptance that its role in this process is an indispensable one and any reforms should aim to build upon this undoubted success.

THE CASE FOR A DEPARTMENT OF EUROPEAN AFFAIRS

In Chapter 5, arguments for a Department of European Affairs were presented. In particular, the most desirable aspect of such a development would be a greater co-ordination and evaluation of European policy within Parliament. Of most value would be the fact that such a Department would be scrutinised by a Departmentally Related Select Committee.

   The primary function of such a Select Committee would undoubtedly be longer term policy developments e.g. enlargement of the EU. It would probably share the same reluctance for scrutiny of legislative proposals as the current Departmentally Related Select Committees do. In this respect the present Select Committee for the European Communities would continue with its important task. However, this task would now be aided by reports and inquiries into policy carried out by not just the new European Affairs Select Committee, but by any relevant Departmentally Related Select Committee.

   Thus, all Departmental Committees need to be encouraged to participate more in European issues where they affect their brief. This is the increased coordination which is proposed. It will benefit not only the scrutiny process, but add to the influence the minister has at the negotiating table. A formulated and thoroughly investigated European policy will strengthen the UK's position in the Council of Ministers.

From the discussion above it is evident that there are currently several areas in which Parliamentary scrutiny could be improved. The specific proposals outlined above and those discussed throughout the course of this work have at their heart the aim of not only making scrutiny more effective but also increasing democratic accountability of the executive in the field of European Affairs (i.e. in the Council of Ministers). It is the establishment of effective control over executive actions that will address the issue of the democratic deficit within the EU. The Select Committee system in both Houses of Parliament is central to this task and for this reason above all must be enhanced.

NATIONAL PARLIAMENTS IN THE EUROPEAN UNION – WHAT NEXT?

Parliamentarianism at a European level

Within this work, the discussion has focussed on the existing arrangements for scrutiny of European legislation. However, in this final part, the discussion will proceed to examine (potentially at least) how the final outcome of the 1996-97 Inter-Governmental conference will affect Westminster's role in the EU.

In its 1995 Report, *The 1996 Inter-Governmental Conference: The Agenda Democracy Efficiency and the Role of National Parliaments*,[1] the Select Committee on European Legislation made the following observation:[2]

> "The question is, will the IGC strengthen the role of National Parliaments *in practice* or will it simply produce empty rhetoric? The last IGC is not an encouraging precedent."

The Select Committee's scepticism is quite understandable if the developments post Maastricht are examined. The Maastricht Declaration on the role of national parliaments was intended to be the guardian of domestic parliaments to ensure their participation in the European legislative process. However as the evidence in both Chapter 6 and 10 suggests the government has not kept to the spirit of the Declaration. In particular, its refusal to extend the Resolution of the House to cover the final stage of the co-decision procedure leads one to question its commitment to the Resolution.

Thus, the issue to consider is whether the balance can be redressed in the 1996-97 Inter-Governmental Conference. Let us first consider what the government's attitude to the role of national parliaments currently is. In the White Paper *A Partnership of Nations*,[3] the government outlined its position

---

1   See HC 239-I (Session 1994-95).
2   *Ibid.* p. xxxv, para. 107.
3   See Cm 3181 (Session 1995-96).

with regard to the IGC. It made the following observation about the role of national parliaments:[4]

> "National parliaments remain the primary focus of democratic legitimacy in the European Union, holding national Ministers in the Council to account. The Government is keen to develop this role and is considering a range of ideas, some of which have been suggested by Parliamentary Committees. These include making the main elements of the Maastricht Declaration 13 (on the role of national parliaments) legally binding by entrenching them in the Treaty; including a minimum period for parliaments to scrutinise Community documents and notably draft legislation (with exceptions for urgent cases); and a greater role for national parliaments in the Justice and Home Affairs Pillar."

From the extract above it would appear that the government is committed to enhancing the participation of national parliaments and indeed making them the focus of democratic accountability in the Union. Indeed, in the next paragraph, the government seem to underline this pledge by make the following observation about the role of the European Parliament:[5]

> "The Government does not feel, however, that the European Parliament needs new powers. Nor do we accept, in a Union of nation states that the European Parliament can displace the primary role of national parliaments."

At the Amsterdam IGC, the Member States agreed to include the Maastricht Declaration on the role of national parliaments in the main body of the Treaty. This is now a legally binding requirement. However, the question of how the role of national parliaments will be guaranteed in the legislative process remains unclear, and must be addressed. The Treaty itself is silent on this point.

This issue is further complicated by the decision of the Member States to amend Article 139b and extend the co-decision procedure by giving further powers to the European Parliament. The potential effect of this will be to increase the Conflict between national parliaments and the European Parliament. Only once the Treaty is implemented will any firm conclusion be reached about the actual impact of these developments.

How can national parliaments have a greater impact?

As has been stressed at many occasions during the course of the book, the aim of scrutiny is to influence the minister. Thus, detailed and timely scrutiny would have a salutary effect on the Council of Ministers and perhaps most importantly would ensure accountability of the Executive which has an ever growing disproportionate power in the European legislative process.

---

4   *Ibid.* p. 15, para. 33.
5   *Ibid.* p. 16, para. 35.

In the quote given above from the White Paper the former government quite correctly made the point that there should be a minimum period for parliaments to scrutinise legislative proposals. This is included in the Amsterdam Treaty. However, national parliaments must cooperate more closely to promote effective scrutiny.

Currently the Conference of European Affairs Committees (CEAC) is the forum for such cooperation. It meets every six months and discusses scrutiny developments in the national parliaments. However, its role is only consultative and it has no mandate from the national parliament. Such a Committee has great potential because to some extent it mirrors the Council of Ministers. It could therefore develop into a body which collectively scrutinises the Council. Something which is currently lacking. Most importantly however, this scrutiny would be under the control of the national parliaments leaving accountability of the minister in their hands.

If any of the above proposals are to be implemented, there needs to the political will among the Member States. As already stated, this appears to be lacking. Currently the EU is pre-occupied with much bigger issues that politically are more important. Furthermore, why should governments put at the top of the agenda the debate and discussion of a process which undoubtedly limits their freedom to act and attempts to make their actions more transparent?

From the above discussion, it is clearly visible that the aims of the UK government at least, do not represent the true picture within the Community. In fact the rhetoric about the desirability of increasing the role played by national parliaments could not be further from the reality of their exclusion in the legislative process. Herein lies the conflict. The argument that increasing participation by national parliaments will address the issue of the democratic deficit within the EU is a strong one. However, such a development would also have an adverse effect on the efficiency of the decision making process. Thus a value judgement needs to be made as to which of these is the more desirable.[6] For this author, the need for effective scrutiny and accountability should be the paramount consideration and not the meeting of arbitrary time limits. There is no point in agreeing legislation quickly merely for it to be unworkable or irrelevant.

CONCLUDING REMARKS

In the course of his research the author received correspondence from Tony Benn MP. He made the following observation:[7]

> "There is no real Parliamentary scrutiny because once a law has been agreed to by ministers in Brussels, Parliament can do nothing about it."

---

6   See also Juliet Lodge *The Weakness of National Parliaments* Parliamentary Brief Vol. 3, No. 9. Summer 1995.
7   Letter from the Right Honourable Tony Benn MP 6 February 1994.

With respect to Mr Benn his view is (currently at least) unduly apocalyptic. His assertion that Parliament can do nothing once the measure has been approved by the Council of Ministers is correct. However, he has missed the point that the influence and input by Parliament comes *before* this approval is given. It is this influence which needs to be protected and nurtured. Unless the role of national parliaments is guaranteed, Mr Benn's view will sadly become a reality.

Thus what is needed is a framework to maintain and develop the scrutiny procedures which are seen in this country. The UK is undoubtedly the leader in scrutiny matters within the EU. Two Chambers scrutinising every proposal is an immense achievement in circumstances which could not be described as conducive to effective scrutiny. Both Houses work very hard to ensure the executive is held to account and the constitutional function of Parliament is preserved.

In twenty-four years Parliament has developed the most advanced scrutiny procedures in the EU. The challenge facing it today is to preserve and ultimately enhance this process. However, paradoxically, this is not within Parliament's domain. The future of the scrutiny process and national parliaments will be on the agenda at the IGC in the year 2000. If development of the EU continues apace then it is undoubtedly true that national parliaments will become peripheral to EU activity. For the UK with its tradition of Parliamentary democracy this will be unacceptable. Thus the UK's continued participation at the heart of the EU is intrinsically linked to Parliament maintaining and enhancing its role in the legislative process. In essence national parliaments must be central to addressing the democratic deficit in the EU and the government has a duty to do everything within its power to ensure that not only do national parliaments remain central to the development of the EU but that their scrutiny function is preserved.

APPENDIX 1

LIST OF WITNESSES

Harry Barnes MP; Tony Benn MP; Andrew F Bennet; Peter Bottomley MP; Bill Cash MP; James Cornford; Eileen Denza; David Doig; Paul Evans; Frank Field MP; Tristan Garel-Jones MP; Mathew Hamlyn; Alan Haslehurst MP; Tom Healy; Jimmy Hood MP; David Liddington MP; David North; Dominic O'Shea; Michael Pownall; C J Poyser; Robert Rogers; Les Saunders; Lord Slynn of Hadley; Ivan Smith; Liam Laurence Smyth; Tim Pratt; Nick Walker; C R M Ward.

APPENDIX 2

STRUCTURE OF THE EUROPEAN UNION

INTRODUCTION

In 1951, the Treaty of Paris established the European Coal and Steel Community (ECSC) with six members – Belgium, Italy, France, Luxembourg, Germany and the Netherlands. In 1957 the same six nations signed the Treaty of Rome which established the European Economic Community (EEC) and the European Atomic Energy Community (EURATOM). In 1968 the institutions of these three organisations merged but to this day their powers and functions are wholly separate.

The original membership of six has by 1997 grown to 15 Member States with twelve official languages being spoken. Today, the European Community (as it has been known since the Single European Act 1986) has extensive law making powers which operate independently of the Parliaments in Member States but does not operate as a federal government, having legislative competence only in the areas prescribed by the Treaty.

However, the emphasis in recent years has shifted in favour of the European Community acting as a single cohesive block when dealing with third countries. For example, the European Community is now a member of the G7 group of countries and in areas such as customs duties has the exclusive power to make agreements with third States. For many, this is viewed as the initial steps to the formation of a United States of Europe.

The areas of competence of the European Community were again enlarged by the Treaty on European Union (the Maastricht Treaty), most notably in the areas of Justice and Home Affairs and the Common Foreign and Security Policy. These two new pillars along with the central pillar of the European Community form the European Union.

COMMUNITY INSTITUTIONS

Following the Maastricht Treaty, the decision making structure of the Community is separated into five institutions – the Council of Ministers, the European Parliament, the Commission, the Court of Auditors and the Court of Justice. Each institution is assigned specific tasks by the Treaty, and this division of power reflects the complex political, legal and economic relationship which is at the core of the Communities objectives.

The Council of Ministers

The Council of Ministers[1] consists of Ministerial representatives from governments of each of the Member States. Depending upon the policy area

---

1   The constitution and principal functions of the Council are set out in Articles 145-154 EC Treaty (as amended by TEU).

under discussion, this will dictate which minister attends.[2] The Council is the principal legislative body within the EC, though the Commission has some legislative powers under the Treaty (see below). Due to criticisms of it being undemocratic and secretive, the Council has following the Edinburgh Inter-Governmental Conference (IGC) published automatically all votes taken by the Council on legislative proposals. Furthermore, the Council publishes detailed documents concerning legislative proposals and holds detailed press briefings following each meeting.[3]

Under the Maastricht Treaty majority voting (whether qualified majority or simple) in the Council is now the norm, though a few areas, taxation being one, are still subject to unanimity. It was the Single European Act 1986 which increased the use of Qualified Majority Voting (QMV) and the Maastricht Treaty which extended it further. The votes of each Member State are weighted so that larger states have 10 votes and smaller ones fewer. A qualified majority consists of 62 votes out of a total of 87 when the Council acts on a Commission proposal. In other cases, the 62 votes must represent a favourable vote from at least 10 Member States. When the Council acts under the Social Protocol. a qualified majority consists of 52 votes out of 77.[4]

One further point to be noted in connection with QMV is the so called "Ioannina Compromise". This came about following the enlargement of the Community in 1995 and reflected primarily the concerns of the UK government. The compromise provides that if a total of 23 to 25 votes indicate their opposition to the adoption by the Council of a decision by qualified majority, the Council will do all within its power to reach within a reasonable time a solution that can be adopted by at least 65 votes.

The Council is assisted in its work by a Committee of Permanent Representatives (COREPER) which consists of the Member States' Ambassadors to the Community. The main task of COREPER is to prepare the work of the Council and carry out tasks assigned to it by the Council. COREPER also splits into smaller Working Groups that discuss some of the more technical aspects of the legislative proposals.[5] Only if COREPER or the Working Group fail to reach agreement on a legislative proposal will the matter be discussed further within the full Council. Otherwise it is adopted without further debate.

---

2   If a major policy area or constitutional matter is under discussion, it will usually be the Foreign Ministers of each Member State who attend.

3   However, televising the Council of Ministers has been ruled out as being impractical. Because of the nature of the negotiations, it was felt television would prevent candid and open debate. In evidence given to the author during his research, a former Foreign Office Minister rejected strongly any further increase in the televising of the Council of Ministers because he viewed it as a cabinet which could only function effectively behind closed doors.

4   The United Kingdom does not participate in policy areas covered by the Social Protocol.

5   See the chapter 1 for a more detailed account of the work of COREPER.

The Presidency of the Council of Minsters is held in accordance with the Treaties by each Member State for a period of six months. During this six month period, the Member State holding the Presidency has the pivotal role within the Community. It is this Member State that sets the agenda for Council meetings and strongly influences the pace of the Councils work. Perhaps most importantly, it is the Member State holding the Presidency that will seek compromise when there is disagreement over legislative proposals.

At the end of each six month Presidency, there is a full meeting of the European Council.[6] This is when the Heads of Government meet to discuss the future direction of the EC. The meetings of the European Council are highly political affairs and are not concerned with the adoption of legislative proposals. They provide the policy direction which will be translated into legislation by the Council of Ministers.

The Commission

The Commission is the Civil Service of the Community and helps to develop the policy adopted by the Council.[7] Furthermore, the Commission also has some legislative powers and will introduce directives in mainly procedural areas. The Commission avoids political discussion, leaving this task to the Council.

There are 20 Commissioners in total – two each from the UK France, Germany, Italy and Spain, and one from each of the remaining Member States. Since the Maastricht Treaty, the European Parliament must give approval to any Commissioner nominated for the Presidency of the Commission. Furthermore, the Parliament will also give its consent to the Commission once it has been nominated by the Member States and this Commission will be appointed for a five year term.

Once appointed, the Commission operates collectively and must speak with one voice on all policy areas.[8] As stated they are politically independent and carry out their duties independently of their national governments. Each Commissioner is given a particular policy responsibility during his or her tenure which they pursue in all Member States and not just their home country.

The functions and duties of the Commission are inter alia:

– to initiate Community action by proposing policies and putting legislative proposals to the Council.

---

6   See Article D EC Treaty (as amended by TEU).

7   See Articles 155-163 EC Treaty (as amended by TEU) for work of the Commission.

8   This is best illustrated by the criticism of Transport Commissioner Neil Kinnock who in a speech in November 1995 questioned the viability of Monetary Union. He claimed to speak in a personal capacity and not as a Commissioner but this was not accepted by Commission President Jacques Santer who rebuked him for this speech.

  – to act as a "guardian" of the Treaties by using its wide powers of super-
    vision and inspection to ensure that Member States apply the provi-
    sions of the Treaties and any subsequent legislation. Perhaps most
    importantly, the Commission has the power to initiate actions in the
    European Court of Justice when a Member State breaches the Treaty
    provisions.
  – to act as an external negotiator on behalf of the Communities in areas
    such as the environment and trade.
  – to implement Community policies in accordance with the Treaty and
    supervise Member States in their implementation of legislation.
  – in the case of legislation subject to the cooperation or co-decision pro-
    cedure, to re-examine the Council's common position on a proposal if
    any amendments are proposed by the European Parliament, and to
    submit a re-examined proposal to the Council.
  – to propose a first draft of and to implement the Budget of the EC.

The European Court of Justice

The Court of Justice[9] is the final arbiter on all legal questions submitted to it
under the EC Treaty. The primary duty of the Court is to ensure that the
Treaty is applied and interpreted correctly by all Member States. It will hear
disputes arising between Community institutions and between institutions
and private firms. All decisions of the ECJ are binding on those concerned.

In recent years, the workload of the Court has increased leading to a delay
in the time taken for a case to be heard. This was the main motivation behind
the establishment of the Court of First instance in the Single European Act.
Since 1988, the Court of First Instance has dealt with cases which are complex or of less general interest. Initially, its competence extended only to areas
such as competition and steel but since the Maastricht Treaty, its competence
has been extended to cover all direct actions by citizens and firms against
Community Institutions. However, it has no competence to hear actions
brought by Member States or Community Institutions, or to give preliminary
rulings on questions from national courts.

The Court of Justice, consists of 16 Judges and 9 advocate-generals who
are appointed for a five year period and they operate independently of all
Member States.

The European Parliament

Since 1979 the Members of the European Parliament have[10] been directly
elected by the universal suffrage. Prior to this, the institution was referred to
only as the "European Assembly" because its members were nominated by
each Member State. Each Member of the European Parliament (MEP) is

---

9   See articles 164-188 EC Treaty (as amended by TEU).
10 See Articles 137-144 EC Treaty (as amended by TEU).

elected for a five year period with elections being held simultaneously in each Member State.

At present there is no common electoral procedure within the Community with each Member State applying its own electoral process.[11] However, since 1982 there have been proposals for a uniform electoral procedure but this has proved to unsuccessful due to lack of agreement in the Council. The proposals of the Parliament are based on proportional representation and thus would change the present electoral arrangements of the UK.[12]

The European Parliament comprises of 626 Members, 87 of whom represent constituencies in the United Kingdom. In the UK, Members of both Houses of Parliament may stand for election to the European Parliament, with those Members representing Northern Ireland constituencies being regularly elected to both.

Any citizen of the European Union may stand for election to the European Parliament in *any* Member State and not just in his or her country of origin. Though the chances of being successfully elected are greatly diminished UK politicians have stood for election with varying degrees of success. David Steel MP unsuccessfully challenged to represent a constituency in Milan in 1989, but the British businessman Sir James Goldsmith represented a constituency in Paris for his anti-federalist party.

Since 1986, and the introduction of the cooperation procedure, there has been a major increase in the role of the European Parliament in the legislative process. The Maastricht Treaty has given the Parliament an even greater say through the co-decision procedure. The Parliament now has a direct influence on the content of legislation, by proposing amendments and can by unanimity reject the Common Position of the Council.[13]

The Treaties provide for other functions to be carried out by the Parliament. For example, it has the power to question both the Council and Commission on matters of policy. By a two-thirds majority, it can require the resignation of the Commission as an entire body (but not individually). In the international sphere, the assent of the Parliament is needed to conclude certain agreements,[14] as is also the case prior to the admission of new Member States.[15]

An area of operation that was widely extended by the Maastricht Treaty came in the area of the European Parliaments investigative powers in cases of maladministration or infringement of Community law which are not subject to judicial proceedings In this context, Article 138e EC Treaty provides for the appointment, by the European Parliament of an Ombudsman to investigate maladministration.

---

11   In the United Kingdom, elections are governed by the European Parliamentary Act 1978.

12   In fact the failure to adopt a uniform electoral system based on proportional representation led to an unsuccessful challenge in the ECJ by the Liberal Party.

13   For a full discussion of the European Parliaments role in the legislative process see chapter 1.

14   See Article 238 EC Treaty (as amended by TEU).

15   *Ibid.* Article 237.

The reason for this increase in the activities of the European Parliament was to counter criticisms that the Community was undemocratic and isolated from the real needs of the peoples of Europe. The Parliament being the only directly elected institution of the EC, had to increase its influence and profile in order to establish its democratic credentials.

The Court of Auditors

The Court of Auditors[16] is now considered as the fifth institution of the EC. It consists of 15 members who are appointed for a six year term by the Council following consultation with the European Parliament. The primary function of the Court of Auditors is to examine the accounts of the Community. Allied to this is the vital task of combating fraud in the Community[17] by ensuring all expenditure is lawful or not wasteful.

The Court of Auditors operates in a wholly autonomous way and has the power to investigate any Community institution or any funding decision. Each year, an annual report is presented with the findings of the Court of Auditors to all the Community institutions in preparation for agreeing the following years budget.

OTHER EUROPEAN COMMUNITY COMMITTEES

The Economic and Social Committee

The Economic and Social Committee[18] consists of 222 members who are appointed for a four year term. The membership is drawn from a variety of European organisations such as Trade Unions, business leaders and a variety of professional occupations. The United Kingdom is represented by 24 members who take their place on the Committee.

The primary function of the Economic and Social Committee is to act as a consultative body for both the Council and the Commission on any Community matter. Thus it is a major source (along with individual pressure groups) of information and ideas for Community policy.

The Committee of the Regions

The Committee of the Regions[19] is a new development, only coming into being since the Maastricht Treaty. The Committee is constituted of representatives of regional and local authorities from all 15 Member States. It has 222

---

16   See Articles 188a and 188b EC Treaty (as amended by TEU).
17   This is an issue that has been fully investigated by the House of Lords. See HL 34 Sixth Report Session 1993-94.
18   See Articles 193-198 EC Treaty (as amended by TEU).
19   See Articles 198a - 198c EC Treaty (as inserted by Article G(67) TEU).

members who are appointed by the Council of Ministers for a four year tenure. The number of members are weighted according to the population of each Member State.

Though independent in its operation, the role of the Committee is purely advisory. It is convened on the request of the Council of Ministers or the Commission, but can if required meet at its own initiative. The Committee may be consulted by the Council or Commission on any policy matter. However, both of these institutions are under an obligation to consult the Committee in the following policy areas: education; public health; the report on economic and social cohesion; cultural "incentive measures"; basic rules governing all the Structural Funds and implementing rules for the Regional Fund.

The Council and Commission may set a time limit in which these opinions are given, but a failure by the Committee to produce a report will not prevent further action. Similarly, though under an obligation to consult, the Council and Commission will not always take onboard the views of the Committee. In essence, the Committee of the Regions is just one part of a wider lobbying process.

APPENDIX 3

THE WORKING METHODS OF THE SELECT COMMITTEE ON EUROPEAN LEGISLATION

The Committee meets every week when the House is sitting, usually at 4 pm on Wednesdays. Though the Committee has the power to meet during an adjournment this has not been exercised for many years.

In preparation for the weekly meeting, a batch af advisory briefs is put on the Letter Board in the Vote Office at about 6 pm in Mondays. A second batch of advisory briefs together with a draft agenda is put on the Letter Board at about 6 pm on Tuesdays. However, it is often the case that last minute briefs are put on the Board at lunch-time on Wednesdays.

On arrival at the meeting each member of the Committee is given a folder which contains an updated copy of the agenda, a fresh copy of each advisory brief and a copy of the relevant Explanatory Memoranda. (This can also be obtained at an earlier stage from the Clerk).

The Members receive no other documents, but can obtain a copy of the instrument for themselves from the Vote Office. The Committee's staff are there to assist the members with any matters relating to the instrument or any other issues concerning the work of the Select Committee.

The Clerk of the Committee has the overall responsibility for the work of the Committee and the conduct of its meetings. It is the role of the Clerk to deal with the procedural advice for the Committee. In his role, the Clerk is assisted by the Assistant to the Clerk who deals with the agenda for meetings and makes the arrangements for any visits. There is also a documents clerk whose function is to prepare the relevant documents for each meeting.

Under the general direction of the Clerk, there are three Clerks/Advisers who are responsible for examining all the instruments coming before the Committee and offering advice to the Committee on how they should be dealt with. Each of the three Clerks/Advisers has responsibility for a particular area of legislation. They specialise as follows:

1. Agriculture, Fisheries and Food
2. Energy, Overseas Development, Employment, Health and Safety and Environment.
3. Treasury, Inland Revenue, Customs and Excise, Trade and Industry and Transport.

The Committee also has the assistance of one of the Speaker's Counsel, whose task is to clarify the likely impact on United Kingdom law of the instrument coming before the committee and give any other legal advice which is required. This is an important role, as the impact of the legislation on UK domestic legislation is often the reason for the document to be recommended for further debate by the Committee.

At deliberative meetings of the Committee, the Clerk and all other relevant adviser are present. These deliberative sessions are always held in private.

For oral evidence sessions which are usually held in Public, similar arrangements apply with the Clerk and adviser being present to assist.

After each meeting, the Committee's decisions are collated and presented to the House, together with explanatory paragraphs in a Report. It is published as soon as possible after the meeting of the Committee and is available to all Members from the Vote Office.

Each week, a list of European Community Documents which have been referred to one of the two European Standing Committees is published by the Public Bill Office. This also refers to the progress of the document and is circulated in Mondays Order Paper.

The support staff are vital to the functioning of the Committee. They do all the necessary preparation which the Members with all their other obligations could never do. They also liaise with the other departments to keep informed of what European documents are likely to be before the Committee in the near future. Furthermore, unlike the Members, the permanent staff do not have a lengthy summer recess, and continue the work of the Committee at this time, but without the weekly meetings.

BIBLIOGRAPHY

PARLIAMENTARY PAPERS AND DEBATES

Chronological Order

House of Lords Reform, Cmnd 3799, (Session 1968-69)
House of Commons – First Report from the Select Committee on European Community Legislation. HC 143 (Session 1972-73).
House of Commons – Second Report from the Select Committee on European Community Legislation. HC 463-I and II (Session 1972-73).
House of Lords – Second Report by the Select Committee on Procedures for Scrutiny of Proposals for European Instruments. HL 194 (Session 1972-73).
House of Commons – Second Special Report from the European Secondary Legislation &c Committee. HL 258-I and II (Session 1974).
House of Commons – First Report from the Select Committee on Procedure. HC 588-I (Session 1977-78).
House of Commons Debates – Standing Committee on European Community Documents. 30 October 1980. Columns 837 – 838.
House of Commons – First Special Report from the Select Committee on European Community Legislation. HC 527 (Session 1983-84).
House of Commons Debates, 29 October 1984. Vol. 65 Columns 798-800. Government Reply to HC 527 (Session 1983-84).
House of Commons – First Special Report from the Select Committee on European Community Legislation. HC 264 (Session 1985-86).
House of Commons – Second Special Report from the Select Committee on European Community Legislation. HC 400 (Session 1985-86).
Second Special Report from the House of Commons Select Committee on European Legislation Session 1985-86 – Observations by the Government. Cm 123 (Session 1985-86).
House of Lords – Select Committee on the European Communities, *Single European Act and Parliamentary Scrutiny*. HL 140 (Session 1985-86).
House of Lords – Report by the Working Group on the Working of the House. HL 9 (Session 1987-88).
Developments in the European Union July – December 1988. Cm 641.
House of Commons – Foreign Affairs Select Committee. Second Report – *The Operation of the Single European Act*. HC 82-I and II (Session 1989-90).
House of Commons – Fourth Report from the Select Committee on Procedure – *The Scrutiny of European Legislation*. HC 622-I and II (Session 1988-89).
Developments in the European Community January – June 1989. Cm 801.
House of Commons Debates – European Community Documents. 1 February 1989. Columns 398-399.
Fourth Report from the House of Commons Select Committee on Procedure Session 1988-89 – *The Scrutiny of European Legislation*. Government Response. Cm 1081 (1989-90).

Developments in the European Community. July – December 1989. Cm 1023.

Developments in the European Community. January – June 1990. Cm 1234.

House of Lords – Select Committee on the European Communities – *Conference of Parliaments of the European Community.* HL 20 (Session 1990-91).

House of Lords – Select Committee on the European Communities. *Political Union: Law- making Powers and Procedures.* HL 80 (Session 1990-91).

Developments in the European Community. July – December 1990. Cmnd 1457.

House of Commons Debates – European Standing Committees. 24 October 1990. Columns 393-400.

House of Commons Debates – European Standing Committees. 22 January 1991. Columns 269-293.

House of Commons Debates – Point of Order Mr Teddy Taylor. 25 March 1991. Columns 722-724.

House of Commons Debates – European Standing Committees. 26 June 1991. Columns 1092-1110.

House of Commons – Select Committee on Procedure. First Report – *Review of Standing Committees.* HC 31 (Session 1991-92).

House of Commons – Select Committee on Procedure. Third Report. The Government's Response to the procedure Committee's Review of European Standing Committees. HC 331 (Session 1991-92).

House of Lords – Report from the Select Committee on the Committee Work of the House. HL 35-I and II (Session 1991-92).

House of Lords – Select Committee on the European Communities – *Implementation and Enforcement of Environmental Legislation.* HL 53-I and II (Session 1991-92).

Developments in the European Community January – June 1991 Cm 1657.

Developments in the European Community July – December 1991. Cm 1857.

Developments in the European Community January – June 1992. Cm 2065.

Developments in the European Union July – December 1992. Cm 2168.

House of Lords – Select Committee on the European Communities – House of Lords Scrutiny of the Inter-Governmental Pillars of the European Union. HL 124 (Session 1992-93).

House of Lords Scrutiny of the Inter-Governmental Pillars of the European Union – *Observations by the Secretary of State for Foreign and Commonwealth Affairs and the Secretary of State for Home Affairs.* Cm 2471 (Session 1992-93).

Developments in the European Union. January – June 1993. Cm 2369.

European Standing Committee A – Minutes of Proceedings HC 737 (Session 1993-94).

European Standing Committee B – Minutes of Proceedings HC 738 (Session 1993-94).

House of Commons – First Special Report from the Select Committee on European Legislation – *Scrutiny after Maastricht.* HC 99 (Session 1993-94).

House of Commons – Second Special Report from the Select Committee on European Legislation – Parliamentary Scrutiny of the Co-Decision Procedure and The Government's Reply to the First Special Report from the

Committee: *Scrutiny after Maastricht*. HC 739 (Session 1993-94). *Developments in the European Union*. July – December 1993. Cm 2525. *Developments in the European Union* January – June 1994. Cm 2675.

House of Lords – Select Committee on the European Communities – *Relations Between the EU and the Maghreb Countries*. HL 58 (Session 1994-95).

House of Lords – Select Committee on the European Communities – *Environmental Issues in Central and Eastern Europe: The Phare Programme*. HL 86 (Session 1994-95).

House of Commons – Select Committee on European Legislation. The 1996 Inter-Governmental Conference: *The Agenda; Democracy and Efficiency; The Role of National Parliaments*. HC 239-I and II (Session 1994-95).

House of Commons – Foreign Affairs Select Committee. European Union: *Preparations for the 1996 Inter-Governmental Conference*. HC 401 (Session 1994-95).

House of Lords – The Select Committee on the European Communities – *Reform of the Sugar Regime*. HL 28 (Session 1994-95).

House of Lords – The Select Committee on the European Communities – *The Right of Establishment of Lawyers*. HL 82 (Session 1994-95).

House of Lords – Select Committee on the European Communities – *EURO-POL*. HL 51-I and II (Session 1994-95).

House of Lords – Select Committee on the European Communities – *European Union Energy Policy*. HL 87 (Session 1994-95).

House of Lords – Select Committee on the European Communities – *1996 Inter-Governmental Conference*. HL 105 (Session 1994-95). *Developments in the European Union*. July – December 1994. Cm 2798. *Developments in the European Union* January – June 1995. Cm 3130.

House of Lords Debates – Debate on EUROPOL. 6 June 1995. Columns 1307 – 1341.

House of Commons – Select Committee on European Legislation – *The Scrutiny of European Business*. HC 51-xxvii (Session 1995-96).

Foreign and Commonwealth Office – *A Partnership of Nations. The British Approach to the European Union Inter-Governmental Conference 1996*. Cm 3181 (1995-96).

House of Lords – Select Committee on the European Communities – *Drinking Water*. HL 31 (Session 1995-96). *Developments in the European Union* July-December 1995. Cm 3250.

House of Lords Debates – Debate on the Right for Establishment of Lawyers. 18 June 1996 Columns 243-256.

House of Lords Debates – EC Proposals: Prompt Scrutiny. 6 November 1995. Columns 1569-1571.

House of Lords Debates – Debate on the Relations between the EU and the Maghreb Countries. 26 June 1996. Columns 928 – 930.

House of Lords Debates – *The Constitution*. 4 July 1996. Columns 1581-1690.

PARLIAMENTARY INFORMATION AND OTHER OFFICIAL PUBLICATIONS

Public Information Office House of Commons London. Factsheet No. 56 – *The House of Commons and European Union.*

Journal and Information Office House of Lords London – Information Sheet No. 2 – *The House of Lords at Work.*

Journal and Information Office House of Lords London. Information Sheet No.4 – *The House of Lords and the European Union.*

Journal and Information Office House of Lords London. Information Sheet No.6 – *House of Lords Sessional Business Statistics Session 1994-95.*

Journal and Information Office House of Lords London. Information Sheet No.7 – *House of Lords Annual Business Statistics Calendar Year 1995.*

Journal and Information Office House of Lords London. Information Sheet No.13 – *House of Lords Membership and attendance Statistics: Session 1994-95.*

European Parliament, Division for Relations with the Parliaments of the Member States, *European Affairs Committees of the Parliaments of the Member States.* June 1995.

Emile Noel, *Working Together – The Institutions of the European Community.* Luxembourg: Office for Official Publications of the European Communities, 1994.

Directorate-General for Information and Public Relations of the European Parliament, *The European Parliament.* Office for Official Publications of the European Communities.

Directorate-General for Information, Communication, Culture and Audiovisual Media of the European Commission, *The European Union.* Office for Official Publications of the European Community.

ARTICLES AND PUBLISHED WORKS

T. St J. N. Bates, *European Community Legislation before the House of Commons,* Statute Law Review 1991, p. 109.

Jane D. N. Bates, *The Conversion of EC Legislation into UK Legislation,* Statute Law Review, 1989, p. 110.

Earl of Carnarvon, Lord Bancroft, Earl of Selborne, Viscount Tenby and Douglas Slater, *Second Chamber: Some remarks on reforming the House of Lords,* (1995).

Commonwealth Parliamentary Association, *The Role of Second Chambers,* The Parliamentarian, October 1982.

Adam Cygan, *The Scrutiny of EU Legislation by the House of Commons after Masstricht,* The King's College Law Journal 1995-96, p. 38.

Eileen Denza, *The Parliamentary Scrutiny of European Legislation,* Statute Law Review 1992, p. 56.

Eileen Denza, *La Chambre Des Lords: Vingt Annees D'enquetes Communautaires,* Revue du Marche commun et de l'Union europeene, No. 371 septembre-octobre 1993.

Right Honourable Lord Hailsham of St Marylebone, British Broadcasting
    Corporation *Elective Dictatorship* Richard Dimbleby Lecture (1976).
Hansard Society *Making the Law* (1992).
Ian Harden, *The Constitution of the European Union*, Public Law 1994, p.609.
Juliet Lodge *The Weakness of National Parliaments*, Parliamentary Brief, Vol. 3
    No. 9, Summer 1995.
Lord Rees-Mogg, *Why we need the Lords*, The Times 7 July 1994.
Jean Louis Scurin, Towards a European Constitution? Problems of Political
    Integration, Public Law 1994, p. 625.
Right Honourable Lord Slynn of Hadley, *Looking at European Community
    Texts*, Statute Law Review 1993, p. 12.
Woodrow Wyatt, *Leave us Lords well alone*, The Times 17 January 1995.
Woodrow Wyatt, *Learning to love the Lords,* The Times 5 December 1995.

GENERAL WORKS

T. St. J.N. Bates *et al* (eds.) *European Community Studies In Memoriam: J.D.B.
    Mitchell* (1983).
The Constitution Unit, *Reform of the Lords,* (1996).
Gavin Drewry (ed.) *The New Select Committees A study of the 1979 Reforms*
    (1985).
Neil Foster, *Blackstones EC Legislation* (Seventh Edition1996-97).
J.A.G. Griffith and Michael Ryle, *Parliament, Functions Practice and Proce-
    dures.* (1989).
Institute for Public Policy Research, *The Constitution of the United Kingdom*
    (1991).
Institute for Public Policy Research, *Reforming the Lords* (1993).
The Labour Party *New Labour, New Life for Britain* (1996).
Erskine May, *Parliamentary Practice* (21st ed., 1989).
Laursen and Pappas (eds.) European Institute of Public Administration, *The
    Changing Role of Parliaments in the European Union* (1995).
Mazey and Richardson (eds.) *Lobbying in the European Community* (1993).
Neil Nugent, *The Government and Politcs of the European Union.* (1994).
O'Keefe and Twomey (eds.) United Kingdom association of European Law,
    Legal Issues of the Maastricht Treaty (1993).
Josephine Shaw, *European Community Law* (1994).
Donald Shell, *The House of Lords* (1988).
Donald Shell and David Beamish (eds.), *The House of Lords at Work* (1993).
Paul Silk and R.H. Walters *How Parliament Works* (1987).
Josephine Steiner and Lorna Woods, *Textbook on EC Law* (5th Edition 1995).
Colin Turpin *British Government and the Constitution* (1995).

INDEX

STUDIES IN LAW - A SERIES OF PUBLICATIONS BY THE CENTRE OF EUROPEAN
LAW, KING'S COLLEGE LONDON

1. R. Müllerson, M. Fitzmaurice and M. Andenas (eds.): *Constitutional Reform and
International Law in Central and Eastern Europe*. 1997 ISBN 90-411-0526-3

2. A. J. Cygan: *The United Kingdom Parliament and European Union Legislation*. 1998
ISBN 90-411-9650-1